KAPLAN

K12 LEARNING
SERVICES

Kaplan
ADVANTAGE

ACT*

English & Reading

① Reading Activel
 - summarize
 - underline/circle
 - ? the Author

② Examine ?

③ Predict, eliminate

LEVEL
HS

Curriculum Development
Caryn Siegel Moss

Contributing Writers
Jennifer Baker, Molly Pont-Brown, Kenneth Kriwanek, Marcella Spruce, Adam Marks

Design
Maurice Kessler

Editorial
Erin Finelli, Emily McCombs, Ray Ojserkis, Linda Peterson

Illustration
Tom Kurzanski

Production
Scott Rayow, Stephanie Thompson

Associate Manager of Traffic and Post-Production
Dustin Helmer

Project Coordinators
Sandra Ogle, Aaron Riccio

Senior Editor
Emily McCombs

Manager of Editorial, Traffic, and Project Management
Mary Beth Garrick

Production Manager
Richard Welch

Art Director
Michael Young

Associate Director of English Language Arts Curriculum
Sajitha Jahangir

Director of Curriculum and Instruction
Deborah Lerman

TABLE OF CONTENTS

Unit 1: *Getting to Know the ACT* **1**

    LESSON A: English Practice Test 1 3

    LESSON B: Reading Practice Test 1 19

    LESSON C: The Landscape of the Tests 33

Unit 2: *ACT Reading I* **49**

    LESSON A: Reading Actively 51

    LESSON B: Examining the Question Stems 65

    LESSON C: Answering the Questions 81

Unit 3: *ACT Reading II* **97**

    LESSON A: Detail Questions 99

    LESSON B: Function Questions 113

    LESSON C: Vocabulary-in-Context Questions . . 131

Unit 4: *ACT Reading III* **147**

    LESSON A: Narrow-Inference Questions 149

    LESSON B: Broad-Inference Questions 165

    LESSON C: Writer's-View Questions 179

Unit 5: *ACT English I* **195**

    LESSON A: The 3-Step Method for
                 ACT English Success 197

    LESSON B: Grammar Questions 213

    LESSON C: Style Questions 229

Unit 6: *ACT English II* **243**

    LESSON A: Sentence-Sense Questions 245

    LESSON B: Punctuation Questions 261

    LESSON C: Writing-Strategy and
                 Organization Questions 277

Unit 7: *ACT Writing* **295**

    LESSON A: Understanding the Essay 297

    LESSON B: Planning Your Essay 307

    LESSON C: Writing and Reviewing Your Essay . . 317

English Practice Test 2 . . . . **327**

Reading Practice Test 2 . . . . **347**

Unit 1
Getting to Know the ACT

Welcome to *ACT Advantage*. This program will help you prepare for the ACT English Test and the ACT Reading Test, which are, respectively, the first and third of the four ACT tests you will take on Test Day. The first step in your climb to the summit of test success is an English Practice Test.

This is not the actual test, so don't worry! This is simply a chance to practice skills that will be on the real test. It will also give you and your teacher a sense of your strengths and weaknesses so that you can better prepare for Test Day.

This test is designed to resemble the ACT English Test, and therefore has the range of topics and difficulty levels that you will see on Test Day. To best accustom yourself to test-like conditions, the teach will administer the test using the same timing rules as the ACT English Test: all 75 questions to be completed in a total of 45 minutes.

All of the questions are multiple choice. Use the Answer Sheet to mark each answer so you can become accustomed to doing so on Test Day.

If you finish all 75 problems before time is called, review your work.

A

English Practice Test 1

When your teacher tells you, carefully tear out this page.

1. Ⓐ Ⓑ Ⓒ Ⓓ	15. Ⓐ Ⓑ Ⓒ Ⓓ	29. Ⓐ Ⓑ Ⓒ Ⓓ
2. Ⓕ Ⓖ Ⓗ Ⓙ	16. Ⓕ Ⓖ Ⓗ Ⓙ	30. Ⓕ Ⓖ Ⓗ Ⓙ
3. Ⓐ Ⓑ Ⓒ Ⓓ	17. Ⓐ Ⓑ Ⓒ Ⓓ	31. Ⓐ Ⓑ Ⓒ Ⓓ
4. Ⓕ Ⓖ Ⓗ Ⓙ	18. Ⓕ Ⓖ Ⓗ Ⓙ	32. Ⓕ Ⓖ Ⓗ Ⓙ
5. Ⓐ Ⓑ Ⓒ Ⓓ	19. Ⓐ Ⓑ Ⓒ Ⓓ	33. Ⓐ Ⓑ Ⓒ Ⓓ
6. Ⓕ Ⓖ Ⓗ Ⓙ	20. Ⓕ Ⓖ Ⓗ Ⓙ	34. Ⓕ Ⓖ Ⓗ Ⓙ
7. Ⓐ Ⓑ Ⓒ Ⓓ	21. Ⓐ Ⓑ Ⓒ Ⓓ	35. Ⓐ Ⓑ Ⓒ Ⓓ
8. Ⓕ Ⓖ Ⓗ Ⓙ	22. Ⓕ Ⓖ Ⓗ Ⓙ	36. Ⓕ Ⓖ Ⓗ Ⓙ
9. Ⓐ Ⓑ Ⓒ Ⓓ	23. Ⓐ Ⓑ Ⓒ Ⓓ	37. Ⓐ Ⓑ Ⓒ Ⓓ
10. Ⓕ Ⓖ Ⓗ Ⓙ	24. Ⓕ Ⓖ Ⓗ Ⓙ	38. Ⓕ Ⓖ Ⓗ Ⓙ
11. Ⓐ Ⓑ Ⓒ Ⓓ	25. Ⓐ Ⓑ Ⓒ Ⓓ	39. Ⓐ Ⓑ Ⓒ Ⓓ
12. Ⓕ Ⓖ Ⓗ Ⓙ	26. Ⓕ Ⓖ Ⓗ Ⓙ	40. Ⓕ Ⓖ Ⓗ Ⓙ
13. Ⓐ Ⓑ Ⓒ Ⓓ	27. Ⓐ Ⓑ Ⓒ Ⓓ	41. Ⓐ Ⓑ Ⓒ Ⓓ
14. Ⓕ Ⓖ Ⓗ Ⓙ	28. Ⓕ Ⓖ Ⓗ Ⓙ	42. Ⓕ Ⓖ Ⓗ Ⓙ

43. Ⓐ Ⓑ Ⓒ Ⓓ   60. Ⓕ Ⓖ Ⓗ Ⓙ

44. Ⓕ Ⓖ Ⓗ Ⓙ   61. Ⓐ Ⓑ Ⓒ Ⓓ

45. Ⓐ Ⓑ Ⓒ Ⓓ   62. Ⓕ Ⓖ Ⓗ Ⓙ

46. Ⓕ Ⓖ Ⓗ Ⓙ   63. Ⓐ Ⓑ Ⓒ Ⓓ

47. Ⓐ Ⓑ Ⓒ Ⓓ   64. Ⓕ Ⓖ Ⓗ Ⓙ

48. Ⓕ Ⓖ Ⓗ Ⓙ   65. Ⓐ Ⓑ Ⓒ Ⓓ

49. Ⓐ Ⓑ Ⓒ Ⓓ   66. Ⓕ Ⓖ Ⓗ Ⓙ

50. Ⓕ Ⓖ Ⓗ Ⓙ   67. Ⓐ Ⓑ Ⓒ Ⓓ

51. Ⓐ Ⓑ Ⓒ Ⓓ   68. Ⓕ Ⓖ Ⓗ Ⓙ

52. Ⓕ Ⓖ Ⓗ Ⓙ   69. Ⓐ Ⓑ Ⓒ Ⓓ

53. Ⓐ Ⓑ Ⓒ Ⓓ   70. Ⓕ Ⓖ Ⓗ Ⓙ

54. Ⓕ Ⓖ Ⓗ Ⓙ   71. Ⓐ Ⓑ Ⓒ Ⓓ

55. Ⓐ Ⓑ Ⓒ Ⓓ   72. Ⓕ Ⓖ Ⓗ Ⓙ

56. Ⓕ Ⓖ Ⓗ Ⓙ   73. Ⓐ Ⓑ Ⓒ Ⓓ

57. Ⓐ Ⓑ Ⓒ Ⓓ   74. Ⓕ Ⓖ Ⓗ Ⓙ

58. Ⓕ Ⓖ Ⓗ Ⓙ   75. Ⓐ Ⓑ Ⓒ Ⓓ

59. Ⓐ Ⓑ Ⓒ Ⓓ

ACT ADVANTAGE
ENGLISH & READING

ENGLISH TEST
45 Minutes—75 Questions

DIRECTIONS: In the five passages that follow, certain words and phrases are underlined and numbered. In the right-hand column, you will find alternatives for the underlined part. In most cases, you are to choose the one that best expresses the idea, makes the statement appropriate for standard written English, or is worded most consistently with the style and tone of the passage as a whole. If you think the original version is best, choose "NO CHANGE." In some cases, you will find in the right-hand column a question about the underlined part. You are to choose the best answer to the question. For each question, choose the alternative you consider best and fill in the corresponding oval on your answer document. Read each passage through once before you begin to answer the questions that accompany it. For many of the questions, you must read several sentences beyond the question to determine the answer. Be sure that you have read far enough ahead each time you choose an alternative.

PASSAGE I

American Jazz

<u>One of the earliest</u> music forms to originate in the
₁
United States was Jazz. Known as truly Mid-American

because of <u>it's</u> having origins in several locations in
₂
middle America, this music developed almost

simultaneously in New Orleans, St. Louis, Kansas City,

and Chicago.

At the start of the 20th century, musicians all along

the Mississippi River familiar with West African folk

music ⬜3⬜ blended it with European classical music

from the early 19th century. This combination was

adopted by artists in the region who began to

1. **A.** NO CHANGE
   B. One of the most earliest
   C. The most early
   D. The earliest

2. **F.** NO CHANGE
   G. its
   H. its's
   J. its'

3. At this point, the writer is considering adding the following phrase:

   —rich with syncopation—

   Given that it is true, would this be a relevant addition to make here?
   A. Yes, because it can help the reader have a better understanding of the music being discussed.
   B. Yes, because it helps explain to the reader why this music became popular.
   C. No, because it fails to explain the connection between this music and the button accordion.
   D. No, because it is inconsistent with the style of this essay to mention specific musical forms.

use minor chords and <u>syncopation, in their own music,</u>
₄
ragtime, and blues. At the same time, brass bands and

gospel choirs adopted Jazz music, and it became a true

blend of cultures. Eventually, a unique music <u>style</u>

<u>developed; based on</u> a blend of the many different
₅

cultures in America at the time. <u>It was American Jazz</u>
₆
<u>and</u> became the first indigenous American style to
₆
affect music in the rest of the world.

[1] One of the true greats of American Jazz was

Cabell "Cab" Calloway III. [2] He was born in New York

in 1907, but his family moved to Chicago during his teen

years. [3] Growing up, Cab <u>made his living</u> working as a
₇

shoe shiner and <u>he was</u> a waiter. [4] During these years,
₈
he also spent time at the racetrack, where he walked

horses to keep them in good shape. ⬚9 [5] After

graduating from high school in Chicago, <u>where</u> Cab got
₁₀
his first performance job in a revue called "Plantation

Days." [6] His strong and impressive voice soon gained

4. F. NO CHANGE
   G. syncopation in their own music,
   H. syncopation, in their own music
   J. syncopation in their own music

5. A. NO CHANGE
   B. style developed based on
   C. style developed based on,
   D. style, developed based on

6. F. NO CHANGE
   G. This style, known as American Jazz,
   H. Being known as American Jazz, it
   J. It being American Jazz first

7. Which of the following alternatives to the underlined portion would NOT be acceptable?
   A. earned his living by
   B. made his living from
   C. made his living on
   D. earned his living

8. F. NO CHANGE
   G. as well
   H. being
   J. OMIT the underlined portion

9. The writer is considering deleting the following clause from the preceding sentence (placing a period after the word racetrack):

   where he walked horses to keep them in good shape

   Should the writer make this deletion?
   A. Yes, because the information is unrelated to the topic addressed in this paragraph.
   B. Yes, because the information diminishes the musical accomplishments and successes of Cab Calloway.
   C. No, because the information explains the reference to the racetrack, which might otherwise puzzle readers.
   D. No, because the information shows how far Cab Calloway came in his life.

10. F. NO CHANGE
    G. it was there that
    H. was where
    J. OMIT the underlined portion

GO ON TO THE NEXT PAGE.

© 2007 Kaplan, Inc.

him <u>popularity in the top Jazz circles</u> of the
11

United States. 12

Many others have followed Cab's lead <u>and have</u>
13
<u>moved from the East Coast to Middle America.</u> Like
13

other folk music forms, American Jazz has a rich history

and unique sound that <u>means it'll stick around for a</u>
14
<u>while.</u>
14

11. **A.** NO CHANGE
    B. popularity: in the top Jazz circles
    C. popularity, in the top Jazz circles,
    D. popularity in the top Jazz circles,

12. Upon reviewing this paragraph and finding that some information has been left out, the writer composes the following sentence incorporating that information:

    He became widely known as "The man in the zoot suit with the reet pleats."

    This sentence would most logically be placed after sentence:
    F. 3.
    G. 4.
    H. 5.
    J. 6.

13. Given that all the choices are true, which one would most effectively tie together the two main subjects of this essay?
    A. NO CHANGE
    B. and have added to the rich tradition of American Jazz.
    C. such as George Duke and Earl Klugh.
    D. and have signed large recording contracts.

14. **F.** NO CHANGE
    G. causes it to be an enduring institution with a timeless appeal.
    H. makes many people enjoy it.
    J. ensures its continued vitality.

Question 15 asks about the passage as a whole.

15. Suppose the writer's goal was to write a brief essay focusing on the history and development of American Jazz music. Would this essay successfully fulfill that goal?
    A. Yes, because the essay describes the origins of American Jazz music and one of its important figures.
    B. Yes, because the essay mentions the contributions American Jazz music has made to other folk music traditions.
    C. No, because the essay refers to other musical forms besides American Jazz music.
    D. No, because the essay focuses on only one American Jazz musician, Cab Calloway.

GO ON TO THE NEXT PAGE.

PASSAGE II

My Grandfather's Internet

My grandfather is possibly the least technologically

capable writer in the world. He refused to use anything
                                          16

but his pen and paper to write until last year. (He said,
                                                      17
he didn't need any keys or mouse pads between his

words and himself.) Consequently, when he has went to
                                             18

buy a computer—because of the knowledge that his
                        19
editor refused to read another hand-written novel—he

resisted connecting it to the Internet for several months.

He said he had no need to find information on a World

Wide Web. 20

Grandpa's editor, however, was clever and, knowing

exactly how my grandfather could use it, described how

the Internet would improve his life. However, Grandpa
                                         21

could get instant feedback, and praise from the
                    22
publishing company, read online reviews, and do

research for his characters much faster. Finally,

Grandpa connected to the Internet, and he hasn't

logged off since.

　Grandpa is fascinated by all the things he can do on

the World Wide Web. He has found that chat rooms are

wonderful places to have long conversations with

16. **F.** NO CHANGE
　　G. world he refused
　　H. world refusing,
　　J. world, and has been refusing

17. **A.** NO CHANGE
　　B. said
　　C. said, that
　　D. said, that,

18. **F.** NO CHANGE
　　G. had went
　　H. went
　　J. goes

19. **A.** NO CHANGE
　　B. due to the fact that
　　C. because
　　D. so

20. Given that all are true, which of the following additions to the preceding sentence (after World Wide Web) would be most relevant?
　　F. that was on his computer.
　　G. when he had a set of encyclopedias right there in his office.
　　H. with other people on it.
　　J. where he might get a computer virus.

21. **A.** NO CHANGE
　　B. Additionally, Grandpa
　　C. Conversely, Grandpa
　　D. Grandpa

22. **F.** NO CHANGE
　　G. feedback and, praise
　　H. feedback and praise
　　J. feedback and praise,

GO ON TO THE NEXT PAGE.

people interesting enough to be characters in his books.

For example, he says, by clicking the "close" button he
23

can just ignore them who aren't interesting. Grandpa's
24

favorite website is Google.com. Google.com is a search

engine that searches millions of sites for whatever word

he types in, which is very convenient when he needs to
25

know how the native people of Africa developed the

game Mancala. For him, Grandpa says that, in merely a
26

few seconds, to be able to find anything he wants is a
26

source of pure joy.
26

    [1] As for his writings, Grandpa uses the Internet not

only for research but also for making them more

creative and checking his word choice. [2] Explaining

his new vocabulary to his editor, Grandpa points to his
27

new computer and admits that an Internet connection

was a good idea after all. [3] I am sure Grandpa hasn't

explored the entire Internet yet, but I am sure he will
28

continue to find new and better ways of using it. 29
28

23. **A.** NO CHANGE
    B. To illustrate,
    C. On the one hand,
    D. On the other hand,

24. **F.** NO CHANGE
    G. the people
    H. it
    J. their talking

25. **A.** NO CHANGE
    B. convenient, when
    C. convenient. When
    D. convenient; when

26. **F.** NO CHANGE
    G. For him, Grandpa says that to be able to find anything he wants, is a source of pure joy for him, in merely a few seconds.
    H. Grandpa says a source of pure joy for him is that he is able to find anything he wants, in merely a few seconds.
    J. Grandpa says that being able to find anything he wants in merely a few seconds is a source of pure joy for him.

27. **A.** NO CHANGE
    B. pointing
    C. having pointed
    D. Grandpa has pointed

28. **F.** NO CHANGE
    G. and he probably won't explore the rest of it either.
    H. and so his editor will have to teach him to find things faster.
    J. and his editor knows just that.

29. Upon reviewing Paragraph 5 and realizing that some information has been left out, the writer composes the following sentence:

    He uses the dictionary and thesaurus websites religiously.

The most logical placement for this sentence would be:
    A. before sentence 1.
    B. after sentence 1.
    C. after sentence 2.
    D. after sentence 3.

GO ON TO THE NEXT PAGE.

Question 30 asks about the essay as a whole.

30. The writer is considering deleting the first sentence of Paragraph 1. If the writer removed this sentence, the essay would primarily lose:
    F. information about aspects of technology that his grandfather does not use.
    G. humor that sets the mood for the piece.
    H. important details about the Internet that his grandfather might enjoy.
    J. a justification for his grandfather's reluctance to use the Internet.

PASSAGE III

Chickasaw Wandering

In the twilight of a cool autumn evening, I walked with
31

a gathering of people to the center of a field in

Oklahoma.

    Although I didn't know more of the people who
32

walked with me, a few of them I did know quite well. We
33

were Chickasaw Indians, and some of us had waited for

years to make this journey across the Chickasaw
34

31. A. NO CHANGE
    B. On
    C. With
    D. From

32. F. NO CHANGE
    G. more of the people whom
    H. most of the people who
    J. most of the people whom

33. The writer wants to balance the statement made in the earlier part of this sentence with a related detail that suggests the unity of the people. Given that all of the following choices are true, which one best accomplishes this goal?
    A. NO CHANGE
    B. we each had our own reasons for being there.
    C. I hoped I would get to know some of them.
    D. I felt a kinship with them.

34. Which of the following alternatives to the underlined portion would NOT be acceptable?
    F. among
    G. over
    H. on
    J. through

GO ON TO THE NEXT PAGE.

territory to the ornately decorated capital of

Tishomingo. 35

For my whole life I had been shown other
                                      36
Chickasaw's pictures — many of them the ancestors of
   36

the people, who walked along with me, to the Festival
        37

that evening. My father and grandmother helped
                                          38
preserve tribal history by collecting books and
                   38
newspaper clippings. Books about the history and
      38
traditions of our tribe were stacked on the bookshelves,

and framed portraits of members of our tribe decorated

the walls of these rooms. When I was growing up, I

would often find my father or grandmother in one of the

rooms, my father reading a book and my grandmother

listening to ancient tribal music.

That room held everything I knew about being a
   39

Chickasaw, and unlike many Chickasaw, my family had
      40
moved away from Oklahoma all the way to Seattle.

---

35. The writer is considering revising the preceding sentence by deleting the phrase "to the ornately decorated capital of Tishomingo" (placing a period after the word *territory*). If the writer did this, the paragraph would primarily lose:
- **A.** information comparing the narrator's own journey to similar ones made by members of other tribes.
- **B.** details describing the destination of the people the narrator is traveling with.
- **C.** details that establish the time and place of the events of the essay.
- **D.** interesting but irrelevant information about the Chickasaw.

36.
- **F.** NO CHANGE
- **G.** pictures in which other Chickasaw were present
- **H.** pictures of other Chickasaw
- **J.** other Chickasaw whose pictures had been taken

37.
- **A.** NO CHANGE
- **B.** people who, walked along with me
- **C.** people, who walked along, with me
- **D.** people who walked along with me

38.
- **F.** NO CHANGE
- **G.** Some of those pictures had been reprinted in books my father and grandmother collected.
- **H.** My grandmother and father proudly displayed these pictures in their homes.
- **J.** Like other Chickasaw, my father and grandmother had each set aside a room in their own home to the tribe.

39.
- **A.** NO CHANGE
- **B.** Her rooms
- **C.** Those rooms
- **D.** This room

40.
- **F.** NO CHANGE
- **G.** Chickasaw unlike
- **H.** Chickasaw, unlike
- **J.** Chickasaw. Unlike

GO ON TO THE NEXT PAGE.

Once a year, the tribe held a Festival and Annual

Meeting that was always well attended.
         41

     Before they moved to Seattle, my grandmother and

father had always attended this event. However, the

tribe owned no land in Seattle on which a ceremonial

house could be built and Chickasaw ceremonies
                                  42

conducted. Since I had never been to Oklahoma, I had
  42

never been to a Chickasaw event or walked in our

territory. Still, I had never even known any other
         43

Chickasaw children. Finally, my father, grandmother,

and I all took a trip to participate in the Festival. As we

walked together through the open plain, hundreds of

crickets chirping softly from the grass. The insects
  44

accompanied our march like the spirits of our ancestors
                         45

singing to us on our way home.

41. Given that all of the choices are true, which one
provides information most relevant to the main
focus of this paragraph?
A. NO CHANGE
B. notable for its exquisite dancing.
C. in south central Oklahoma.
D. that lasted several days.

42. F. NO CHANGE
G. Chickasaw ceremonies were conducted there.
H. there were Chickasaw ceremonies conducted there.
J. the conducting of Chickasaw ceremonies.

43. A. NO CHANGE
B. Meanwhile
C. In fact,
D. On the other hand,

44. F. NO CHANGE
G. crickets, which chirped
H. crickets that chirped
J. crickets chirped

45. A. NO CHANGE
B. just as
C. as like
D. such as

PASSAGE IV

Topping the Washington Monument

During the midday hours of December 6, 1884,
                                      46

engineers and workers braced themselves for the days
  46   47
dangerous mission. Winds that rushed past the workers

at speeds of nearly 60 miles per hour threatened to
                                       48

46. F. NO CHANGE
G. 1884, and engineers
H. 1884. Engineers
J. 1884; engineers

47. A. NO CHANGE
B. days'
C. day's
D. days's

48. F. NO CHANGE
G. had been threatened
H. will have threatened
J. threatens

GO ON TO THE NEXT PAGE.

postpone <u>and delay</u> the capstone ceremony marking the
⁴⁹
placement of the capstone atop the Washington

Monument. 50

   Eighty-five years of fundraising and planning had

brought about this moment. In 1799, <u>attorney and</u>
⁵¹
<u>Congressman</u> John Marshall proposed a monument
⁵¹
to honor the young nation's Revolutionary War

hero and first president. 52 Architect Robert

<u>Mills, who planned</u> the monument that would
⁵³

memorialize Washington. <u>Meanwhile, the</u> monument
⁵⁴
would be in the form of a 500-foot obelisk made of

marble and topped with a 100-pound capstone of

aluminum.

   In 1861, construction on the monument was halted

because supplies and men were needed to fight the Civil

War. During the war, the monument stood only 176 feet

49.
A. NO CHANGE
B. to a later time
C. by delaying
D. OMIT the underlined portion

50. The writer is considering deleting the following from the preceding sentence:

> marking the placement of the capstone atop the Washington Monument.

If the writer were to delete this phrase, the essay would primarily lose:
F. a minor detail in the essay's opening paragraph.
G. an explanation of the term *capstone ceremony*.
H. the writer's opinion about the significance of the capstone ceremony.
J. an indication of the capstone ceremony's significance to the American people.

51.
A. NO CHANGE
B. attorney, and Congressman
C. attorney and Congressman,
D. attorney, and Congressman,

52. If the writer were to delete the preceding sentence, the paragraph would primarily lose:
F. an explanation of Washington's heroic acts of war.
G. details about what John Marshall thought the monument he envisioned should look like.
H. background information about why Washington was being honored with a monument.
J. biographical information about John Marshall.

53.
A. NO CHANGE
B. Mills, planner of
C. Mills planned
D. Mills creating

54.
F. NO CHANGE
G. Therefore, the
H. However, the
J. The

A

GO ON TO THE NEXT PAGE.

tall and the ground around it served as grazing land for

livestock used to feed the Union army. Fifteen years

passed before work <u>resumed</u> on the monument. The
₅₅

workers had the entire monument's history in their

minds during <u>they're attempt to place its</u> capstone.
₅₆

<u>The crowd cheered as, attached to the top of the</u>
₅₇
<u>monument, the capstone was hoisted up.</u> More than
₅₇

eight <u>decades and more than 80 years</u> of planning
₅₈

and building <u>come to a conclusion</u> and the Washington
₅₉
Monument was finally complete. 60

55. **A.** NO CHANGE
    B. started
    C. began
    D. restarted again

56. **F.** NO CHANGE
    G. they're attempt to place it's
    H. their attempt to place its
    J. their attempt to place it's

57. **A.** NO CHANGE
    B. As the crowd cheered, the capstone was hoisted up and attached to the top of the monument.
    C. As the crowd cheered, attached to the top of the monument, the capstone was hoisted up.
    D. The capstone was hoisted up as the crowd cheered and attached to the top of the monument.

58. **F.** NO CHANGE
    G. decades amounting to more than 80 years
    H. decades–over 80 years–
    J. decades

59. Which of the following alternatives would be LEAST acceptable in terms of the context of this sentence?
    A. reached completion,
    B. come to a halt,
    C. came to an end,
    D. ended

Question 60 asks about the essay as a whole.

60. Suppose the writer had intended to describe the entire process of designing and building the Washington Monument. Would this essay successfully fulfill the writer's goal?
    F. Yes, because it offers such details as the materials used to make the capstone and shaft of the monument.
    G. Yes, because it explains in detail each step in the design and construction of the monument.
    H. No, because it focuses primarily on one point in the development of the monument rather than on the entire process.
    J. No, because it is primarily a historical essay about the early stages in the development of the monument.

GO ON TO THE NEXT PAGE.

PASSAGE V

Why Lions Roar

Research by biologists and environmental scientists has found several reasons that lions roar. Lions, which live in groups called prides, are very social creatures that communicate with one another in many ways. Roaring,
₆₁

the sound most often associated with lions, perform
₆₂
several key functions within the pride.

One of these defense involves protecting the pride's
₆₃
land. When prides take large pieces of land and claim them as their own, they will roar to keep away intruders, those are usually other lions. This "No
₆₄

Trespassing" warning serves to keep the peace because
₆₅
it helps prevent competing prides from fighting over food or for mates.

Lions also roar to stay in contact with one another
₆₆
when members of a pride are separated by long distances. Like all large cats, lions have intense hearing,
₆₇
which makes it possible for them to hear other members of their pride from great distances. Frequently, everyday
₆₈

61. A. NO CHANGE
 B. Roaring
 C. Roaring:
 D. Roaring is

62. F. NO CHANGE
 G. perform,
 H. performs,
 J. performs

63. A. NO CHANGE
 B. One of these, defense,
 C. One of these being defense,
 D. One of these is defense and it

64. F. NO CHANGE
 G. most often these are
 H. and are typically
 J. usually

65. Which of the following alternatives to the underlined portion would be the LEAST acceptable?
 A. although
 B. in that
 C. since
 D. as

66. F. NO CHANGE
 G. It's also the case that roaring is employed
 H. In addition, roaring is a way
 J. Roaring is also used

67. A. NO CHANGE
 B. cunning
 C. acute
 D. vivid

68. F. NO CHANGE
 G. Quite regularly, everyday
 H. Many times, everyday
 J. Everyday

GO ON TO THE NEXT PAGE.

activities like hunting <u>call upon animals' sharp</u>
₆₉

<u>instincts;</u> in order to reunite, the pride members roar to
₆₉

find one another.

 Finally, lions use roars to attract potential mates.
 ₇₀

During mating season, males will try to attract females

from the pride by roaring, displaying their manes, <u>they</u>
₇₁

<u>rub</u> against females, and fighting one another. Often a
₇₁

male that does not belong to a pride will try to enter the

pride and mate with females inside the pride. When this

occurs, the <u>alpha or, dominant, male</u> instructs all the
₇₂

other males in the pride to roar toward the outsider.

<u>The outsider is scared during his preparation for the</u>
₇₃

<u>fight partly by the roaring.</u> The combined roaring of the
₇₃

males <u>make</u> the pride sound much larger than it
₇₄

actually is.

 Future research on lions will help us understand

more about the reasons they roar. What is already

<u>clear, is that</u> often the lion's roar is meant to be heard.
₇₅

Whether communicating with one another or

threatening intruders, lions roar to get attention.

69. Given that all of the choices are true, which is the best replacement for the underlined selection to provide a logical reason for the action described in the second clause of the sentence?
   A. NO CHANGE
   B. disperse a pride over large areas of land
   C. require the pride to travel some distance
   D. involve the entire pride.

70. F. NO CHANGE
    G. Nevertheless,
    H. Second,
    J. Thus,

71. A. NO CHANGE
    B. rubbing
    C. rubbed
    D. rub

72. F. NO CHANGE
    G. alpha, or dominant, male
    H. alpha or dominant male,
    J. alpha or, dominant male

73. A. NO CHANGE
    B. The purpose of the roaring is to help scare the outsider during his preparation for the fight.
    C. Fear in the outsider is raised, during preparation for the fight, by the roaring.
    D. The roaring helps scare the outsider during his preparation for the fight.

74. F. NO CHANGE
    G. have the effect of making
    H. are intended to make
    J. makes

75. A. NO CHANGE
    B. clear is that,
    C. clear is, that
    D. clear is that

END OF TEST.

STOP! DO NOT TURN THE PAGE UNTIL TOLD TO DO SO.

lesson B *Reading Practice Test 1*

The next step in your climb to the summit of test success is a Reading Practice Test.

Like the English Practice Test, this is a chance to practice skills that will be necessary on the actual test. It will also give you and your teacher a sense of your strengths and weaknesses so that you can better prepare for Test Day.

Like the real ACT Reading Test, the Reading Practice Test has 40 questions to be completed in a total of 35 minutes. The questions cover the same range of topics that you will see on Test Day, so that you may familiarize yourself with the subject matter of the test.

All of the questions are multiple choice. Use the Answer Sheet to mark each answer so you can become accustomed to doing so on Test Day.

If you finish all 40 problems before time is called, review your work.

B

DO NOT TURN THE PAGE UNTIL TOLD TO DO SO.

B

READING TEST

35 Minutes—40 Questions

DIRECTIONS: This test contains four passages, each followed by several questions. After reading each passage, select the best answer to each question and fill in the corresponding oval on your answer document. You may refer to the passages while answering the questions.

Passage I

PROSE FICTION: This passage is adapted from Nathaniel Hawthorne's short story "Rappaccini's Daughter."

Giovanni still found no better occupation than to look down into the garden beneath his window. From its appearance, he judged it one of those botanic gardens that were of an earlier date
5　in Padua than elsewhere in Italy or in the world. Or, not improbably, it might once have been the pleasure-place of an opulent family; for there was the ruin of a marble fountain in the center, sculptured with rare art, but so woefully shattered
10　that it was impossible to trace the original design from the chaos of remaining fragments. The water, however, continued to gush and sparkle into the sunbeams as cheerfully as ever. A little gurgling sound ascended to the young man's window,
15　and made him feel as if the fountain were an immortal spirit that sung its song unceasingly and without heeding the vicissitudes around it, while one century embodied it in marble and another scattered the perishable embellishments
20　on the soil. All about the pool into which the water subsided grew various plants that seemed to require a plentiful supply of moisture for the nourishment of gigantic leaves, and, in some instances, flowers gorgeously magnificent. There
25　was one shrub in particular, set in a marble vase in the midst of the pool, that bore a profusion of purple blossoms, each of which had the luster and richness of a gem; and the whole together made a show so resplendent that it seemed enough to
30　illuminate the garden, even had there been no sunshine. Every portion of the soil was peopled with plants and herbs, which, if less beautiful, still bore tokens of assiduous care, as if all had their individual virtues, known to the scientific mind
35　that fostered them. Some were placed in urns, rich with old carving, and others in common garden pots; some crept serpent-like along the ground or climbed on high, using whatever means of ascent was offered them. One plant had wreathed itself
40　round a statue of Vertumnus, which was thus quite veiled and shrouded in a drapery of hanging foliage, so happily arranged that it might have served a sculptor for a study.

While Giovanni stood at the window he
45　heard a rustling behind a screen of leaves, and became aware that a person was at work in the garden. His figure soon emerged into view, and showed itself to be that of no common laborer, but a tall, emaciated, sallow, and sickly-looking
50　man, dressed in a scholar's garb of black. He was beyond the middle term of life, with gray hair, a thin, gray beard, and a face singularly marked with intellect and cultivation, but which could never, even in his more youthful days, have
55　expressed much warmth of heart.

Nothing could exceed the intentness with which this scientific gardener examined every shrub that grew in his path: it seemed as if he were looking into their inmost nature, making
60　observations in regard to their creative essence, and discovering why one leaf grew in this shape and another in that, and why such and such flowers differed among themselves in hue and perfume. Nevertheless, in spite of this deep
65　intelligence on his part, there was no approach to intimacy between himself and these vegetable existences. On the contrary, he avoided their actual touch or the direct inhaling of their odors with a caution that impressed Giovanni most
70　disagreeably; for the man's demeanor was that of one walking among malignant influences, such as savage beasts, or deadly snakes, or evil spirits, which, should he allow them one moment of license, would wreak upon him some terrible
75　fatality. It was strangely frightful to the young man's imagination to see this air of insecurity in a person cultivating a garden, that most simple and innocent of human toils, and which had been alike the joy and labor of the unfallen parents
80　of the race. Was this garden, then, the Eden of the present world? And this man, with such a perception of harm in what his own hands caused to grow—was he the Adam?

The distrustful gardener, while plucking

GO ON TO THE NEXT PAGE.

85   away the dead leaves or pruning the too luxuriant growth of the shrubs, defended his hands with a pair of thick gloves. Nor were these his only armor. When, in his walk through the garden, he came to the magnificent plant that hung its purple
90   gems beside the marble fountain, he placed a kind of mask over his mouth and nostrils, as if all this beauty did but conceal a deadlier malice; but, finding his task still too dangerous, he drew back, removed the mask, and called loudly, but in
95   the infirm voice of a person affected with inward disease.

1. Of the plants mentioned in the passage, which of the following did Giovanni find to be the most exceptional?

   A. The plant wreathed around the statue
   B. The plant that crept along the ground
   C. The plant with the gigantic leaves
   D. The plant with the purple blossoms

2. In order to ensure that he is safe from the plants, the gardener:

   I.   handles them only indirectly.
   II.   avoids looking directly at them.
   III.   avoids breathing their odors.

   F. I and II only
   G. I and III only
   H. II and III only
   J. I, II, and III

3. It can reasonably be inferred from the passage that the gardener, as compared with Giovanni, is a:

   A. more religious man.
   B. less cautious man.
   C. more cautious man.
   D. less religious man.

4. Which of the following actions performed by the gardener disturbs Giovanni?

   I.   Indicating disregard or disapproval of the plants
   II.   Avoiding directly inhaling the odors of the plants
   III.   Looking at the inmost nature of the plants

   F. I only
   G. II only
   H. III only
   J. I and II only

5. As described in the third paragraph, the gardener's actions suggest that he is a man who:

   A. is very alert.
   B. knows all there is to know about plants.
   C. loves nature.
   D. resembles Adam.

6. The narrator suggests that the plant with "a profusion of purple blossoms" (lines 26-27) could:

   F. sprout gems.
   G. produce light.
   H. overrun the garden.
   J. grow very quickly.

7. The narrator takes the point of view of:

   A. a gardener.
   B. Giovanni.
   C. a scientist.
   D. an unknown third party.

8. When Giovanni questions whether the garden is "the Eden of the present world" and whether the gardener is Adam (lines 80–83), he is expressing his belief that the gardener:

   F. goes about his work with great care.
   G. has every reason to be distressed by the plants.
   H. should treat the plants with reverence.
   J. should not appear so afraid of the plants.

9. According to the passage, Giovanni characterizes the area beneath his window as a:

   A. botanic garden.
   B. center for rare art.
   C. place for people with plants.
   D. pleasure-place for the community.

10. In the third paragraph (lines 56–83), the author suggests that the gardener's relationship with the plants was partly characterized by:

   F. the gardener's impatience with the plants.
   G. the gardener's interest in understanding the plants.
   H. the gardener's desire to harm the plants.
   J. the gardener's anger toward the plants.

B

GO ON TO THE NEXT PAGE.

Passage II

SOCIAL SCIENCE: The following passage is excerpted from a magazine article discussing scientific research on traditional methods of predicting the timing and character of the Indian monsoon.

Can traditional rules of thumb provide accurate weather forecasts? Researchers in Junagadh, India, are trying to find out. Most farmers in the region grow one crop of peanuts
5 or castor per year. In a wet year, peanuts give the best returns, but if the rains are poor, the more drought-tolerant castor is a better bet. In April and May, before the monsoon comes, farmers decide what to plant, buy the seed, prepare the soil, and
10 hope for the best. An accurate forecast would be extremely helpful.

Little wonder, then, that observant farmers have devised traditional ways to predict the monsoon's timing and character. One such rule of
15 thumb involves the blooming of the Cassia fistula tree, which is common on roadsides in southern Gujarat. According to an old saying which has been documented as far back as the 8th century, the monsoon begins 45 days after C. fistula's
20 flowering peak. Since 1996, Purshottambhai Kanani, an agronomist at Gujarat Agricultural University, has been collecting data to test this rule. He records the flowering dates of trees all over the university's campus and plots a
25 distribution to work out when the flowering peak occurs. While not perfect, C. fistula has so far done an admirable job of predicting whether the monsoon will come early or late.

Similarly, with help from local farmers,
30 Dr. Kanani has been investigating a local belief regarding the direction of the wind on the day of Holi, a Hindu festival in spring. The wind direction at certain times on Holi is supposed to indicate the strength of the monsoon that year.
35 Wind from the north or west suggests a good monsoon, whereas wind from the east indicates drought. Each year before Holi, Dr. Kanani sends out postcards to over 400 farmers in Junagadh and neighbouring districts. The farmers note the wind
40 direction at the specified times, and then send the postcards back.

In years of average and above-average monsoons (1994, 1997, 1998, and 2001), the wind on Holi tended to come from the north and west.
45 In the drier years of 1995 and 1996, the majority of farmers reported wind from the east (Dr. Kanani did not conduct the study in 1999 and 2000). As with the C. fistula results, the predictions are not especially precise, but the trend is right.

50 Dr. Kanani first became interested in traditional methods in 1990, when an old saying attributed to a 10th-century sage named Bhadli—that a storm on a particular day meant the monsoon would come 72 days later—proved
55 strikingly correct. This prompted Dr. Kanani to collect other rules from old texts in Gujarati and Sanskrit.

Not all of his colleagues approve. Damaru Sahu, a meteorologist at Gujarat Agricultural
60 University and a researcher for India's director-general of meteorology, says that traditional methods are "OK as a hobby." But, he goes on, they cannot be relied upon, and "may not be applicable to this modern age." Yet Dr. Sahu concedes that
65 meteorological science has failed to provide a useful alternative to traditional methods. For the past 13 years, he notes, the director-general for meteorology has predicted "normal monsoons" for the country. Every year, the average rainfall
70 over the whole country is calculated, and this prediction is proved correct. But it is no use at all to farmers who want to know what will happen in their region.

Dr. Kanani hopes that his research will put
75 traditional methods on a proper scientific footing. He and his colleagues have even set up a sort of peer-review forum for traditional meteorology. Each spring, he hosts a conference for 100 local traditional forecasters, each of whom presents a
80 monsoon prediction with supporting evidence— the behaviour of a species of bird, strong flowering in a certain plant, or the prevailing wind direction that season. Dr. Kanani records these predictions and publishes them in the local press.

85 He has also started a non-governmental organization, the Varsha Vigyan Mandal, or Rain Science Association, which has over 400 members. Its vice-president, Dhansukh Shah, is a scientist at the National Directorate of Meteorology in Pune.
90 By involving such mainstream meteorologists as Dr. Shah in his work, Dr. Kanani hopes to bring his unusual research to the attention of national institutions. They could provide the funding for larger studies that could generate
95 results sufficiently robust to be published in peer-reviewed science journals.

GO ON TO THE NEXT PAGE.

ACT ADVANTAGE
ENGLISH & READING

11. According to the passage, all of the following traditional methods of weather prediction have been scientifically tested EXCEPT:

A. wind direction during the Hindi festival of Holi.

B. the behavior of certain bird species.

C. the flowering Cassia fistula trees.

D. a 10th-century prediction connecting storm activity to later monsoons.

12. When the author uses the phrase "useful alternative" (lines 65-66), she means that:

F. modern meteorology rarely provides an accurate forecast.

G. equipment needed for accurate forecasting is too expensive for many in India.

H. modern meteorology doesn't give as specific predictions as traditional methods do.

J. today's science cannot explain why traditional methods work so well.

13. The main purpose of the last three paragraphs (lines 58–96) is to:

A. discuss the efforts to gain acceptance for traditional weather prediction methods from a skeptical scientific community.

B. suggest that both traditional and scientific methods can coexist because they serve very different functions.

C. remind us that traditional methods have been around too long to be easily eclipsed by modern science.

D. introduce us to a general respect for ancient knowledge in the sciences.

14. The author's attitude toward traditional methods of weather forecasting may reasonably be described as:

F. curious as to their development.

G. cautious hopefulness that they are useful.

H. skeptical regarding their real scientific value.

J. regretful of the "fad" of interest in these methods.

15. Based on information in the passage, which of the discussed methods gives the most advanced prediction of monsoon arrival?

A. The behavior of the birds

B. The flowering of the C. fistula tree

C. The wind direction on Holi

D. Bhadli's prediction based on storms

16. The function of the second paragraph in relation to the passage as a whole is most likely to provide:

F. a reason that farmers need techniques to predict monsoons earlier.

G. examples of the inexact nature of predictions made from traditional methods.

H. an explanation of the ancient saying that the rest of the passage will examine.

J. an introduction to the modern research of traditional methods.

17. According to the passage, the purpose of Dr. Kanani's springtime conferences is to:

A. record the traditional methods of weather prediction before they disappear.

B. help gain acceptance for traditional methods in the academic community.

C. publish the methods in the local press.

D. facilitate the exchange of ideas between farmers from far-flung regions of India.

18. Based on the details from the passage, it can be inferred that the reason farmers rely on traditional methods to predict the weather is that:

F. traditional methods are more accessible to rural populations.

G. "normal" monsoons can still be very different from each other.

H. they need to anticipate the local conditions for the coming growing season.

J. traditional methods get the basic trends right.

19. The author uses the term "admirable job" (line 27) to indicate that:

A. the flowering of the C. fistula tree provides remarkably predictive data on the coming monsoon.

B. precision isn't everything.

C. predictions based on the peak of C. fistula's flowering do provide some reliable answers.

D. sometimes rules of thumb are better than complex formulas.

20. According to Damaru Sahu, traditional weather prediction:

F. can be curiously accurate.

G. has a defined place in meteorology.

H. is useful in some ways, despite its lack of scientific foundation.

J. appeals to an instinct different than the rational brain.

B

Passage III

HUMANITIES: The following passage is adapted from *A Guitar Serenade* by J. Miller Kelley III.

We know the guitar as the essence of modern rock and roll, but it is actually over 5,000 years old and evolved from other ancient stringed instruments. Stringed instruments exist in nearly
5　every civilization, but the guitar is distinguished by its flat-backed body with a separate neck. The musician plays the guitar by pressing the strings on the neck with one hand while plucking or strumming with the other.

10　The ancient origins of the guitar are obscure. The modern guitar seems to have come from Spain, but its earlier roots are open to debate. Archeologists have located ancient Central Asian tablets showing priests playing a possible ancestor
15　of the guitar. Early references to Persian stringed instruments refer to these as *tars*—a possible basis for the word *guitar*. The Greeks also played an instrument known as a *kithara*. Although the name strongly resembles our word *guitar*, the
20　*kithara* was more of a lyre, a type of ancient harp, than a proper guitar.

As Central Asians migrated to medieval Spain, they brought stringed instruments similar to the guitar with them, and these instruments
25　melded with local European instruments. During the Middle Ages, the lute, known as the *qitara* in Arabic, was popular in France and Germany. Traveling troubadours could carry their lutes with them and perform their tales while visiting royal
30　listeners. The lute was also perfect for chivalrous knights who wished to serenade their lady loves discretely.

The sound of the lute was too soft to be a true band instrument, however. Scholars also
35　theorize that the Spanish thought of the lute as an instrument of the Moorish conquerors or the lower classes. So the Spanish royalty and upper class favored a new instrument, known as the *vihuela*, which had the curved body and flat back
40　characteristic of the modern guitar.

By the late 18th century, Europeans developed the six-string classical guitar. The guitar became a respectable instrument for concerts, especially in Spain. Even in other countries that favored the
45　piano for important performances, composers were familiar with the guitar. For those who could not afford a piano or wanted a more convenient instrument, the guitar was perfect for composing. Carl Maria Von Weber, Rossini, Verdi, and Franz
50　Schubert wrote many of their pieces on guitars.

During the Victorian Era, the piano became the instrument of choice among the rising middle class. More families could now afford this large instrument and provide it the necessary parlor
55　space. Music in Western Europe and America was enjoyed in the privacy of the home. The invention of the automobile, however, was about to change all of that.

With the growing popularity of mass-
60　produced cars in the 1920s, Americans became more mobile. Teenagers, a growing demographic, wanted music they could take along with them. Part of the appeal of the guitar has always been its easy portability. Young suitors could hop in
65　their jalopies with their guitars and head over to the nearest women's college. America's love affairs with cars and guitars fed into each other. Think of how many rock odes to cars you have heard. Another advantage of the guitar is its ease
70　of play. Although it requires a real virtuoso to play solos, almost anyone can strum the few chords necessary to accompany a popular song. Guitars could provide ready entertainment at picnics and other gatherings. The serenading lover was back
75　in romantic fashion—now with wheels.

Although guitars steadily gained popularity, they really burst on the scene in the late 1950s and 1960s, as the baby boomers came of age. This generation created and admired guitar-playing
80　rock stars. Nylon strings, cheaper and easier to restring, replaced gut strings in 1946 and facilitated this guitar boom. Les Paul, Gibson, and Fender electrified the guitar to make it a fit weapon for the rock-and-roll revolution. The
85　singer-songwriter traveled from town to town to perform for screaming crowds of teenagers. Guitars now loudly howled the angst and protest of this new generation.

Today, guitars continue to evolve. The guitar
90　is still the instrument of choice for rock and roll and is featured in such diverse music genres as pop, classical, jazz, and reggae. During the last few decades, the rise of hip-hop and rap has crowned "beat" over guitar melody. What this means for the
95　guitar remains to be seen. The guitar has proved very resilient in its thousands of years of history. Only time will tell whether new tastes are a bridge or a coda for the long-lived guitar.

GO ON TO THE NEXT PAGE.

ACT ADVANTAGE
ENGLISH & READING

© 2007 Kaplan, Inc.

B

21. The passage suggests that the guitar became more popular than the piano after the 1920s because:

   A. the rise in availability of automobiles created demand for a portable instrument.
   B. the advent of mass production made guitars affordable for the middle class.
   C. the piano did not fit the sound of rock and roll, so a new instrument was needed.
   D. the invention of nylon made guitar strings cheaper and easier to replace.

22. The passage implies that the lute was "perfect for chivalrous knights...to serenade their lady loves discretely" (lines 30–32) because:

   F. troubadours introduced the lute to European courts.
   G. it was popular from Persia to France.
   H. its sound evoked the romance of the East.
   J. it was portable and had a subtle sound.

23. The main purpose of the passage is to:

   A. show the influence of technology on music.
   B. illustrate how music travels across cultures.
   C. discuss various precursors of the modern guitar.
   D. describe the history and popularity of the guitar.

24. According to the passage, the lute was:

   F. first played in ancient Greece.
   G. considered a noble instrument in Spain.
   H. called the *qitara* in Arabic.
   J. known for its robust sound.

25. Which of the following instruments is NOT mentioned as a direct ancestor of the modern guitar?

   A. The *vihuela* of Spain
   B. The *tar* of Persia
   C. The Moorish *qitara*
   D. The *kithara* of Greece

26. It can be inferred from the passage that the guitar's "roots are open to debate" (line 12) because:

   F. no examples of early guitars survived the Middle Ages.
   G. it is unclear whether either the *tar* or the *qitara* is an ancestor of the guitar.
   H. the history of the guitar was not well documented in Europe.
   J. evidence of early stringed instruments has been found in more than one place.

27. According to the passage, the earliest known predecessor of the guitar appeared in:

   A. Greece.
   B. Spain.
   C. Persia.
   D. France.

28. According to the passage, Les Paul's contribution to the history of music was:

   F. using nylon instead of gut for guitar strings.
   G. helping to create the electric guitar.
   H. popularizing the singer-songwriter.
   J. using the guitar in a range of genres.

29. According to the passage, which of the following contributed to the popularity of the guitar in the 20th century?

   I. Although difficult to master, guitar fundamentals are easy to learn.

   II. Composers such as Verdi and Schubert brought the instrument to prominence.

   III. The guitar is more portable than the piano and took music out of the parlor.

   A. I only
   B. I and III only
   C. II and III only
   D. I, II, and III

30. According to the passage, the development of the guitar could best be summarized by which of the following?

   F. Stringed instruments were carried from Asia to Europe, evolving as they crossed cultures.
   G. Spanish nobility needed a replacement for the lute; the modern guitar was the result.
   H. The guitar has been virtually unchanged since the Persian *tar* of 5,000 years ago.
   J. All changes were slight until the breakthrough of the electric guitar in 1946.

B

GO ON TO THE NEXT PAGE.

Passage IV

NATURAL SCIENCE: This passage is adapted from a Wikipedia.com entry on particle accelerators. It describes two different devices used to accelerate subatomic particles.

In linear accelerators, particles are accelerated in a straight line, with the target at the end of the line. Low energy accelerators such as cathode ray tubes and X-ray generators use a
5   single pair of electrodes with a DC voltage of a few thousand volts between them. In an X-ray generator, the target is one of the electrodes.

Higher energy accelerators use a linear array of plates to which an alternating high energy field
10 is applied. As the particles approach a plate, they are accelerated toward it by an opposite polarity charge applied to the plate. As they pass through a hole in the plate, the polarity is switched so that the plate now repels the particles, which are now
15 accelerated by it toward the next plate. Normally, a stream bunches particles that are accelerated, so a carefully controlled AC voltage is applied to each plate to repeat this for each bunch continuously.

As the particles approach the speed of light,
20 the switching rate of the electric fields becomes so high as to operate at microwave frequencies, and so microwave cavities are used in higher energy machines instead of simple plates. High energy linear accelerators are often called linacs.

25 Linear accelerators are very widely used—every cathode ray tube contains one, and they are also used to provide an initial low-energy kick to particles before they are injected into circular accelerators. They can also produce
30 proton beams, which can produce "proton–heavy" medical or research isotopes as opposed to the "neutron-heavy" ones made in reactors.

In circular accelerators, the accelerated particles move in a circle until they reach
35 sufficient levels of energy. The particle track is bent into a circle using dipole magnets. The advantage of circular accelerators over linacs is that components can be reused to accelerate the particles further, as the particle passes a
40 given point many times. However, they suffer a disadvantage in that the particles emit synchrotron radiation.

When any charged particle is accelerated, it emits electromagnetic radiation. As a particle
45 traveling in a circle is always accelerating towards the center of the circle, it continuously radiates. This has to be compensated for by some

of the energy used to power the accelerating electric fields, which makes circular accelerators
50 less efficient than linear ones. Some circular accelerators have been deliberately built to generate this radiation (called synchrotron light) as X-rays—for example, the Diamond Light Source being built at the Rutherford Appleton Laboratory
55 in England. High energy X-rays are useful for X-ray spectroscopy of proteins, for example.

Synchrotron radiation is more powerfully emitted by lighter particles, so these accelerators are invariably electron accelerators. Consequently,
60 particle physicists are increasingly using heavier particles such as protons in their accelerators to achieve higher levels of energy. The downside is that these particles are composites of quarks and gluons, which makes analyzing the results of their
65 interactions much more complicated.

The earliest circular accelerators were cyclotrons, invented in 1929 by Ernest O. Lawrence. Cyclotrons have a single pair of hollow "D"-shaped plates to accelerate the particles, and
70 a single dipole magnet to curve the track of the particles. The particles are injected in the center of the circular machine and spiral outwards toward the circumference.

Cyclotrons reach an energy limit because
75 of relativistic effects at high energies, whereby particles gain mass rather than speed. As the Special Theory of Relativity means that nothing can travel faster than the speed of light does in a vacuum, the particles in an accelerator normally
80 travel very close to the speed of light. In high energy accelerators, there is a diminishing return in speed as the particle approaches the speed of light. The effect of the energy injected using the electric fields is therefore to increase their mass
85 markedly, rather than their speed. Doubling the energy might increase the speed a fraction of a percent closer to that of light, but the main effect is to increase the relativistic mass of the particle.

Cyclotrons no longer accelerate electrons
90 when they have reached an energy of about 10 million electron volts. There are ways to compensate for this to some extent—namely the synchrocyclotron and the isochronous cyclotron. They are nevertheless useful for lower energy
95 applications.

To push the energies even higher—into billions of electron volts—it is necessary to use a synchrotron. This is an accelerator in which the particles are contained in a doughnut-shaped
100 tube, called a storage ring. The tube has many magnets distributed around it to focus the

GO ON TO THE NEXT PAGE.

particles and curve their track around the tube, and microwave cavities similarly distributed to accelerate them. The size of Lawrence's first cyclotron was a mere four inches in diameter. Fermilab now has a ring with a beam path of four miles.

105

31. The main idea of the passage is that:
- **A.** linear accelerators are more efficient than circular accelerators.
- **B.** particles in accelerators cannot travel at the speed of light.
- **C.** linear and circular accelerators have important, but different, uses.
- **D.** cyclotrons are a useful type of circular accelerator.

32. The passage states that magnets affect particles by:
- **F.** influencing the direction particles travel.
- **G.** creating curved particles.
- **H.** increasing the acceleration of particles.
- **J.** causing an increase in the particles' energy levels.

33. The passage states that which of the following causes an increase in particle mass?
- **A.** A particle reaching the speed of light
- **B.** Acceleration of a particle in a vacuum
- **C.** Using heavier particles
- **D.** Injecting energy using electric fields

34. As it is used in line 63, the word *quarks* most nearly refers to:
- **F.** objects made up of electrons.
- **G.** objects made up of radiation.
- **H.** components of protons.
- **J.** components of gluons.

35. Which of the following statements would the author most likely agree with?
- **A.** Linear accelerators are of limited use.
- **B.** Using particles such as protons in such experiments is not possible, since they are composites of quarks and gluons.
- **C.** Circular accelerators have improved little since Lawrence's first cyclotron.
- **D.** Depending on the desired result, both linear and circular accelerators are valuable tools.

36. According to the passage, which of the following CANNOT be a result of using a circular accelerator?
- **F.** Particles that emit electromagnetic radiation
- **G.** Reuse of components to accelerate particles
- **H.** Particles that emit synchrotron radiation
- **J.** An initial low kick of energy in particles

37. According to the passage, what is one effect of particles passing through the hole in the plate of higher energy accelerators?
- **A.** The mass of the particles increases.
- **B.** The charge of the particles changes.
- **C.** The particles lose energy.
- **D.** The particles are repelled and accelerated toward the next plate.

38. The passage suggests that the greatest difference between a cyclotron and a synchrotron is that:
- **F.** cyclotrons are not useful.
- **G.** synchrotrons accelerate particles in a circle.
- **H.** synchrotrons can overcome limitations that cyclotrons cannot.
- **J.** synchrotrons are capable of causing particles to curve more closely to the edge of the tube.

39. How does the information about the size of Lawrence's first cyclotron and the size of Fermilab's ring function in the passage?
- **A.** It suggests that, over time, there has been progress in improving the size and capabilities of particle accelerators.
- **B.** It proves that cyclotrons are important for particle acceleration because they were invented by Lawrence.
- **C.** It indicates that the inventors at Fermilab were more capable than Lawrence was.
- **D.** It emphasizes the difference between cyclotrons and synchrotrons.

40. What is the main idea of the ninth paragraph (lines 74–88)?
- **F.** Cyclotrons can accelerate particles to nearly the speed of light.
- **G.** As the speed of particles in an accelerator approaches the speed of light, they gain more mass than speed.
- **H.** The speed of particles diminishes when particles get close to the speed of light.
- **J.** Energy limits are reached in cyclotrons because the mass of the particles becomes too high.

B

END OF TEST.

STOP! DO NOT TURN THE PAGE UNTIL TOLD TO DO SO.

The Landscape of the Tests

ReKAP

Review the information in this unit. Then fill in the blanks with what you have learned.

1. On the ACT English Test, I will have _____45_____ minutes to answer _____75_____ questions.

2. On the ACT Reading Test, I will have _____35_____ minutes to answer _____40_____ questions.

3. All of the questions on the ACT English Test and ACT Reading Test are in a _____Multiple choice_____ format.

Know Where the Points Are

Each year, college admissions officers use ACT scores to compare applicants. The ACT test that is administered in any given year is never used again. How, then, can admissions officers compare their applicants' scores if the tests they took were not identical?

The answer is simple. The ACT is written to follow clearly defined specifications that are used each time a new test is created. The *ACT Advantage* program has been designed with those specifications in mind. Throughout the course of the program you will be exposed to the same content that will be on the actual ACT English and Reading Tests.

You will receive two sub-scores for the ACT Reading Test (Arts/ Literature and Social Studies/Sciences), and two sub-scores for the ACT English Test (Usage/Mechanics and Rhetorical Skills).

ACT English Test

Topic	# of Questions	Approximate Point Value
Grammar	12	5.8
Style	12	5.8
Sentence Structure	18	8.6
Punctuation	10	4.8
Writing Strategy	12	5.7
Organization	11	5.3
Total	**75**	**36**

ACT Reading Test

Topic	# of Questions	Point Value
Prose Fiction	10	9
Humanities	10	9
Social Studies	10	9
Natural Sciences	10	9
Total	**40**	**36**

Test-Taking Tips

You will learn strategies and methods throughout this program to help you succeed on Test Day. What follows are several tips that you can also use to your advantage.

Guessing

There is no penalty for incorrect answers on the ACT. Therefore, you should answer every question, even if you have to guess.

Answer the Easy Questions First

All of the questions on the ACT English Test and the ACT Reading Test are worth the same number of points. Don't spend too much time on any one question. If you get bogged down on one or two difficult questions, you might run out of time before you have a chance to answer some questions that may be relatively easy for you.

keep in mind

Place a "?" in the margin next to any questions you skip so you won't forget to return to them later.

Keep Track of Time and Leave Time to Check Your Work

Bring a watch in case your seat doesn't allow you a clear view of a clock. Check the time after every few questions. Be sure to pace yourself. Everyone makes simple mistakes once in a while. Plan ahead so you will have enough time to check your answers.

English Test Practice Unit 1

When your teacher tells you, carefully tear out this page.

1. Ⓐ Ⓑ Ⓒ Ⓓ   15. Ⓐ Ⓑ Ⓒ Ⓓ

2. Ⓕ Ⓖ Ⓗ Ⓙ

3. Ⓐ Ⓑ Ⓒ Ⓓ

4. Ⓕ Ⓖ Ⓗ Ⓙ

5. Ⓐ Ⓑ Ⓒ Ⓓ

6. Ⓕ Ⓖ Ⓗ Ⓙ

7. Ⓐ Ⓑ Ⓒ Ⓓ

8. Ⓕ Ⓖ Ⓗ Ⓙ

9. Ⓐ Ⓑ Ⓒ Ⓓ

10. Ⓕ Ⓖ Ⓗ Ⓙ

11. Ⓐ Ⓑ Ⓒ Ⓓ

12. Ⓕ Ⓖ Ⓗ Ⓙ

13. Ⓐ Ⓑ Ⓒ Ⓓ

14. Ⓕ Ⓖ Ⓗ Ⓙ

Reading Test Practice Unit 1

When your teacher tells you, carefully tear out this page.

1. Ⓐ Ⓑ Ⓒ Ⓓ

2. Ⓕ Ⓖ Ⓗ Ⓙ

3. Ⓐ Ⓑ Ⓒ Ⓓ

4. Ⓕ Ⓖ Ⓗ Ⓙ

5. Ⓐ Ⓑ Ⓒ Ⓓ

6. Ⓕ Ⓖ Ⓗ Ⓙ

7. Ⓐ Ⓑ Ⓒ Ⓓ

8. Ⓕ Ⓖ Ⓗ Ⓙ

9. Ⓐ Ⓑ Ⓒ Ⓓ

10. Ⓕ Ⓖ Ⓗ Ⓙ

C

ENGLISH TEST
9 Minutes—15 Questions

DIRECTIONS: In the passage that follows, certain words and phrases are underlined and numbered. In the right-hand column, you will find alternatives for the underlined part. In most cases, you are to choose the one that best expresses the idea, makes the statement appropriate for standard written English, or is worded most consistently with the style and tone of the passage as a whole. If you think the original version is best, choose "NO CHANGE." In some cases, you will find in the right-hand column a question about the underlined part. You are to choose the best answer to the question. For each question, choose the alternative you consider best and fill in the corresponding oval on your answer document. Read each passage through once before you begin to answer the questions that accompany it. For many of the questions, you must read several sentences beyond the question to determine the answer. Be sure that you have read far enough ahead each time you choose an alternative.

PASSAGE I

[1]

More than half of the world's <u>currently living plant</u>
₁
and animal species live in tropical rainforests. Four square miles of a Central American rainforest can be home to up to 1,500 different species of flowering plants, 700 species of trees, 400 species of birds, and 125 species of mammals. Of these mammals, the sloth is one of the most unusual.

[2]

Unlike most mammals, the sloth is usually upside down. A sloth does just about everything upside down, including sleeping, eating, mating, and giving birth. <u>Its' unique</u> anatomy allows the sloth to spend most of
₂
the time hanging from one tree branch or another, high in the canopy of a rainforest tree. About the size of a large domestic <u>cat, the</u> sloth hangs from its unusually
₃
long limbs and long hook-like claws.

1. **A.** NO CHANGE
   B. currently existing plant
   C. living plant
   D. plant

2. **F.** NO CHANGE
   G. It's unique
   H. Its unique
   J. Its uniquely

3. **A.** NO CHANGE
   B. cat; the
   C. cat. The
   D. cat, but the

GO ON TO THE NEXT PAGE.

Specially designed for limbs, the sloth's muscles seem
to cling to things.
                                                                    4

[3]

In fact, a sloth's limbs are so specific adapted to
                                               5
upside-down life that a sloth is essentially incapable

of walking on the ground. Instead, they must crawl or
                                          6
drag itself with its massive claws. This makes it easy

to see why the sloth rarely leaves its home in the trees.

Because it can not move swiftly on the ground, the sloth
7
is an excellent swimmer.

[4]

8 A sloth can hang upside down and, without

moving the rest of its body turn its face 180 degrees
                             9

so that it was looking at the ground. A sloth
            10
can rotate its forelimbs in all directions, so it

can easily reach the leaves that make up its diet.

The sloth can also roll itself up into a ball in order

to protect and defend itself from predators.
   11

4. F. NO CHANGE
    G. The sloth's muscles seem to cling to things
        for specially designed limbs.
    H. The muscles in a sloth's limbs seem to be
        specially designed for clinging to things.
    J. OMIT the underlined portion.

5. A. NO CHANGE
    B. so specific and
    C. so specified
    D. so specifically

6. F. NO CHANGE
    G. Instead, it
    H. However, they
    J. In addition, it

7. A. NO CHANGE
    B. Despite
    C. Similarly,
    D. Though

8. The author wants to insert a sentence here to help
    connect paragraph 3 and paragraph 4. Which
    of the following sentences would best serve that
    purpose?
    F. Of course, many other animals are also
        excellent swimmers.
    G. Another unique characteristic of the sloth is
        its flexibility.
    H. In addition to swimming, the sloth is an
        incredible climber.
    J. Flexibility is a trait that helps the sloth
        survive.

9. A. NO CHANGE
    B. body turns
    C. body, it has the capability of turning
    D. body, turn

10. F. NO CHANGE
    G. had been looking
    H. will have the ability to be looking
    J. can look

11. A. NO CHANGE
    B. protect, and defend itself
    C. protects itself
    D. protect itself

GO ON TO THE NEXT PAGE.

The howler monkey, another inhabitant of the
rainforest, is not as flexible as the sloth.
                                    12

[5]

The best defense a sloth has from predators such as jaguars and large snakes, though, is its camouflage. During the rainy season, a sloth's thick brown or gray fur is usually covered with a coat of blue-green algae.
                                                    13
Which helps it blend in with its forest surroundings.
13
Another type of camouflage is the sloth's incredibly slow movement: it often moves less than 100 feet during a 24-hour period.

[6]

It is this slow movement that earned the sloth its name. *Sloth* is also a word for laziness or an aversion to work. But even though it sleeps an average of 15 hours a day, the sloth isn't necessarily lazy. It just moves, upside down, at its own slow pace through its world of rainforest trees. 14

12. F. NO CHANGE
    G. Another inhabitant of the rainforest, the howler monkey, is not as flexible as the sloth.
    H. Not as flexible as the sloth is the howler monkey, another inhabitant of the rainforest.
    J. OMIT the underlined portion.

13. A. NO CHANGE
    B. algae, which
    C. algae, being that it
    D. algae

14. The author is considering deleting the last sentence of paragraph 6. This change would:
    F. diminish the amount of information provided about the habits of the sloth.
    G. make the ending of the passage more abrupt.
    H. emphasize the slothful nature of the sloth.
    J. make the tone of the essay more consistent.

Question 15 asks about the essay as a whole.

15. The author wants to insert the following description:

    An observer could easily be tricked into thinking that a sloth was just a pile of decaying leaves.

    What would be the most appropriate placement this sentence?
    A. After the last sentence of paragraph 1
    B. After the third sentence of paragraph 2
    C. Before the last sentence of paragraph 5
    D. Before the first sentence of paragraph 6

GO ON TO THE NEXT PAGE.

READING TEST

9 Minutes—10 Questions

DIRECTIONS: There is one passage in this test, followed by 10 questions. After reading the passage, choose the best answer to each question and fill in the corresponding oval on your answer document. You may refer to the passage as often as necessary.

Passage I

HUMANITIES: This passage is adapted from the article "Looking With: The Photography of Annie Leibovitz" by Camilla J. Hutton.

Photography is the most visible exception to male dominance in artistic endeavors. From Julia Margaret Cameron to Dorothea Lange to Cindy Sherman, some of the biggest names in
5 photography are those of women.

Scholars, art critics, and feminists provide different explanations for the rapid advances women have made in this genre. Some say that since the invention of photography coincided with
10 the inception of the women's suffrage movement, liberated women felt confident enough to join this new wide-open field, which was unfettered by centuries of academic tradition. Others suggest that female photographers can penetrate
15 deeper into society: women might be welcomed into homes where men would be perceived as intruders, and subjects of either gender might feel more comfortable revealing their innermost selves to a woman. Feminist art theory emphasizes the
20 power dynamic inherent in the gaze. In most mainstream art throughout history, the artist and the audience are male—women only appear as the object of the male gaze. A female photographer changes that paradigm, providing fresh insight
25 into her subject matter.

Annie Leibovitz is one of the world's most famous living photographers. In her long and varied and career, she has taken hundreds of iconic photographs of rock stars, actors,
30 politicians, and ordinary people. Leibovitz began as a painter, studying at the San Francisco Art Institute. After taking her first photographs, however, the camera's ability to capture the innermost life of a subject captivated her. When
35 she worked on a kibbutz in Israel as part of a work-study program, Leibovitz brought her camera with her. The photographs she took there became her first published pieces when they caught the eye of the art editor at *Rolling Stone* magazine.

40 Leibovitz became a celebrity photographer within a year. *Rolling Stone* provided her with regular assignments, and by 1973, the magazine promoted her to chief photographer. Leibovitz considered herself a photojournalist until a
45 critical early assignment photographing John Lennon. Her experience photographing Lennon—surprisingly open despite his extraordinary fame—changed her focus. Leibovitz became better known as a portrait photographer than as a
50 photojournalist. Unrestrained by the objectivity required for journalism, Leibovitz allowed her opinions to influence her photographs and infuse them with feeling.

Vivid colors and surprising, yet intimate,
55 poses became a trademark of Leibovitz's work. Both attributes are on full display in Leibovitz's memorable 1980 photograph of John Lennon and Yoko Ono: A naked Lennon curls in a fetal position around a fully-clothed Ono. Lennon seems to
60 draw sustenance from Ono, while she basks in his glorious, unconditional love. Hours later, Lennon was murdered outside his apartment building in New York City. Leibovitz's portrait, the last photograph of Lennon before his death, remains
65 the definitive image of the beloved musician.

Later assignments with *Vanity Fair* allowed Leibovitz access to a spectrum of celebrities. Instantly recognizable, Leibovitz became a star in her own right. Her remarkable photographs
70 and worldwide renown have won her advertising contracts with Gap, American Express, and Honda. Detractors have asserted that she is too commercial to be a fine artist, but Leibovitz's work endures.

75 In an extraordinary anthology, Leibovitz turned her keen eye on her gender. Entitled *Women*, Leibovitz's collection examines the astonishing, ordinary, transcendent, and mundane. According to critic Susan Sontag's
80 introduction, the assembled photographs address the "question" of women. What Leibovitz brings to her photographs is the "commanding notion of the sheer interestingness of the subject."

GO ON TO THE NEXT PAGE.

The photographs illustrate, challenge, and
85 deconstruct the stereotypes that society continues
to perpetuate. A Muslim woman shares the page
with showgirls, celebrities co-exist with coal
miners, and one woman is identified simply
as a victim of abuse. Although by no means
90 exhaustive, *Women* is perhaps the most candid
examination of the subject in recent times.
Whether it is Leibovitz's feminine identity, or her
own unique, sensitive powers of perception, she
moves beyond the traditional pattern of the gaze
95 and looks with, rather than at, the people in her
photographs.

1. The passage most fully supports which of the
following conclusions about Annie Leibovitz?
   A. Her photographs reflect the objectivity of a
      photojournalist.
   B. She will be remembered most for pursuing a
      sense of celebrity herself.
   C. Her portrait work has established her as a
      culturally significant photographer.
   D. Her most common theme is the exploration
      of women's roles in society.

2. According to the passage, Leibovitz is sometimes
criticized for her:
   F. subjectivity.
   G. strange poses.
   H. commercial achievements.
   J. tiresome examination of a single theme.

3. Which of the following methods does the author
utilize in developing the second paragraph?
   A. A presentation of factual data concerning
      feminist art
   B. A series of hypotheses explaining the unique
      abilities of women in photography
   C. A list of shortcomings found in the work of
      male photographers
   D. A historical account of art theory

4. The details in lines 46–53 ("Her experience...with
feeling.") are used to illustrate:
   F. the restrictions of photojournalism
      compared with portrait photography.
   G. the primary reason for Leibovitz's worldwide
      renown and popularity.
   H. the difficulty of Leibovitz's transition to
      portrait photography.
   J. the various challenges facing a celebrity
      photographer.

5. The author states that Leibovitz has moved past
"the traditional pattern" (line 94), is because her
photography:
   A. utilizes innovative color schemes.
   B. explores subjects who had previously not
      been photographed.
   C. represents a new interpretation of
      portraiture.
   D. focuses on the everyday lives of ordinary
      women.

6. The author's main point in the fifth paragraph is
that Leibovitz:
   F. was able to capture something amazing in
      her photography.
   G. was the last person to photograph John
      Lennon.
   H. considered Lennon and Ono her favorite
      subjects.
   J. shot the greatest photograph ever taken.

7. The author's primary intention in citing the
opinions of a critic (lines 79–83) is to:
   A. place Leibovitz's work in historical
      perspective.
   B. emphasize the broad critical acclaim
      Leibovitz enjoys.
   C. dispute the claim that Leibovitz is "too
      commercial."
   D. provide an analytical view of Leibovitz's
      skill.

8. The author offers the anthology, *Women*, as an
example of:
   F. contemporary art doubling as social
      activism.
   G. a group of photos with a single-minded
      theme.
   H. photography's ability to raise important
      social questions.
   J. the power of contrasting various subjects
      with each other.

9. According to the passage, which of the following
is not a possible explanation for the larger role
played by women in photography as opposed to
the other arts?
   A. A woman's ability to comfort an intimidated
      subject.
   B. The presence of institutionalized traditions.
   C. A historical confluence of artistic invention
      and social development.
   D. The difference between male and female
      perspectives.

GO ON TO THE NEXT PAGE.

10. The author's attitude towards Leibovitz's artistic development can best be described as:
    F. unimpressed.
    G. admiring.
    H. detached.
    J. scared.

END OF TEST.

STOP! DO NOT TURN THE PAGE UNTIL TOLD TO DO SO.

KAP Wrap

Think back to a test on which you did really well. What sort of information did you have about the test before you took it?

Now think back to a test you did not do well on. How would knowing about the test have helped you to prepare better?

Unit 2
ACT Reading I

Thinking KAP

Describe how you get ready for school every morning. What is your routine?
What steps do you follow every day?

Strategy Instruction

The 3-Step Method for ACT Reading Comprehension

In the Thinking KAP activity, you described a series of steps that you follow every day to meet the challenge of getting ready for your school day. In this unit, you will learn a series of steps to meet the challenge of the ACT Reading Test. You briefly saw the 3-Step Method for ACT Reading Comprehension in Unit 1. In this unit, you will learn how to perform each step of the method, beginning with the first.

Step 1: Read Actively

To get the most from each passage, you need to read actively.

Summarize Each Paragraph

The first part of Step 1 is to summarize each paragraph. Think of each summary statement as a headline—it pulls together the details from the paragraph into one central idea. It is important to record your summary statements. When you go to answer the questions, your notes will serve as a table of contents—they'll show you where to look for the answers.

Read the first paragraph of a passage about England's Sweet Track and review the summary statement.

> About 50 miles west of Stonehenge, buried in the peat bogs of the Somerset flatlands in southwestern England, lies the oldest road known to humanity. Dubbed the Sweet Track after its discoverer, Raymond Sweet, this painstakingly constructed 1,800-meter road dates back to the early Neolithic period, some 6,000 years ago. Thanks primarily to the overlying layer of acidic peat, which has kept the wood moist, inhibited the growth of decaying bacteria, and discouraged the curiosity of animal life, the road is remarkably well-preserved. Examination of its remains has provided extensive information about the people who constructed it.

Summary Statement: *S.T. is old, well preserved road; tells much about people who made it.*

On the ACT Reading Test, you can record your summary statements in the margins or in the spaces between paragraphs. Use abbreviations and phrases to save yourself time.

Try It Out!

Read the next five paragraphs of the passage about England's Sweet Track and record summary statements.

The design of the Sweet Track indicates that its builders possessed extraordinary engineering skills. In constructing the road, they first hammered pegs into the soil in the form of upright X's. They slid single rails beneath the pegs so that the rails rested firmly on the soft surface of the bog. Then they placed planks in the V-shaped space formed by the upper arms of the pegs. This method of construction—allowing the underlying rail to distribute the weight of the plank above and thereby prevent the pegs from sinking into the marsh—is remarkably sophisticated, testifying to a surprisingly advanced level of technology.

builders good skills

Summary Statement: *The S. T. builders used there own method of construction.*

Furthermore, in order to procure the materials for the road, several different types of trees were felled, debarked, and split. This suggests that the builders possessed high-quality tools and that they knew the differing properties of various roundwoods. It appears also that the builders were privy to the finer points of lumbering, since they maximized the amount of wood extracted from a given tree by slicing logs of large diameter radially and logs of small diameter tangentially.

good intelligent

Summary Statement: *different types of trees*

keep in mind

Don't just write down details. Write down what sums up the details.

Studies of the Sweet Track further indicate a high level of social organization among its builders. This is supported by the observation that the road seems to have been completed in a very short time; tree-ring analysis confirms that the components of the Sweet Track were probably all felled within a single year. Moreover, the fact that such an involved engineering effort could be orchestrated in the first place hints at a complex social structure.

social organization quick

Summary Statement: *Higher level*

Excavation of the Sweet Track has provided evidence that the people who built it comprised a community devoted to land cultivation. It appears that the road was built to serve as a footpath linking two islands—islands that provided sources of timber, cropland, and pastures for the community that settled the hills to the south.

Community

Summary Statement: _____

The quality of the pegs indicates that the workers knew to fell trees in a way to encourage the rapid growth of long, straight, rod-link shoots from the remaining stumps, to be used as pegs. This method, called coppicing, is the earliest known example of woodland management.

Summary Statement: *Coppicing equals*

A

Question the Author

The second part of Step 1 is to **Question the Author**. Understanding the content of a passage on the ACT is not sufficient. To answer questions about a passage on the ACT, you must also be able to identify the **main idea** and the **author's purpose**.

Question the Author	
Main Idea:	What does the author want me to know?
Author's Purpose:	Why does the author want me to know this?

Read the excerpt from a passage about engineering below and review the main idea and author's purpose.

> To reengineer anything—be it a straight pin or a Las Vegas resort—we first must understand failure. Failures provide incontrovertible proof that we have done something wrong. That is invaluable information. Imagine that the *Titanic* had not struck the iceberg on her maiden voyage. The example of that "unsinkable" ship would have emboldened shipbuilders to model larger and larger ocean liners after her. Eventually, the *Titanic*, or one of those derivative vessels, would probably have encountered an iceberg with obvious consequences. Thus, the failure of the *Titanic* contributed much more to the design of safe ocean liners than her success would have. That is the paradox of engineering—and reengineering.

Main Idea: *Failures like Titanic help improve reengineering.*

Author's Purpose: *to argue that failures can be more important than successes in engineering*

Try It Out!

Look back at your summary statements for "Sweet Track" on pages 52–53. Use Question the Author to identify the main idea and the author's purpose.

Main Idea: S.T. is old but had good skills people worked on it

Author's Purpose: _____

Try It Out!

Read the excerpt below adapted from Willa Cather's novel, *O Pioneers!*, which is set on the Nebraska prairie. Record summary statements and then use Question the Author to identify the main idea and the author's purpose.

> "I want you to see Emil, Carl. He is so different from the rest of us!"
>
> "How different?"
>
> "Oh, you'll see! I'm sure it was to have children like Emil, to give them a chance, that Father left Sweden."
>
> "Is he going to farm here with you?"
>
> "He shall do whatever he wants to," Alexandra declared. "He is going to have a real chance; that's what I've worked for!"

Summary Statement: _____

> Alexandra looked at Carl with her calm, deliberate eyes. "Why are you dissatisfied with yourself?" she asked earnestly.
>
> Her visitor winced and paused. "You see," he said, "measured by your standards here, I'm a failure. I couldn't buy even one of your cornfields. I've enjoyed many things in New York, but I've got nothing to show for it."
>
> "But you show for it yourself, Carl. I'd rather have had your freedom than my land."

Summary Statement: _____

keep in mind

Always read the introduction above the passage. It often contains the main idea or other helpful information about the passage.

> Carl shook his head mournfully. "Freedom so often means that one isn't needed anywhere. Here you have a background of your own; you would be missed. But in the cities there are thousands of rolling stones like me. We're all alike, paying exorbitant rent for a few square feet of space near the heart of things; we have no ties, we know nobody, we own nothing. When people die, they scarcely know where to bury them."

Summary Statement: _____

> Alexandra was silent. He knew that she understood what he meant. At last she said slowly, "And yet I would rather have Emil grow up like that than like his other brothers. We pay a high rent, too, though we pay differently. We grow hard and heavy. We don't move lightly and easily as you do, and our minds get stiff. If the world were no wider than my cornfields, I wouldn't feel that it was worthwhile to work. No, I would rather have Emil like you. I felt that as soon as you came."

Summary Statement: _____

Main Idea: _____

Author's Purpose: _____

A

The 3-Step Method for ACT Reading Comprehension

STEP 1: Read actively.

- **Summarize each paragraph.**

- **Question the Author.**

STEP 2: Examine the question stems.

- Identify the question type.

- Determine the correct strategy.

STEP 3: Answer the questions.

- Find the important information.

- Predict and eliminate.

Question the Author	
Main Idea:	What does the author want me to know?
Author's Purpose:	Why does the author want me to know this?

Read the text below and answer the following questions.

Passage I

NATURAL SCIENCE: This passage from a textbook about the solar system discusses research examining the possibility of life on Mars.

When the first of the two Viking Landers touched down on Martian soil on July 20, 1976, and began to send camera images back to Earth, the scientists at Jet Propulsion Laboratory could
5 not suppress a certain nervous anticipation, like people who hold tickets to a lottery they have a one-in-a-million chance of winning. The first photographs that arrived, however, did not contain any evidence of life. What was
10 revealed was merely a barren landscape littered with rocks and boulders. The view resembled nothing so much as a flat section of desert. In fact, the winning entry in a contest at J.P.L. for the photograph most accurately predicting what
15 Mars would look like was a snapshot taken from a particularly arid section of the Mojave Desert.

The scientists were soon ready to turn their attentions from visible life to microorganisms. The twin Viking Landers carried experiments
20 designed to detect organic compounds. Researchers thought it possible that life had developed on early Mars just as it is thought to have developed on Earth, through the gradual chemical evolution of complex organic molecules.
25 To detect biological activity, Martian soil samples were treated with various nutrients that would produce characteristic by-products if life forms were active in the soil. The results from all three experiments were inconclusive. In the
30 fourth experiment, a soil sample was heated to look for signs of organic material, but none were found—an unexpected result because scientists thought organic compounds from the steady bombardment of the Martian surface by
35 meteorites would be present.

The absence of organic materials, some scientists speculated, was the result of intense ultraviolet radiation penetrating the atmosphere of Mars and destroying organic compounds in the
40 soil. Although Mars' atmosphere was at one time rich in carbon dioxide and thus thick enough to protect its surface from the harmful rays of the sun, the carbon dioxide had gradually left the atmosphere and been converted into rocks. This
45 means that even if life had gotten a start on early Mars, it could not have survived the exposure to ultraviolet radiation when the atmosphere thinned. Mars never developed a protective layer of ozone as Earth did.

50 Despite the disappointing Viking results, there are those who still believe in the possibility of life on Mars. They point out that the Viking data cannot be considered the final word on Martian life because the two landers only sampled
55 limited—and uninteresting—sites. The Viking landing sites were not chosen for what they might tell of the planet's biology. They were chosen primarily because they appeared to be safe for landing a spacecraft. The landing sites were
60 on parts of the Martian plains that appeared relatively featureless from orbital photographs.

The type of terrain that these researchers suggest may be a possible hiding place for active life has an earthly parallel: the ice-free region of
65 southern Victoria Land, Antarctica, where the temperatures in some dry valleys average below zero. Organisms known as endoliths, a form of blue-green algae that has adapted to this harsh environment, were found living inside certain
70 translucent, porous rocks in these Antarctic valleys. The argument based on this discovery is that if life did exist on early Mars, it is possible that it escaped worsening conditions by similarly seeking refuge in rocks. Skeptics object, however,
75 that Mars in its present state is simply too dry, even compared with Antarctic valleys, to sustain any life whatsoever.

1. The main purpose of the passage is to:

   A. argue that life never existed on Mars.
   B. promote the idea that life almost certainly exists on other planets.
   C. discuss an attempt to find life on another planet.
   D. explain how life may have survived in rocks on Mars.

2. The main point of the second paragraph (lines 17–35) is that:

   F. scientists were disappointed by the inconclusive results of their experiments.

   G. theories about how life developed on Earth were shown to be flawed.

   H. there was no experimental confirmation that life exists on Mars.

   J. meteorite bombardment of the Martian surface is less constant than scientists had predicted.

A

Shared Practice

■ *Use Step 1 of the 3-Step Method for ACT Reading Comprehension for the passage and questions below.*

Passage II

HUMANITIES: The following passage is adapted from the article "A Colorful Haven: The Heidelberg Project," by Jan de los Santos (*The Kriwanek Press*, April 2003, Vol. 10, Issue 2, p. 96).

Detroit, known as the home of America's automobile industry and the birthplace of Motown music, earned its reputation as a prosperous and progressive city. Beginning in the
5 1950s, though, Detroit began to gain notoriety due to racial tension and crime. By the 1980s, it had become a symbol of urban decay. The 1967 riots, the closing of automobile factories, and other factors contributed to poverty. A middle-class
10 exodus from Detroit's inner city to the suburbs left abandoned buildings in its wake. In 1999, the city recorded over 16,000 empty houses.

The city lacked the funds to demolish the abandoned buildings, leaving them to become
15 magnets for drug dealers and other criminals. Detroit's adolescent residents became so disillusioned, in fact, that they immolated their own neighborhoods, setting bonfires throughout the city to show their seething fury. In the mid-
20 80s, arson became a tradition. The night before Halloween became known as "Devil's Night," and fires were set throughout the city. In an effort to rejuvenate the city, Detroit's leaders razed decayed buildings and instituted "Angel's Night"
25 patrols to combat the pre-Halloween bonfires. Despite these endeavors, Detroit lacked the tax base for a real urban renewal. Large portions of the city remained barren, and the crime rate remained among the worst in the nation.

30 Heidelberg, one of Detroit's blighted neighborhoods, lost 71 percent of its housing stock between 1960 and 2000, according to the Heidelberg Legal Counsel. One resident of the neighborhood, Tyree Guyton, decided he could
35 no longer stand it. He believed that the dark, gutted, and decayed buildings were more than just a reflection of Detroit's affliction—they were the rotten foundations on which these calamities were built. He thought that these uninspiring
40 surroundings created a cloud of despair that hovered over the remaining residents.

In 1986, Guyton took matters into his own hands. He—along with his wife and grandfather—applied found objects to the
45 facades of the buildings and constructed massive roadside sculptures. He created a multicolored wonderland out of the ramshackle houses, pockmarked streets, and vacant lots that formed the municipal landscape of Heidelberg. Beginning
50 with one city block and expanding throughout the neighborhood, Guyton took a place that others had given up on and infused it with vibrancy and hope. Art critics see the rhythms of jazz in Guyton's juxtapositions of vividly colored polka
55 dots, urban detritus, and contrasting stripes. Guyton derives his art—both his literal materials and his inspiration—from fellow city dwellers.

The Heidelberg Project strives to break the apathy that plagued the neighborhoods
60 by astonishing residents and visitors. The extraordinary art installations are completely accessible public art; all are welcome to enjoy the living sculptures for free and at all hours. The presence of viewers also helps to discourage some
65 of the criminal elements from remaining in the abandoned structures.

Guyton's project grew beyond the installations in Heidelberg. Cities like Mt. Vernon invited Guyton to rehabilitate parks and other public
70 spaces. Guyton also established an arts-education program at his old school, Bunche Elementary. Bunche students designed a garbage truck for the 2002 Detroit Thanksgiving Day Parade and a community arts center. As part of their work on
75 his projects, Guyton demands commitment and self-examination from these young artists.

Guyton's art is not all sunshine and polka dots. He has tackled controversial themes that many would prefer to avoid. One example,
80 nicknamed the Doll House, is dedicated to victims of child abuse. Guyton affixed mutilated and broken dolls to the structure's exterior to vividly illustrate the lives broken by neglect, maltreatment, and abuse. On another installation,
85 shoes embellished the facade of a derelict house, symbolizing the "soles/souls" of those lost to urban violence. By bringing harsh issues to the foreground, Guyton forces others to confront

90 these formidable realities. His art provides a
healing sense of social change.

Perhaps out of a desire to avoid these
controversial issues, critics campaigned to
dismantle the Heidelberg Project. Asserting
that the luridly colored facades were an eyesore
95 and that the materials constituted unhygienic
garbage, they filed complaints with the city.
The mayor may also have had another motive:
ultimately, the Heidelberg Project was a symbol
of his failure to lead Detroit into a renaissance.
100 Whatever the motivation, the city designated the
structures "illegal dump sites" and sent bulldozers
to annihilate most of Guyton's installations first in
1991 and again in 1999.

Despite attempts to destroy Guyton's vision,
105 the Heidelberg Project continues to grow. The
Heidelberg Legal Counsel went to court to defend
the project against demolition. Guyton persisted
and Heidelberg became the third largest tourist
attraction in Detroit. Possibly sensing a shift in
110 attitudes, Detroit's new administration began to
embrace Guyton and his efforts.

Perhaps Guyton's greatest triumph is that he
has forced people to acknowledge the dilemmas
of urban decay. Faced with an overwhelming
115 environment of despondency and desolation,
Guyton fought back with color, optimism,
and aspirations. His community is no longer
anonymous and invisible. Whether people adore
or despise Guyton's installations, at least they are
120 talking about Heidelberg.

1. According to the passage, "Devil's Night" became
a Detroit tradition during:

A. the early 1950s.
B. the late 1960s.
C. the mid-1980s.
D. the 1990s.

hint *In which paragraph is "Devil's Night" discussed?*

2. The primary purpose of this passage is to:

F. convince the reader that city efforts are essential to large-scale urban renewal.
G. explain how Guyton highlighted neighborhood problems while the city failed to do so.
H. describe the roots of Detroit's growing poverty and rising crime rates since 1950.
J. offer criticism of Guyton's work in relation to other contemporary installation art.

hint *Use Question the Author to identify the author's purpose.*

3. The passage suggests that before the 1950s, Detroit was known for its:

A. racial tension and crime.
B. prosperity and industry.
C. poverty and middle-class exodus.
D. installation art and color.

hint *Where do you find information about the history of Detroit?*

4. The purpose of the eighth paragraph (lines 91–103) is to:

F. question the motives of city government in destroying Guyton's work.
G. argue for greater funding for urban artwork in decayed neighborhoods.
H. discuss the themes of several Heidelberg installations.
J. illustrate the numerous hazards posed by the Heidelberg Project.

hint *Use your summary statements to help you answer the question.*

5. In the passage, the author indicates that each of the following is a reason the city wanted to bulldoze the Heidelberg Project EXCEPT:

   A. it was a lurid eyesore.
   B. it wanted to clear lots for renewal.
   C. it called attention to the city's failures.
   D. it was built of unhygienic garbage.

> **hint** *Use your summary statements to find the paragraph about the city's efforts to demolish the Heidelberg Project.*

6. The main idea of the passage is that:

   F. Guyton's art brought attention to one of Detroit's decayed neighborhoods.
   G. cities should take a more active role in regulating urban artwork.
   H. Detroit has been in a state of economic decline since the 1950s.
   J. colorful artwork can distract people from desolate environments.

> **hint** *Use Question the Author to identify the main idea.*

7. According to the passage, Tyree Guyton first began building art installations in:

   A. Bunche Elementary School.
   B. the neighborhood of Heidelberg.
   C. abandoned auto factories.
   D. the city of Mt. Vernon.

> **hint** *Use your summary statements to locate the correct paragraph for this question.*

8. The main idea of the first paragraph is that:

   F. artists like Guyton offer the best hope at private renewal for depressed communities.
   G. over the past 50 years, Detroit has been characterized by decay and loss of industry.
   H. with its loss of housing, Heidelberg is unusual in the otherwise prosperous Detroit.
   J. urban decline must be addressed through civic action rather than by individuals.

> **hint** *What does the author want me to know?*

A

KAP Wrap

Think about your favorite movie. What notes would you write about the movie to summarize it? What is the main idea? What was the screenwriter's purpose in writing the script?

A

Thinking KAP

Imagine that you are the coach of a professional sports team that is preparing for a big playoff game. How might you determine what your opponents are likely to do in the game? How could you use this information to improve your team's chances for success?

Strategy Instruction

Step 2: Examine the Question Stems

In the Thinking KAP activity, you put yourself in the shoes of a professional sports team coach anticipating a big game. A coach needs to identify the type of problem a team faces and develop a strategy to counter the opposing team. Step 2 of the 3-Step Method for ACT Reading Comprehension will help you determine the best strategy for each question you must answer on the ACT Reading Test.

The question stem is the part of the question that comes before the answer choices.

Identify the Question Type

The first part of Step 2 involves identifying the question type. Before you can identify the question type, you need to understand what the question is asking. Restating the question stem in your own words will ensure that you understand the question.

Try It Out!

Read each question stem below and restate it in your own words.

1.   The purpose of the passage is to convey the idea that:

    Restate: _____

    _____

2.   The author believes the sinking of the Titanic contributed more to the safety of ocean travel than its success would have because:

    Restate: _____

    _____

B

Two Categories of Questions: Broad and Narrow

The questions on the ACT Reading Test fall into two categories. Broad questions ask about the *whole passage*. Narrow questions ask about specific *parts of the passage*. Knowing if a question is a broad question or a narrow question will help you know where to look for the answers. To answer broad questions, you will use your summary statements, the main idea, and the author's purpose. To answer narrow questions, you will use your summary statements to help you locate relevant information in the passage.

Restate each question stem below in your own words and determine if it is broad or narrow.

1. The central purpose of the passage is to:

   Restate: _____

   _____

   Broad or narrow? _____

2. According to the passage, how long ago was the Sweet Track constructed?

   Restate: _____

   _____

   Broad or narrow? _____

The information you gathered during Step 1 will help you answer both broad and narrow questions.

Question Types

Once you determine if a question falls into the broad or narrow category, you can identify the specific question type. The table below lists the specific types of questions you will see on the ACT Reading Test.

ACT Reading Test Question Types

Broad Question Types	It asks you to:	Example
Inference (Broad) including **Main Idea** and **Author's Purpose**	deduce something about the whole passage not specifically stated by the author.	The passage suggests that Alexandra wants Emil to:
Writer's View	describe the author's attitude.	Her depiction of the conversation between Carl and Alexandra suggests that the author sympathizes with:

Narrow Question Types	It asks you to:	Example
Function	describe why the author does something in a specific part of the passage.	The question "Why are you dissatisfied with yourself?" (lines 8-9) helps establish that Alexandra:
Inference (Narrow)	deduce something about a part of the passage not specifically stated by the author.	Carl's comments in lines 10-12 ("You see … show for it.") suggest that he feels:
Detail	find specific information from the passage.	According to the passage, Carl has recently lived in which of the following cities?
Vocabulary-in-Context	define a word or a phrase as it is used in the passage.	As used in line 11, the word *standards* most nearly means:

keep in mind

Notice that inference questions come in two varieties—broad and narrow.

B

Read the questions below for the passage about England's Sweet Track on pages 52–53. Restate each question in your own words and determine if it is broad or narrow. Then identify the question type.

1.   Based on his discussion of the community that built the Sweet Track, which of the following statements would the author be most likely to make?

Restate: _____

_____

Broad or narrow? _____   **Question Type:** _____

2.   The author notes the use of tree-ring analysis in order to illustrate that:

Restate: _____

_____

Broad or narrow? _____   **Question Type:** _____

keep in mind

The more you know about the types of questions on the test, the more likely you are to be successful.

3.   According to the passage, how long ago was the Sweet Track constructed?

Restate: _____

_____

Broad or narrow? _____   **Question Type:** _____

4.   As used in line 22, the word *orchestrated* most nearly means:

Restate: _____

_____

Broad or narrow? _____   **Question Type:** _____

Determine the Correct Strategy

The second part of Step 2 is to determine the correct strategy for each question. Specific question types call for specific strategies. In Units 3 and 4, you will learn a strategy for each type of question on the ACT Reading Test.

B

The 3-Step Method for ACT Reading Comprehension

 STEP 1: Read actively.

- **Summarize each paragraph.**

- **Question the Author.**

 STEP 2: Examine the question stems.

- **Identify the question type.**

- **Determine the correct strategy.**

 STEP 3: Answer the questions.

- Find the important information.

- Predict and eliminate.

B

Read the text below and answer the following questions.

Passage I

NATURAL SCIENCE: This passage from a textbook about the solar system discusses research examining the possibility of life on Mars.

When the first of the two Viking Landers touched down on Martian soil on July 20, 1976, and began to send camera images back to Earth, the scientists at Jet Propulsion Laboratory could
5 not suppress a certain nervous anticipation, like people who hold tickets to a lottery they have a one-in-a-million chance of winning. The first photographs that arrived, however, did not contain any evidence of life. What was
10 revealed was merely a barren landscape littered with rocks and boulders. The view resembled nothing so much as a flat section of desert. In fact, the winning entry in a contest at J.P.L. for the photograph most accurately predicting what
15 Mars would look like was a snapshot taken from a particularly arid section of the Mojave Desert.

The scientists were soon ready to turn their attentions from visible life to microorganisms. The twin Viking Landers carried experiments
20 designed to detect organic compounds. Researchers thought it possible that life had developed on early Mars just as it is thought to have developed on Earth, through the gradual chemical evolution of complex organic molecules.
25 To detect biological activity, Martian soil samples were treated with various nutrients that would produce characteristic by-products if life forms were active in the soil. The results from all three experiments were inconclusive. In the
30 fourth experiment, a soil sample was heated to look for signs of organic material, but none were found—an unexpected result because scientists thought organic compounds from the steady bombardment of the Martian surface by
35 meteorites would be present.

The absence of organic materials, some scientists speculated, was the result of intense ultraviolet radiation penetrating the atmosphere of Mars and destroying organic compounds in the
40 soil. Although Mars' atmosphere was at one time rich in carbon dioxide and thus thick enough to protect its surface from the harmful rays of the sun, the carbon dioxide had gradually left the atmosphere and been converted into rocks. This
45 means that even if life had gotten a start on early Mars, it could not have survived the exposure to ultraviolet radiation when the atmosphere thinned. Mars never developed a protective layer of ozone as Earth did.

50 Despite the disappointing Viking results, there are those who still believe in the possibility of life on Mars. They point out that the Viking data cannot be considered the final word on Martian life because the two landers only sampled
55 limited—and uninteresting—sites. The Viking landing sites were not chosen for what they might tell of the planet's biology. They were chosen primarily because they appeared to be safe for landing a spacecraft. The landing sites were
60 on parts of the Martian plains that appeared relatively featureless from orbital photographs.

The type of terrain that these researchers suggest may be a possible hiding place for active life has an earthly parallel: the ice-free region of
65 southern Victoria Land, Antarctica, where the temperatures in some dry valleys average below zero. Organisms known as endoliths, a form of blue-green algae that has adapted to this harsh environment, were found living inside certain
70 translucent, porous rocks in these Antarctic valleys. The argument based on this discovery is that if life did exist on early Mars, it is possible that it escaped worsening conditions by similarly seeking refuge in rocks. Skeptics object, however,
75 that Mars in its present state is simply too dry, even compared with Antarctic valleys, to sustain any life whatsoever.

1. According to the passage, the surface of Mars most resembles:

   A. the ice valleys of Antarctica.
   B. a very dry section of a desert.
   C. that of Earth's moon.
   D. that of Earth, if it lacked its ozone layer.

Restate: _____

_____

Broad or narrow? _____

Question Type: _____

2. What is the main idea of the passage as a whole?

    F. The Viking Landers and the Jet Propulsion Laboratory were representative of the most advanced space travel technology in the 1970s.

    G. Experiments have confirmed that no life exists on Mars now, though scientists still debate whether life existed there in the past.

    H. The experiments run by each Viking Lander were the most scientifically advanced experiments available, even though their results were inconclusive.

    J. While no signs of life on Mars have yet been found, there is still debate over whether life might exist on that planet.

Restate: _____

_____

Broad or narrow? _____

Question Type: _____

B

Shared Practice

■ *Use Steps 1 and 2 of the 3-Step Method for ACT Reading Comprehension for the passage and questions below.*

Passage II

HUMANITIES: This passage is excerpted from the catalog of a museum exhibition on arms and armor. The passage provides examples of the connections between art and weaponry throughout the ages.

From the beginning, arms and art were essential and interrelated elements in the life of mankind. Weapons for the hunt, such as spears, throwing clubs, and bows and arrows, were
5 necessary tools in the daily struggle for survival. Art, meanwhile, seems to have begun primarily as hunting magic. By painting images of game animals on cave walls and carving them on spear-throwers and arrow-straighteners, hunters
10 attempted to use supernatural means to secure an abundant supply of meat and hides for food and clothing.

Since arms were literally a matter of life and death, either as weapons designed to kill or as
15 armor designed to protect from harm, it was crucial that they be constructed for maximum effect and with the greatest technical efficiency; in many cases, this process resulted in functional beauty. To further enhance the aesthetic and
20 ideological values of arms—and not least of all to emphasize their significance as status symbols for their owners—arms of all periods were embellished with a wide range of designs in every technique known to the decorative arts.

25 In classical antiquity, too, there was a close relationship between art and arms. The patron deity of the arts in ancient Greece, for instance, was Pallas Athena, who was represented as helmeted, armored, and carrying a shield and
30 a spear. Athena's weapons were of supernatural origin: she was born fully armed from the brow of Zeus.

Significantly, there was also one among the Olympian gods who worked with his hands at
35 a human craft, the divine smith Hephaestos—known as Vulcan to the Romans—who not only created dazzling jewelry for the goddesses but also manufactured impenetrable and splendidly decorated armor for the god of war Ares, or Mars,
40 as well as for the mortal hero Achilles.

Evidence of the artistry brought to weapons in ancient times is abundant. In *The Iliad*, Homer describes the shield of Achilles as a mirror of the world "in imperishable bronze, some tin, and
45 precious gold and silver." When Mycenae was excavated in 1875 by Heinrich Schliemann, he found swords and daggers decorated with superb multicolored inlays in the technique vividly described by Homer. They were of such artistic
50 finesse that they would even have met with the approval of Hephaestos.

Under the influence of Christianity, during the so-called Dark Ages, the idea of the divine craftsman was transformed into a human figure:
55 the legendary Wayland the Smith. Wayland worked in gold as well as in steel, fashioning jewels so temptingly beautiful as to sway the virtue of princesses and forging sword blades painstakingly wrought from interwoven strands of
60 iron and steel. The craft of the smith was believed to hold a powerful magic, and the prestige of even the greatest of Celtic or Germanic heroes was enhanced if they were apprenticed to smiths.

For centuries, master craftsmen remained
65 nameless, but when awakening artistic self-esteem in the Renaissance let artists step out of the shadows of anonymity, the greatest names such as Leonardo da Vinci, Hans Holbein, Albrecht Durer, and Benvenuto Cellini, were
70 found quite matter-of-factly among those of designers and manufacturers of arms.

1. According to the passage, art most likely began:
    A. as a means of obtaining clothing.
    B. mainly as hunting magic.
    C. during the Renaissance.
    D. in classical antiquity.

    hint *What paragraph discusses the origins of art and armsmaking?*

2. The central purpose of the passage is to:
    F. compare the relative importance of art to that of armsmaking in various eras.
    G. describe the high level of artistry brought to armsmaking throughout history.
    H. show how the influence of Christianity affected the practice of armsmaking.
    J. analyze the interplay between the Renaissance ideals of beauty and function in the design of arms.

    hint *Use Question the Author to identify the author's (central) purpose.*

3. Which of the following is NOT used in the passage as an example of the interplay between artistry and weaponry?
    A. Images of game animals carved into spear-throwers
    B. Homer's description of Achilles' shield
    C. The work of Heinrich Schliemann
    D. The work of Wayland the Smith

    hint *Look at all of the answer choices to find the one that is correct.*

B

4. As it is used in line 10, the word *secure* most nearly means:

    F.   create.
    G.   make safe.
    H.   obtain.
    J.   guard.

hint ▷ *Find the important information by reading the whole sentence in which this word appears.*

5. In the second paragraph (lines 13-24), the author states that arms were embellished as a way of:

    A.   lending legitimacy to the causes for which wars were fought.
    B.   distinguishing them from purely ceremonial objects.
    C.   enhancing their effectiveness in battle.
    D.   suggesting the importance of those who possessed them.

hint ▷ *Read the whole sentence from this paragraph that discusses decorating arms.*

6. Information in the passage suggests that the author regards Wayland the Smith as:

    F.   a figure whose work stands in stark contrast to that of the divine craftsmen of ancient lore.
    G.   a figure of legend, one who embodied the ideal of skilled craftsmanship.
    H.   an exception to the rule of the armorer as a creator of useful yet decorative objects.
    J.   a figure who was symbolic of the decline in status of armsmaking in the Dark Ages.

hint ▷ *Compare the characterization of Wayland the Smith in the second to last paragraph to the characterization of other legendary arms-makers earlier in the passage.*

B

7. According to the passage, which deity did the ancient Greeks believe was an armsmaker?

    A. Pallas Athena
    B. Zeus
    C. Hephaestos
    D. Ares

> **hint** ▷ *Use your summary statements to locate the important information.*

8. The main point of the last paragraph (lines 64-71) is that during the Renaissance:

    F. great artists generally shunned the creation of arms.
    G. most master arms-makers were more concerned with appearance than with function.
    H. great artists demanded anonymity when they turned their skills to arms-making.
    J. some of the greatest and well-known artists were also arms-makers.

> **hint** ▷ *Refer to your summary statements for help answering paragraph-level questions.*

B

KAP Wrap

Think back to your favorite movie again. Imagine that you could interview the writer or director of the movie. What broad questions would you ask the writer or director of the movie? What narrow questions would you ask?

B

Answering the Questions

ReKAP

Review the strategies from Lessons A and B. Then fill in the blanks to show what you have learned.

1. The 3-Step Method for ACT Reading Comprehension:

    Step 1: Read _____.

    *   _____ each paragraph.
    *   Question the _____.

    Step 2: Examine the _____ stems.

    *   Identify the question _____.
    *   Determine the correct _____.

    Step 3: Answer the questions.

    *   Find the important information.
    *   Predict and eliminate.

2. Question the Author:

    *   Main _____: _____ does the author want me to know?
    *   _____ Purpose: _____ does the author want me to know this?

Strategy Instruction

Step 3: Answer the Questions

Once you have completed Steps 1 and 2 of the 3-Step Method for ACT Reading Comprehension, you are ready to answer the questions.

Find the Important Information

You will learn more about how to find the important information for specific question types in Units 3 and 4.

The first part of Step 3 is to find the important information in the passage. Important information is what you need to answer the questions. Rely on your notes to quickly find the important information. Use the summary statements that you wrote for each paragraph to locate the information you need to answer each question.

Try It Out!

Look at the questions below and refer back to the passage about England's Sweet Track on pages 52–53. For each question, use your summary statements to find the paragraph that is most likely to contain the important information.

1. The author notes the use of tree-ring analysis in order to illustrate that:

   Based on my summary statements, the answer to this question will be found in paragraph _____.

2. According to the passage, how long ago was the Sweet Track constructed?

   Based on my summary statements, the answer to this question will be found in paragraph _____.

Predict and Eliminate

The last part of Step 3 is to predict and eliminate. By using **Predicting** and **Eliminating**, you will avoid being tricked by distracting wrong answer choices.

Predicting
• Use the important information to predict an answer.   • Find the answer choice that most closely matches your prediction.

Look at the questions below and refer back to the passage about England's Sweet Track on pages 52–53. Use Predicting to answer each question.

When you make a prediction, cover the answer choices with your hand to prevent yourself from being distracted by incorrect answer choices.

1.   The author notes the use of tree-ring analysis in order to illustrate that:

   Prediction: *The Sweet Track was built quickly, showing the social organization of the builders.*

   A.   tree-ring analysis techniques have improved drastically in the past 20 years.
   B.   the Sweet Track was constructed quickly.
   C.   Sweet's reconstruction of the Sweet Track was inaccurate.
   D.   the builders of the Sweet Track used sophisticated tools.

2.   According to the passage, how long ago was the Sweet Track constructed?

   Prediction: _____

   _____

   F.   50 years
   G.   1,800 years
   H.   1,970 years
   J.   6,000 years

Eliminating

For some questions, you will not be able to find a match for your prediction—your prediction may be incorrect, or it may simply be worded differently from the correct answer choice. For other questions, there will not be enough information in the question stem to allow you to make a prediction. In both of these situations, use Eliminating to determine the correct answer.

Even if you eliminate only one choice, you increase your odds of selecting the correct answer.

Eliminating

Eliminate answer choices in the categories below.

- **Out of Scope**—These choices are unrelated—or only weakly related—to the passage.

- **Extreme**—These choices make sweeping statements and use extreme language like "always" or "never."

- **Distortion**—These choices take details from the passage and twist them to change their meaning.

- **Misused Detail**—These choices use details from the passage but are unrelated to the question.

Try It Out!

Look at the question below for which the prediction is incorrect. Refer back to the passage about England's Sweet Track on pages 52–53. Use Eliminating and your notes to determine the correct answer.

1. The author notes the use of tree-ring analysis in order to illustrate that:

   Prediction: _the road is at least 6,000 years old._

   A. tree-ring analysis techniques have improved drastically in the past 20 years.
      Eliminate? _yes_   **Category:** _____

   B. the Sweet Track was constructed quickly.
      Eliminate? _no_   **Category:** _(correct)_

   C. Sweet's reconstruction of the Sweet Track was inaccurate.
      Eliminate? _yes_   **Category:** _____

   D. the builders of the Sweet Track used sophisticated tools.
      Eliminate? _yes_   **Category:** _____

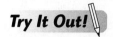

Try It Out!

Look at the questions below for which it is not possible to make predictions. Refer back to the passage about England's Sweet Track on pages 52–53. Use Eliminating and your notes to determine the correct answer to each question.

1. Which of the following statements would the author be most likely to make?

   A. The builders' methods were critical to ensuring the preservation of the Sweet Track.

   Eliminate? _____ **Category:** _____

   B. The society that built the Sweet Track was the most advanced society of the Neolithic period.

   Eliminate? _____ **Category:** _____

   C. The builders of the Sweet Track were more skilled than many archaeologists had expected.

   Eliminate? _____ **Category:** _____

   D. The society that built the Sweet Track did not display skill in woodland management.

   Eliminate? _____ **Category:** _____

keep in mind

If you find yourself unable to predict the correct answer, eliminate your way to the right answer.

2. All of the following are discussed as design features of the Sweet Track EXCEPT:

   F. pegs that were hammered into the soil in a specific form.

   Eliminate? _____ **Category:** _____

   G. planks that had their weight evenly distributed onto an underlying rail.

   Eliminate? _____ **Category:** _____

   H. logs that were sliced radially to prevent them from sinking into the marsh.

   Eliminate? _____ **Category:** _____

   J. rails that rested firmly on the bog, despite its soft surface.

   Eliminate? _____ **Category:** _____

Test Practice Unit 2

When your teacher tells you, carefully tear out this page.

1. Ⓐ Ⓑ Ⓒ Ⓓ   15. Ⓐ Ⓑ Ⓒ Ⓓ

2. Ⓕ Ⓖ Ⓗ Ⓙ   16. Ⓕ Ⓖ Ⓗ Ⓙ

3. Ⓐ Ⓑ Ⓒ Ⓓ   17. Ⓐ Ⓑ Ⓒ Ⓓ

4. Ⓕ Ⓖ Ⓗ Ⓙ   18. Ⓕ Ⓖ Ⓗ Ⓙ

5. Ⓐ Ⓑ Ⓒ Ⓓ   19. Ⓐ Ⓑ Ⓒ Ⓓ

6. Ⓕ Ⓖ Ⓗ Ⓙ   20. Ⓕ Ⓖ Ⓗ Ⓙ

7. Ⓐ Ⓑ Ⓒ Ⓓ

8. Ⓕ Ⓖ Ⓗ Ⓙ

9. Ⓐ Ⓑ Ⓒ Ⓓ

10. Ⓕ Ⓖ Ⓗ Ⓙ

11. Ⓐ Ⓑ Ⓒ Ⓓ

12. Ⓕ Ⓖ Ⓗ Ⓙ

13. Ⓐ Ⓑ Ⓒ Ⓓ

14. Ⓕ Ⓖ Ⓗ Ⓙ

C

DO NOT TURN THE PAGE UNTIL TOLD TO DO SO.

C

READING TEST

18 Minutes—20 Questions

DIRECTIONS: There are two passages in this test. Each passage is followed by several questions. After reading a passage, choose the best answer to each question and fill in the corresponding oval on your answer document. You may refer to the passages as often as necessary.

Passage I

SOCIAL SCIENCE: The following passage is excerpted from "Nonviolence: A Force More Powerful than Electricity" by Peter M. Loveless. The passage discusses how nonviolent methods can effect political change.

In 1936, Mohandas Gandhi was asked if nonviolent resistance was a form of direct action. "It is not one form," he answered. "It is the only form....It is the greatest...force in the world....It is
[5] a force which is more positive than electricity, and more powerful than even ether."

Nonviolence is a political force that has helped shape history. In many cases it receives less attention than violent conflict such as war
[10] or guerrilla activity. Yet it has often produced momentous change. Governments as entrenched as South Africa's apartheid government, the British occupation of India, and communist Poland have crumbled in the face of ordinary,
[15] unarmed people.

How is it possible for people to bring about such change when confronting powerful opponents? There are various factors that contribute to the success of nonviolence.

[20] First, it is important to understand how governments rule. Political power involves a relationship between the rulers and the workers. Local governments, schools, and businesses rely on the cooperation of the people to run smoothly.
[25] Even the most rigid states depend on this cooperation, although they may secure it through invisible forces such as fear or loyalty.

Sometimes people in a society are willing to obey the government due to a sense of
[30] helplessness or anxiety. Rulers can then behave as they wish. Subjects may withdraw their consent to be governed, however, and this can lead to the disintegration of power.

If there is widespread disobedience in a
[35] society, rulers will often inflict punishments. Maintaining control in this way requires that some citizens—often a police force or army willing to crush resistance—remain loyal to the government. In many cases, however, people
[40] refuse to give in to this kind of force.

Another important factor in nonviolence is the number of people willing to take action. Once a campaign of disobedience becomes widespread, it gains momentum and can become a significant
[45] force. As more people become involved in disobedience, it becomes harder for a government to control them with violence or imprisonment.

As author Gene Sharp writes, "The theory that power derives from violence, and that victory
[50] necessarily goes to the side with the greater capacity for violence, is false." To attain victory through nonviolence, however, people must understand the methods that are at their disposal. These tools can be divided roughly into three
[55] classes.

The first kind is symbolic or persuasive action. Protest marches, vigils, speeches, posters, banners, and the like may be used to gain support for a cause.

[60] Another method is refusal to cooperate—a passive, but powerful, form of resistance. When citizens disagree with a law, they may disobey it. Workers may go on strike. This happened when Lech Walesa led the Polish people out of the grasp
[65] of Soviet control in the 1980s. By bringing an economy to its knees, strikes can result in the total collapse of a regime. Similarly, people can join boycotts or refuse to pay taxes, and government officials, police, and soldiers can all disobey
[70] orders. In the end, the entire system that props up a ruler's power can be taken apart. Then the ruler is no more powerful than any other individual.

The third category of nonviolent action is intervention. People may intervene in order to
[75] disrupt a situation that they think is causing

GO ON TO THE NEXT PAGE.

harm. Methods include sit-ins and peaceful direct action. People may act in ways that they know will lead to their imprisonment, which in turn focuses negative publicity on their opponents. One famous
80 example of this occurred in 1955 in Montgomery, Alabama, when Rosa Parks refused to give up her seat on a bus to a white passenger.

It is often assumed that nonviolence methods take longer to succeed than violent approaches.
85 In fact, the reverse may be true; in some cases, nonviolence has brought about change in a matter of weeks or days.

As Leo Tolstoy wrote, "Violence can never destroy what is accepted by public opinion.
90 On the contrary, public opinion need only be diametrically opposed to violence to destroy its every action."

Once a path of nonviolence is chosen, it is crucial to stick to that path. To shift to the use of
95 violence is to adopt the tools of the oppressive regime. The use of violence can dissuade ordinary people from supporting a cause. Valuable allies may turn away. And, in the face of a heavily armed opponent, violence is unlikely to succeed. In
100 contrast, nonviolent resistance has been described as "political jujitsu." Nonviolence uses the force and weight of an opposing regime against itself in order to bring about the regime's defeat.

1. As it is used in line 44, the word *momentum* most nearly means:
- **A.** power.
- **B.** time.
- **C.** involvement.
- **D.** adherence.

2. The quote by Tolstoy (lines 88–92) can best be paraphrased as:
- **F.** "An individual can be intimidated by violence, but the public cannot."
- **G.** "Violence will always run counter to public opinion."
- **H.** "Violent actions will never succeed without popular consent."
- **J.** "Violence cannot sway public opinion, but opinion can disarm violence."

3. The passage suggests that violent conflict may be perceived by some as more effective than nonviolent resistance because:
- **A.** years have passed since Gandhi brought recognition to nonviolence.
- **B.** violence and guerrilla action often receive more attention.
- **C.** while causing greater suffering, violent resistance is usually faster.
- **D.** a violent victory is more decisive than a nonviolent victory.

4. According to the passage, which of the following is NOT a tool of nonviolent resistance?
- **F.** Refusal to cooperate
- **G.** Intervention
- **H.** Symbolic action
- **J.** Diametric opposition

5. According to the passage, nonviolent resistance is called "political jujitsu" (line 101) because jujitsu is a martial art that:
- **A.** causes incapacitation without doing real harm.
- **B.** uses the strength of opponents against themselves.
- **C.** centers more on self-discipline than on combat.
- **D.** has frequently been used in guerrilla warfare.

6. It is most reasonable to infer that the author of the passage believes that:
- **F.** the media should give nonviolence and guerrilla actions equal attention.
- **G.** in some situations, violence is the most direct route to change.
- **H.** nonviolence is a powerful tool that enables ordinary people to change history.
- **J.** to succeed, nonviolence requires a strong leader like Gandhi or Parks.

7. According to the passage, if a group shifts from the path of nonviolent resistance to a course of violence, it can expect to fail because:
- **A.** it will lose support from ordinary people.
- **B.** too much energy will be wasted in changing tactics.
- **C.** public opinion never favors guerrilla resistance.
- **D.** violence is rarely able to achieve political goals.

GO ON TO THE NEXT PAGE.

8. The main purpose of the passage is to:
   F. discuss the mechanisms and powerful outcomes of nonviolence.
   G. examine the three primary tools of nonviolent resistance.
   H. explain the relationship between governments and their subjects.
   J. give case studies of several famous examples of nonviolence.

9. The main idea of the passage is that:
   A. governments require the cooperation of the people in order to rule.
   B. against powerful opponents, nonviolence is more effective than violence.
   C. nonviolence often takes longer to achieve results than violent resistance.
   D. while nonviolence is effective, violence often brings more attention to a cause.

10. The main point of the fourth paragraph (lines 20–27) is that:
   F. governments cannot rule effectively without the consent of the people.
   G. cooperation is not needed by federal, colonial, or other non-local governments.
   H. rigid states gain cooperation through intimidation and patriotism.
   J. by virtue of their size, all states possess a degree of absolute institutional power.

Passage II

NATURAL SCIENCE: The following passage appeared in *Planets* magazine as "Titanic Journey" by Emilio Vargas (© Planets, Inc., 2005).

On December 25, 2004, a tiny probe hardly larger than a family car was released in space. Three weeks later, in the most distant landing ever made by a human-built spacecraft, it descended
5 by parachute onto the surface of Titan. Scientists cheered as it beamed back to Earth an array of images and sound recordings of one of the solar system's most mysterious bodies.

The largest of Saturn's 47 moons, Titan has
10 long intrigued scientists. Larger than Mercury, it is the second-largest moon in the solar system, after Jupiter's moon, Ganymede. More significantly though, Titan is the only moon in the solar system to harbor an atmosphere. It is surrounded by a
15 thick, orange-brown layer of nitrogen, methane, and other organic compounds. Titan's atmosphere is thought to be similar to the atmosphere of Earth billions of years ago, when primeval life began. As a result, it promises to reveal much about how
20 Earth was formed and how life emerged on our planet.

On Earth, the presence of nitrogen and methane would be signs of life. Titan, however, is far too cold—a chilly minus 289°F (minus
25 178°C)—for water to appear in liquid form. Without liquid water, no known life form can exist. Yet scientists are curious about the presence of organic compounds on Titan.

Organic compounds form when sunlight
30 destroys methane. On Earth, methane is continuously re-supplied by life—it is released from peat bogs, rice paddies, and cattle and other farm animals. Yet, if we rule out the presence of life forms on Titan, what is the source of methane
35 and organic compounds in Titan's atmosphere? Scientists suspect there may be oceans of methane on or below Titan's surface.

These oceans are of special interest because, while the chances of life existing on Titan today
40 are remote, it is possible that the oceans indicate that some life forms appeared there long ago. Once, Titan may have been much warmer than it is today, with water flowing over its surface in liquid form, prompting microscopic organisms
45 to emerge. Billions of years from now, life could appear there once again, as our Sun is expected to grow to 50 times its current size. Over that time, Earth would become too hot for life. On Titan, however, the frozen surface mixture of water
50 and ammonia would melt and life could begin to flourish.

The presence of oceans is one of many questions the probe, named Huygens after the Dutch astronomer who first spotted Titan in 1655,
55 may answer. Launched from Cape Canaveral in 1997 on a ship called the *Cassini*, the Cassini-Huygens mission is a joint project between NASA, the European Space Agency (ESA), and the Italian Space Agency (ASI).

60 In order to travel the 3.3 billion kilometers to the planet Saturn, the *Cassini-Huygens* made use of "gravity-assist." This is the mutual gravitational pull between a planet and a spacecraft that gives a spacecraft an extra boost as it passes by. After
65 two swing-bys of Venus, one of Earth itself, and one of Jupiter, Cassini had gained enough orbital momentum to charge into the outer reaches of the solar system.

Although only 2.7 meters across, *Huygens* is

GO ON TO THE NEXT PAGE.

70 packed with scientific instruments. During the
seven years it took to reach Saturn, ESA scientists
"woke up" the probe every six months to check
that everything was working. Much like a crab,
Huygens has a hard exterior shell. *Huygens'* shell
75 can bear temperatures of up to 18,000°C. This was
crucial when the time came for the precarious
descent through Titan's atmosphere.

As it descended onto Titan, *Huygens'* camera
at first revealed only haze over the distant surface.
80 But by the time it had landed, sharp details
came into focus. The pictures beamed to Earth
by *Huygens* via the *Cassini* delighted scientists.
Images showed a range of features similar to
Earth's: river terrains, highlands, basins, and large
85 boulders on flat ground. Some pictures showed
thick ripples like drainage channels leading into a
dark lake or sea—described by one scientist as "a
lake of tar."

"It looks like something has flowed at some
90 time to make those channels," mission scientist
Andrew Ball told the BBC, "but is it something that
has solidified?"

If Titan has liquid running across its surface,
it could be the only place in the solar system other
95 than Earth that does. Instead of water, though, the
liquid on Titan would be methane or ethane. This
might fall like rain from the moon's dense skies.
Sound recordings from Titan seem to indicate
some kind of showers.

100 Cassini continues to orbit Saturn and will
do so 70 times during its four-year study of the
beautiful ringed planet and its moons. Scientists
will remain busy for years analyzing the data
Cassini sends to Earth, including hundreds of
105 images of the alien, yet familiar, landscape of
Titan.

11. According to the passage, the author believes
which of the following regarding the possibility of
life on Titan?
   A. The surface of Titan is too hot to ever support
      life.
   B. Audio recordings from *Huygens* will provide
      evidence of life.
   C. Organic compounds suggest the presence of
      simple organisms.
   D. While currently highly improbable, life
      might exist if conditions change.

12. It can be inferred from the passage that the
presence of organic compounds in Titan's
atmosphere is unusual because:
   F. such compounds are usually only found in
      oceans.
   G. the moon cannot support life that produces
      such compounds.
   H. it implies there is a supply of methane that is
      being broken down.
   J. the moon is the only other body known to
      have such compounds.

13. The passage compares the *Huygens* to a crab to
show that the probe:
   A. is resistant to extreme temperatures.
   B. was designed to be amphibious.
   C. has a durable, protective skin.
   D. moves on six articulated legs.

14. The primary purpose of this passage is to:
   F. discuss the Huygens-Cassini mission and
      some questions it may answer.
   G. raise the possibility that life may exist on
      moons within the solar system.
   H. show how successful missions can raise
      public opinion of space exploration.
   J. argue for increased funding for NASA and
      foreign aerospace agencies.

15. Which of the following is NOT mentioned as a
feature of Titan?
   A. its extreme temperature.
   B. its organic atmosphere.
   C. its small size.
   D. its discovery in 1655.

16. As it is used in line 18, the word *primeval* most
nearly means:
   F. principal.
   G. ancient.
   H. rustic.
   J. pristine.

17. The passage suggests that the descent of *Huygens*
onto Titan was "precarious" because of the:
   A. methane storms.
   B. rocky terrain.
   C. gusting winds.
   D. high temperatures.

GO ON TO THE NEXT PAGE.

18. Based on details in the passage, it can be inferred that the *Cassini* served what purpose in the mission to Titan?

    F. It sheltered the *Huygens* during the perilous descent onto the moon.

    G. It carried the *Huygens* to Titan and relayed broadcasts back to Earth.

    H. It studied the atmosphere of Titan while *Huygens* explored its surface.

    J. It made audio recordings to accompany the images from the *Huygens*.

19. According to the passage, Titan is unique among moons in our solar system because:

    A. it is larger than some planets.

    B. it harbors an atmosphere.

    C. liquid water is present on its surface.

    D. it has a constant subzero climate.

20. Many images from Titan suggest that:

    F. the environment is totally unlike Earth's.

    G. the moon is completely icebound.

    H. liquid has flowed on the moon's surface.

    J. the landscape is desolate and rocky.

END OF TEST.

STOP! DO NOT TURN THE PAGE UNTIL TOLD TO DO SO.

KAP Wrap

Think back to your favorite movie one more time. Think of two major characters and of what might happen to them after the movie ends. Make a prediction about an experience that one of the characters might have and describe what events from the movie allow you to make that prediction. Next, describe an experience that the second character will likely *not* have and explain what events from the movie allow you to eliminate this possibility.

Unit 3
ACT Reading II

Thinking KAP

Look at the questions below. Circle the questions that you could easily look up the answer to in a book or on the Internet.

1. How many miles is the earth from the sun?

2. What would happen if we found out the sun was going to stop shining in 50 years?

3. How do most people feel when they look down on the city of Paris from atop the Eiffel Tower?

4. How many years did it take to build the Eiffel Tower?

5. What qualities does it take to be a successful professional athlete?

6. Who holds the record in Major League Baseball for the most regular-season home runs?

A

Strategy Instruction

Detail Questions

Detail questions ask you about specific points in the passage. What makes detail questions easy to answer is that the answers to the questions appear directly in the passage. What makes this type of question difficult to answer is that there are lots of details in the passage to choose from.

Identifying Detail Questions

Detail questions represent about 1/3 of all questions on the ACT Reading Test. You should expect to see 13 or 14 of them per test.

Detail questions will normally give you enough clues that, if you use your notes, you will know where to find the answers in the passage. You can identify detail questions by looking for concrete references to the passage in the question stems. Detail questions will sometimes provide additional help by referring to a specific line, sentence, or paragraph—beware, though, not every question with a line reference is a detail question. Some detail questions use the word NOT or the word EXCEPT. Others include lists with Roman numerals. The following are common phrases indicating detail questions:

- According to the author …

- According to the passage …

- In the passage …

- In the third paragraph, the author states …

Try It Out!

Read the question stems below. Circle the detail questions.

1. The central purpose of the passage is to:

2. According to the passage, art most likely began:

3. As it is used in line 6, *secure* most nearly means:

4. In the second paragraph (lines 10–12), the author states that arms were decorated as a way of:

5. The last paragraph mentions famous artists in order to show how arms making:

6. Which of the following is NOT used in the passage as an example of the interplay between artistry and weaponry?

Answering Detail Questions

In the Thinking KAP activity, you circled the questions you could easily look up the answer to in a book or on the Internet. The questions you circled were similar to detail questions on the ACT Reading Test in that you could do research to find the answers. Detail questions are the only question type on the ACT for which you can find the answer solely by doing research—you will be able to find the answers stated directly in the passage. The other types of questions on the ACT will require you to use not only research, but also reasoning.

During Step 3 of the 3-Step Method for ACT Reading Comprehension, you will find the important information you need to answer the question. For detail questions, you will do research to find specific support for the correct answer choice. You will use **Track It Down**.

Track It Down
• **Track down** and **reread** the part of the passage that contains the answer.   • **Point out** the important information.

Keep in mind

With each detail question, you should be able to put your finger on a specific part of the passage that will lead to the correct answer.

First you must track down the spot in the passage where you will find specific support for the correct answer. When a question gives you a specific line or paragraph number, it's easy to track it down. When the question does not tell you where to look for the answer, use your summary statements like a table of contents—they will help you identify the paragraph that contains the answer. Next, you should reread the lines or paragraph containing the answer.

Finally, physically place your finger on the important information. Pointing it out will save you time as you go back and forth between the passage and the question.

Predicting with Detail Questions

After you use Track It Down, remember to make a prediction based on the text you have read. With detail questions, your prediction may be a direct quote from the passage itself. Remember, you are researching, not reasoning!

Read the excerpted passage about sunspots. Then use Track It Down and Predicting to answer the detail question.

Sunspots are poorly understood. Observations have revealed that the swirly smudges represent areas of intense magnetic activity where the sun's radiative energy has been blocked, and that they are considerably cooler than bright regions of the sun. Scientists have not been able, however, to
5   determine just how sunspots are created or what effect they have on the solar constant (a misnomer that refers to the sun's total radiance at any instant).

The latter question, at least, now seems to have been resolved by data from the Solar Maximum Mission satellite, which has monitored the solar constant since 1980, the peak of the last solar cycle. As the number of
10 sunspots decreased through 1986, the satellite recorded a gradual dimming of the sun. Over the past year, as sunspots have proliferated, the sun has brightened. The data suggest that the sun is 0.1 percent more luminous at the peak of the solar cycle, when the number of sunspots is greatest, than at its nadir, according to Richard C. Willson of Jet Propulsion Laboratory and Hugh
15 S. Hudson of the University of California at San Diego.

The data show that sunspots do not themselves make the sun shine brighter. Quite the contrary. When a sunspot appears, it initially causes the sun to dim slightly, but after a period of weeks or months, islands of brilliance called faculas usually emerge near the sunspot and more than compensate
20 for its dimming effect. Willson says faculas may represent regions where energy that is initially blocked beneath a sunspot finally breaches the surface.

Main Idea: _____

Author's Purpose: _____

Detail questions usually contain tempting wrong answer choices that distort or misuse details from the passage.

1. According to the passage, scientists looking at data from the *Solar Maximum Mission* (line 8) have discovered which of the following about the relationship between sunspot activity and solar luminosity?

    Track down and reread the part of the passage that contains the answer.

    Point out the important information.

    Prediction: _____

    A. At the peak of sunspot activity, the solar constant decreases in magnitude.
    B. At the peak of sunspot activity, the solar constant increases in magnitude.
    C. At the low point of sunspot activity, the sun is 0.1 percent brighter than it is at the peak of such activity.
    D. Scientists have yet to demonstrate a relationship between sunspot activity and solar luminosity.

Eliminating with Specific Kinds of Detail Questions

There are two specific kinds of detail questions for which you will need to use Eliminating rather than Predicting—NOT and EXCEPT questions and Roman numeral questions. NOT and EXCEPT questions ask you to identify the answer choice that is *not* true, so you will not be able to make a prediction. For these questions, you will still use Track It Down. However, you will base your research on the answer choices rather than on the question stem. After you read the question stem, read each answer choice and track it down. Eliminate answer choices that you find to be supported as true in the passage. The one answer choice that you cannot track down and verify as true is the correct answer choice.

Roman numeral questions list three numbered statements. You must select the answer choice that lists the statements that are true. For these questions, you will still use Track It Down. However, instead of making a prediction, you will use the important information to determine whether each numbered statement is true or false. You will then eliminate answer choices that include false numbered statements.

The correct answer choice will not always be a word-for-word match to the text. Look for answer choices that are synonymous with the text.

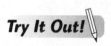

Look at the questions below and refer back to the passage about sunspots on page 104. Use Track It Down and Eliminating to answer each question.

1. Which of the following is NOT cited as an aspect of sunspots or sunspot activity?
   A. Sunspots represent areas of strong magnetic activity.
   B. Sunspots themselves are cooler than bright areas of the sun.
   C. The number of sunspots declined from 1980 to 1986.
   D. Islands of brilliance, known as *faculas*, cause sunspots to emerge.

2. According to the passage, scientists studying data from the *Solar Maximum Mission* satellite have discovered which of the following?
   I.   How sunspots are created
   II. How the number of sunspots affects the solar constant
   III. Why the number of sunspots began to increase after 1986
   F. I only
   G. II only
   H. I and II only
   J. I, II, and III

The 3-Step Method for ACT Reading Comprehension

 ### STEP 1: Read actively.

- **Summarize each paragraph.**

- **Question the Author.**

 ### STEP 2: Examine the question stems.

- **Identify the question type.**

- **Determine the correct strategy.**

 ### STEP 3: Answer the questions.

- **Find the important information.**

- **Predict and eliminate.**

A

Track It Down
• **Track down** and **reread** the part of the passage that contains the answer.
• **Point out** the important information.

Read the text below and answer the following questions.

Passage I

NATURAL SCIENCE: This passage from a textbook about the solar system discusses research examining the possibility of life on Mars.

When the first of the two Viking Landers touched down on Martian soil on July 20, 1976, and began to send camera images back to Earth, the scientists at Jet Propulsion Laboratory could
5 not suppress a certain nervous anticipation, like people who hold tickets to a lottery that they have a one-in-a-million chance of winning. The first photographs that arrived, however, did not contain any evidence of life. What was
10 revealed was merely a barren landscape littered with rocks and boulders. The view resembled nothing so much as a flat section of desert. In fact, the winning entry in a contest at J.P.L. for the photograph most accurately predicting what
15 Mars would look like was a snapshot taken from a particularly arid section of the Mojave Desert.

The scientists were soon ready to turn their attentions from visible life to microorganisms. The twin Viking Landers carried experiments
20 designed to detect organic compounds. Researchers thought it possible that life had developed on early Mars just as it is thought to have developed on Earth, through the gradual chemical evolution of complex organic molecules.
25 To detect biological activity, Martian soil samples were treated with various nutrients that would produce characteristic by-products if life forms were active in the soil. The results from all three experiments were inconclusive. In the
30 fourth experiment, a soil sample was heated to look for signs of organic material, but none were found—an unexpected result because scientists thought organic compounds from the steady bombardment of the Martian surface by
35 meteorites would be present.

The absence of organic materials, some scientists speculated, was the result of intense ultraviolet radiation penetrating the atmosphere of Mars and destroying organic compounds in the
40 soil. Although Mars' atmosphere was at one time rich in carbon dioxide and thus thick enough to protect its surface from the harmful rays of the sun, the carbon dioxide had gradually left the atmosphere and been converted into rocks. This
45 means that even if life had gotten a start on early Mars, it could not have survived the exposure to ultraviolet radiation when the atmosphere thinned. Mars never developed a protective layer of ozone as Earth did.

50 Despite the disappointing Viking results, there are those who still believe in the possibility of life on Mars. They point out that the Viking data cannot be considered the final word on Martian life because the two landers only sampled
55 limited—and uninteresting—sites. The Viking landing sites were not chosen for what they might tell of the planet's biology. They were chosen primarily because they appeared to be safe for landing a spacecraft. The landing sites were
60 on parts of the Martian plains that appeared relatively featureless from orbital photographs.

The type of terrain that these researchers suggest may be a possible hiding place for active life has an earthly parallel: the ice-free region of
65 southern Victoria Land, Antarctica, where the temperatures in some dry valleys average below zero. Organisms known as endoliths, a form of blue-green algae that has adapted to this harsh environment, were found living inside certain
70 translucent, porous rocks in these Antarctic valleys. The argument based on this discovery is that if life did exist on early Mars, it is possible that it escaped worsening conditions by similarly seeking refuge in rocks. Skeptics object, however,
75 that Mars in its present state is simply too dry, even compared with Antarctic valleys, to sustain any life whatsoever.

1. According to the passage, the fact that the carbon dioxide on Mars "had gradually left the atmosphere and been converted into rocks" (lines 43-44) resulted in:

Track down and reread the part of the passage that contains the answer.

Point out the important information.

Prediction: _____

- **A.** radiation that was the cause of the destruction of all life on Mars.
- **B.** an atmosphere unable to protect the planet from intense ultraviolet radiation.
- **C.** an atmosphere thick enough to protect Mars' surface from the harmful rays of the Sun.
- **D.** the development of a protective layer of ozone much like the one on Earth.

2. Each of the following is discussed as an action performed by a Viking Lander on Mars EXCEPT:

Track down and reread the part of the passage that contains the answer.

Point out the important information.

Eliminate the answer choices that are supported as true in the passage.

F. taking photographs of the surface.
G. treating the soil with nutrients.
H. heating a soil sample.
J. taking samples from translucent, porous rocks.

Shared Practice

■ *Use the 3-Step Method for ACT Reading Comprehension—including Track It Down and Predicting or Eliminating—for the passage and questions below.*

Passage II

SOCIAL SCIENCE: The following passage is an adapted excerpt from "Gossip and the Evolution of Language" by Duncan Pauleta.

Gossip has always gotten bad press. The word suggests idleness, malice, and tale-telling. But can gossip be a useful educational tool? Can it be a method of truth seeking? This is how many
5 scientists have started to see gossip. Research now points to gossip's importance in the growth of human societies and the development of language.

For many years the question of how and
10 why humans first learned to speak has been a puzzle. In 1998, researchers studying fossils found that the hole in the skull that allows nerves to connect with tongue muscles was big enough to allow speech 400,000 years ago. So humans may
15 have started speaking much earlier than anyone thought.

Early speech was probably slower and simpler than modern speech. But what did our ancestors chat about? According to psychologist Robin
20 Dunbar, the answer to this question could explain how the unique situation of humans among the world's species contributed to the development of language.

Around the time early humans were
25 developing the ability to speak, they were migrating to new areas. Facing new dangers, our ancestors started to live together in larger groups. Scientists have noted that species living in big groups have bigger brains. In any large grouping,
30 it is crucial for an individual to form a network of bonds with others in the group. This necessity may be the spur for greater brain development.

Dunbar believes that humans had to learn to speak in order to adapt to life in larger groups.
35 Studies of primate behavior show that a key way in which monkeys and apes develop social bonds is through grooming. Primates may spend as much as one-fifth of each day combing through each other's hair with their fingers and picking

40 out bits of twig and insects. Grooming is not just about health and hygiene. It is a way of showing friendship and loyalty. It releases the body's natural stress-reducing chemicals. Monkeys' and apes' "grooming partners" often come to each
45 other's aid when they are in danger.

Yet once humans started living in groups of 150 or more, a quicker method of bonding than grooming was needed. According to Dunbar, speech was our response to this need. And the
50 prime function of speech was not to discuss the best hunting ground or dangers from prey, but to gossip. "If being human is all about talking," Dunbar says, "it's the tittle-tattle of life that makes the world go round."

55 Early humans probably talked about topics that are surprisingly familiar to modern ears: who was behaving well or badly, who was in a dispute, who was "courting" whom, the weather, families, sickness, and health.

60 Social scientists believe that gossip has many redeeming qualities in the present age, too. According to the new thinking, gossip teaches us how to live in the culture we belong to, and how to adhere to, or test, our society's rules. Gossip works
65 by narrative—it tells stories about other people and their experiences that everyone can learn from.

One anthropologist analyzed the conversations of a male rowing team as they drove
70 to practice each morning. A flurry of negative gossip arose when a new member joined the team and repeatedly skipped practice. The gossip stigmatized the lazy team member, but it also underpinned the strength of the team. The men
75 began talking a lot about good team members, telling positive stories, and reinforcing their own senses of purpose.

Gossip can be useful for college students. In one study, students were asked to report gossip
80 they had heard. Sixty-four percent said that they had learned something from the stories. Another study showed that in about 54 percent of cases the reason for telling a gossipy story was "truth

seeking." By analyzing an anecdote and its details,
85 people hope to discover exactly what happened
and learn from it.

"The intent is pretty similar to that of a
social scientist," says Charles Walker, Ph.D,
who conducted the study. "They want to get to
90 the bottom of a story, to find out the truth of the
matter."

Even that well-known drain on businesses,
office gossip, can be a healthy thing. Workers can
learn from each other's mistakes and successes.
95 For instance, an employee might not know how
to approach her boss to ask for maternity leave
until she hears stories of how other women have
done the same. Walker describes office gossip
as a "handbook" that is just as important as the
100 handbook you receive when you start a new job.

1. According to the passage, fossil evidence shows
that humans of 400,000 years ago:
   A. were physically capable of speech.
   B. lived in groups of 150 or more.
   C. bonded primarily through grooming.
   D. had developed large brains for networking.

hint ▷ *Locate the part of the passage that
refers to humans of 400,000 years ago.*

2. The main purpose of the passage is to:
   F. discuss the role of gossip from the origin of
language to the present day.
   G. argue that language developed to promote
stronger social bonding.
   H. illustrate the positive role of gossip as a form
of "truth seeking."
   J. draw parallels between human and primate
social behaviors.

hint ▷ *Use Question the Author to make a
prediction.*

3. In paragraph 6 (lines 46–54), the author
cites Dunbar to illustrate that gossip, unlike
conversations about hunting grounds or prey,
served:
   A. primarily as a means of social bonding.
   B. to set humans apart from other primates.
   C. as an early form of "truth seeking."
   D. as evidence of humans' larger brains.

hint ▷ *This question indicates the paragraph to
examine.*

4. According to the passage, primates such as
monkeys and apes:
   F. live in large groups to counter the dangers of
migration.
   G. model how humans groom for hygiene and
stress reduction.
   H. use grooming to express friendship and
loyalty.
   J. demonstrate a form of nonverbal gossip
within groups.

hint ▷ *Look for information about monkeys
and apes in the passage.*

5. As used in line 32, the word *spur* most nearly means:

    A. prompt.
    B. barb.
    C. impediment.
    D. branch.

hint *Look for clues to the meaning of the word within the sentence.*

6. According to the passage, office gossip can have a positive effect when it:

    F. is motivated by a desire to find the truth of a matter.
    G. helps employees learn from each other's mistakes and successes.
    H. promotes friendship and loyalty in the workplace.
    J. expands social networks and bonds.

hint *Which paragraph discusses the effects of office gossip?*

7. Each of the following is discussed as an example of beneficial modern-day gossip EXCEPT:

    A. office workers learning through anecdotes.
    B. social scientists analyzing narratives for meaning.
    C. college students seeking to discover the truth in stories.
    D. rowers using gossip to affirm team purpose.

hint *Eliminate answer choices that are supported as true in the text.*

8. According to the passage, which of the following contributed to the development of speech?

    I. Migrations and new dangers made social networks essential to survival.
    II. Speech, specifically gossip, offered a quick means of bonding.
    III. Evolutionary pressure led humans to develop speech-capable brains.

    F. I only
    G. III only
    H. I and II only
    J. I, II, and III

hint *Determine whether each numbered statement is true or false.*

KAP Wrap

You use both research and reasoning to find answers and reach conclusions all of the time in your everyday life. Think back on the past week. Write about three instances in which you did research to find information you needed in your everyday life. For at least one of these instances, describe how the steps you took were similar to or different from Track It Down.

A

Thinking KAP

Think about how a tomato contributes to a salad. Now think about how a salad contributes to a meal. In the case of the tomato and the salad, which is the part and which is the whole? In the case of the salad and the meal, which is the part and which is the whole? How is the relationship of the tomato to the salad similar to the relationship of the salad to the meal? How is it different?

B

Function Questions

Function questions ask you to think about the author's motivation and subsequent decisions. What makes function questions easy to answer is that your notes will help you. What makes this type of question difficult to answer is that you will not be able to put your finger directly on the correct answer in the passage.

keep in mind

Function questions represent about 1/6 of all questions on the ACT Reading Test. You should expect to see 6 or 7 of them per test.

Identifying Function Questions

Function questions use distinctive phrasing that make them easy to identify. Sometimes they even use the word *function*. The following are examples of function questions:

- The phrase xxxx serves to:
- The placement of xxxx in quotation marks is meant to:
- Xxxx helps establish that:
- The primary function of xxxx is most likely to:
- The author refers to xxxx to illustrate that:
- The author does xxxx in order to:
- The function of xxxx in relation to the passage as a whole is to:

Try It Out!

Read the question stems below. Circle the function questions.

1. It is most likely that the author mentions Athena (lines 7–8) in order to demonstrate:
2. The central purpose of the passage is to:
3. As it is used in line 20, *secure* most nearly means:
4. The main function of the fourth paragraph (lines 42–44) in relation to the passage as a whole is to indicate that:
5. In the second paragraph (lines 16–18), the author states that arms were decorated as a way of:
6. The last paragraph mentions famous artists in order to show how armsmaking:

B

Answering Function Questions

During Step 3 of the 3-Step Method for ACT Reading Comprehension, you will find the important information you need to answer the questions. For function questions, you will use both research and reasoning to **Think Like the Author**.

Think Like the Author

- **Find** and **reread** the part of the passage referenced in the question.

- **Ask** yourself **why** the author included this part of the passage.

- **Consider how** the part contributes to the whole.

A function question may ask you about a particular punctuation mark, word, quote, paragraph, or event. You must first find and reread the part of the passage to which the question refers. This is similar to what you do for detail questions when you track down the part of the passage that contains the answer.

Next, you must ask yourself why the author included that part of the passage. What was her motivation? What impact was she seeking to achieve?

Finally, consider how the part contributes to the whole. For some function questions, you may be considering how a very small part, such as a word, contributes to a whole sentence or paragraph. For other function questions, you will consider how a larger part, such as an entire paragraph, contributes to the whole passage. Like the salad in the Thinking KAP Activity, some text, such as a paragraph, may be the whole in one situation and the part in another. No matter what the size of the part referenced in the question, you will always go one step higher and consider how it contributes to a larger whole.

Predicting with Function Questions

After you use Think Like the Author, remember to make a prediction based on your conclusion about why the author did what she did.

keep in mind

An author's-purpose question asks you why the author wrote the piece. A function question asks you why the author included a certain part of the piece.

B

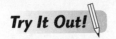

Try It Out!

Passage I

HUMANITIES: This passage is adapted from the article "Looking With: The Photography of Annie Leibovitz" by Camilla J. Hutton.

Photography is the most visible exception to male dominance in artistic endeavors. From Julia Margaret Cameron to Dorothea Lange to Cindy Sherman, some of the biggest names in photography are those of women.

5 Scholars, art critics, and feminists provide different explanations for the rapid advances women have made in this genre. Some say that since the invention of photography coincided with the inception of the women's suffrage movement, liberated women felt confident enough to join this new wide-open field, which was unfettered by centuries of academic tradition. Others suggest that female photographers can penetrate deeper into society:
10 women might be welcomed into homes where men would be perceived as intruders, and subjects of either gender might feel more comfortable revealing their innermost selves to a woman. Feminist art theory emphasizes the power dynamic inherent in the gaze. In most mainstream art throughout history, the artist and the audience are male—women only appear as the
15 object of the male gaze. A female photographer changes that paradigm, providing fresh insight into her subject matter.

Annie Leibovitz is one of the world's most famous living photographers. In her long and varied and career, she has taken hundreds of iconic photographs of rock stars, actors, politicians, and ordinary people. Leibovitz
20 began as a painter, studying at the San Francisco Art Institute. After taking her first photographs, however, the camera's ability to capture the innermost life of a subject captivated her. When she worked on a kibbutz in Israel as part of a work-study program, Leibovitz brought her camera with her. The photographs she took there became her first published pieces when they
25 caught the eye of the art editor at *Rolling Stone* magazine.

Leibovitz became a celebrity photographer within a year. *Rolling Stone* provided her with regular assignments, and by 1973, the magazine promoted her to chief photographer. Leibovitz considered herself a photojournalist until a critical early assignment photographing John Lennon. Her experience
30 photographing Lennon—surprisingly open despite his extraordinary fame—changed her focus. Leibovitz became better known as a portrait photographer than as a photojournalist. Unrestrained by the objectivity required for journalism, Leibovitz allowed her opinions to influence her photographs and infuse them with feeling.

35 Vivid colors and surprising, yet intimate, poses became a trademark of Leibovitz's work. Both attributes are on full display in Leibovitz's memorable 1980 photograph of John Lennon and Yoko Ono: A naked Lennon curls in a fetal position around a fully-clothed Ono. Lennon seems to draw sustenance from Ono, while she basks in his glorious, unconditional love. Hours later,
40 Lennon was murdered outside his apartment building in New York City. Leibovitz's portrait, the last photograph of Lennon before his death, remains the definitive image of the beloved musician.

Later assignments with *Vanity Fair* allowed Leibovitz access to a spectrum of celebrities. Instantly recognizable, Leibovitz became a star in
45 her own right. Her remarkable photographs and worldwide renown have won her advertising contracts with Gap, American Express, and Honda.

Detractors have asserted that she is too commercial to be a fine artist, but Leibovitz's work endures.

In an extraordinary anthology, Leibovitz turned her keen eye on her
50 gender. Entitled *Women*, Leibovitz's collection examines the astonishing, ordinary, transcendent, and mundane. According to critic Susan Sontag's introduction, the assembled photographs address the "question" of women. What Leibovitz brings to her photographs is the "commanding notion of the sheer interestingness of the subject." The photographs illustrate, challenge,
55 and deconstruct the stereotypes that society continues to perpetuate. A Muslim woman shares the page with showgirls, celebrities co-exist with coal miners, and one woman is identified simply as a victim of abuse. Although by no means exhaustive, *Women* is perhaps the most candid examination of the subject in recent times. Whether it is Leibovitz's feminine identity,
60 or her own unique, sensitive powers of perception, she moves beyond the traditional pattern of the gaze and looks with, rather than at, the people in her photographs.

Main Idea: _____

Author's Purpose: _____

B

1. The passage most fully supports which of the following conclusions about Annie Leibovitz?
   A. Her photographs reflect the objectivity of a photojournalist.
   B. She will be remembered most for pursuing a sense of celebrity herself.
   C. Her portrait work has established her as a culturally significant photographer.
   D. Her most common theme is the exploration of women's roles in society.

2. According to the passage, Leibovitz is sometimes criticized for her:
   F. subjectivity.
   G. strange poses.
   H. commercial achievements.
   J. tiresome examination of a single theme.

3. Which of the following methods does the author utilize in developing the second paragraph?
   A. A presentation of factual data concerning feminist art
   B. A series of hypotheses explaining the unique abilities of women in photography
   C. A list of shortcomings found in the work of male photographers
   D. A historical account of art theory

4. The details in lines 29–34 ("Her experience...with feeling.") are used to illustrate:
   F. the restrictions of photojournalism compared with portrait photography.
   G. the primary reason for Leibovitz's worldwide renown and popularity.
   H. the difficulty of Leibovitz's transition to portrait photography.
   J. the various challenges facing a celebrity photographer.

5. The author states that Leibovitz has moved past "the traditional pattern" (line 61), is because her photography:
   A. utilizes innovative color schemes.
   B. explores subjects who had previously not been photographed.
   C. represents a new interpretation of portraiture.
   D. focuses on the everyday lives of ordinary women.

6. The author's main point in the fifth paragraph is that Leibovitz:
   F. was able to capture something amazing in her photography.
   G. was the last person to photograph John Lennon.
   H. considered Lennon and Ono her favorite subjects.
   J. shot the greatest photograph ever taken.

7. The author's primary intention in citing the opinions of a critic (lines 51–54) is to:
   A. place Leibovitz's work in historical perspective.
   B. emphasize the broad critical acclaim Leibovitz enjoys.
   C. dispute the claim that Leibovitz is "too commercial."
   D. provide an analytical view of Leibovitz's skill.

8. The author offers the anthology, *Women*, as an example of:
   F. contemporary art doubling as social activism.
   G. a group of photos with a single-minded theme.
   H. photography's ability to raise important social questions.
   J. the power of contrasting various subjects with each other.

B

9. According to the passage, which of the following is not a possible explanation for the larger role played by women in photography as opposed to the other arts?

    A. A woman's ability to comfort an intimidated subject.
    B. The presence of institutionalized traditions.
    C. A historical confluence of artistic invention and social development.
    D. The difference between male and female perspectives.

10. The author's attitude towards Leibovitz's artistic development can best be described as:

    F. unimpressed.
    G. admiring.
    H. detached.
    J. scared.

B

The 3-Step Method for ACT Reading Comprehension

 STEP 1: Read actively.

- *Summarize each paragraph.*

- *Question the Author.*

 STEP 2: Examine the question stems.

- *Identify the question type.*

- *Determine the correct strategy.*

 STEP 3: Answer the questions.

- *Find the important information.*

- *Predict and eliminate.*

Think Like the Author

- **Find** and **reread** the part of the passage referenced in the question.
- **Ask** yourself **why** the author included this part of the passage.
- **Consider how** the part contributes to the whole.

B

Read the text below and answer the following questions.

Passage I

NATURAL SCIENCE: This passage from a textbook about the solar system discusses research examining the possibility of life on Mars.

When the first of the two Viking Landers touched down on Martian soil on July 20, 1976, and began to send camera images back to Earth, the scientists at Jet Propulsion Laboratory could
5   not suppress a certain nervous anticipation, like people who hold tickets to a lottery they have a one-in-a-million chance of winning. The first photographs that arrived, however, did not contain any evidence of life. What was
10 revealed was merely a barren landscape littered with rocks and boulders. The view resembled nothing so much as a flat section of desert. In fact, the winning entry in a contest at J.P.L. for the photograph most accurately predicting what Mars would look like was a snapshot taken from a
15 particularly arid section of the Mojave Desert.

The scientists were soon ready to turn their attentions from visible life to microorganisms. The twin Viking Landers carried experiments
20 designed to detect organic compounds. Researchers thought it possible that life had developed on early Mars just as it is thought to have developed on Earth, through the gradual chemical evolution of complex organic molecules.
25 To detect biological activity, Martian soil samples were treated with various nutrients that would produce characteristic by-products if life forms were active in the soil. The results from all three experiments were inconclusive. In the
30 fourth experiment, a soil sample was heated to look for signs of organic material, but none were found—an unexpected result because scientists thought organic compounds from the steady bombardment of the Martian surface by
35 meteorites would be present.

The absence of organic materials, some scientists speculated, was the result of intense ultraviolet radiation penetrating the atmosphere of Mars and destroying organic compounds in the
40 soil. Although Mars' atmosphere was at one time rich in carbon dioxide and thus thick enough to protect its surface from the harmful rays of the sun, the carbon dioxide had gradually left the atmosphere and been converted into rocks. This
45 means that even if life had gotten a start on early Mars, it could not have survived the exposure to ultraviolet radiation when the atmosphere thinned. Mars never developed a protective layer of ozone as Earth did.

50 Despite the disappointing Viking results, there are those who still believe in the possibility of life on Mars. They point out that the Viking data cannot be considered the final word on Martian life because the two landers only sampled limited—and uninteresting—sites. The Viking
55 landing sites were not chosen for what they might tell of the planet's biology. They were chosen primarily because they appeared to be safe for landing a spacecraft. The landing sites were on parts of the Martian plains that appeared
60 relatively featureless from orbital photographs.

The type of terrain that these researchers suggest may be a possible hiding place for active life has an earthly parallel: the ice-free region of southern Victoria Land, Antarctica, where the
65 temperatures in some dry valleys average below zero. Organisms known as endoliths, a form of blue-green algae that has adapted to this harsh environment, were found living inside certain translucent, porous rocks in these Antarctic
70 valleys. The argument based on this discovery is that if life did exist on early Mars, it is possible that it escaped worsening conditions by similarly seeking refuge in rocks. Skeptics object, however, that Mars in its present state is simply too dry,
75 even compared with Antarctic valleys, to sustain any life whatsoever.

B

1. The main function of the fourth paragraph (lines 50–60) in relation to the passage as a whole is to indicate that:

Find and reread the part of the passage referenced in the question.

Ask yourself why the author included this part of the text.

Consider how the part contributes to the whole.

Prediction: _____

A. the Viking Mission was unsuccessful due to poor selection of landing sites.
B. the results of the Viking Mission do not necessarily prove that Mars is devoid of life.
C. the detection of life on Mars was not a primary objective of the Viking Mission.
D. scientists were not expecting the Viking Mission to discover life on the Martian plains.

2. The author discusses endoliths (lines 66-71) primarily in order to:

Find and reread the part of the passage referenced in the question.

Ask yourself why the author included this part of the text.

Consider how the part contributes to the whole.

Prediction: _____

F. give an example of an organism that lives in an ice-free region of Antarctica.

G. prove that life exists on Mars despite its harsh environment.

H. illustrate the argument that life may have survived on Mars by hiding in rocks.

J. show the similarities between a life form from Earth and life forms scientists expect to find on Mars.

Shared Practice

■ *Use the 3-Step Method for ACT Reading Comprehension—including Think Like the Author and Predicting—for the passage and questions below.*

Passage II

SOCIAL STUDIES: The following passage is excerpted from a discussion of the origin of the Cold War between the United States and the Soviet Union.

Revisionist historians maintain that it was within the power of the United States, in the years during and immediately after the Second World War, to prevent the Cold War with the Soviet

5 Union. Revisionists suggest that the prospect of impending conflict with the Soviets could have been avoided in several ways. The United States could have officially recognized the new Soviet sphere of influence in Eastern Europe instead of

10 continuing to call for self-determination in those countries. A much-needed reconstruction loan could have helped the Soviets recover from the war. The Americans could have sought to assuage Soviet fears by giving up the United States'
monopoly on the atomic bomb and turning their

15 weapons over to an international agency (with the stipulation that future nuclear powers do the same).

This criticism of the post-war American

20 course of action fails to take into account the political realities in America at the time, and it unfairly condemns the American policy-makers who did consider each of these alternatives and found them to be unworkable. Recognition of a

25 Soviet Eastern Europe was out of the question. Roosevelt had promised self-determination to the Eastern European countries, and the American people, having come to expect this, were furious when Stalin began to shape his spheres of

30 influence in the region. The president was in particular acutely conscious of the millions of Polish-Americans who would be voting in the upcoming election.

35 Negotiations had indeed been conducted by the administration with the Soviets about a reconstruction loan, but Congress refused to approve it unless the Soviets made enormous concessions tantamount to restructuring their system and withdrawing from Eastern Europe.

40 This, of course, made Soviet rejection of the loan a foregone conclusion. As for giving up the

bomb—the elected officials in Washington would have been in deep trouble with their constituents had that plan been carried out. Polls showed that

45 82 percent of the American people understood that other nations would develop bombs eventually, but that 85 percent thought that the United States should retain exclusive possession of the weapon. Policy-makers have to abide by

50 certain constraints in deciding what is acceptable and what is not. They, and not historians, are in the best position to perceive those constraints and make the decisions.

Revisionist historians tend to eschew this type

55 of political explanation of America's supposed failure to reach a peaceful settlement with the Soviets in favor of an economic reading of events. They point to the fact that in the early post-war years American businessmen and government

60 officials cooperated to expand American foreign trade vigorously and to exploit investment opportunities in many foreign countries. In order to sustain the lucrative expansion, revisionists assert, American policy-makers were obliged to maintain an "Open Door" foreign policy, the

65 object of which was to keep all potential trade opportunities open. Since the Soviets could jeopardize such opportunities in Eastern Europe and elsewhere, they had to be opposed. Hence, the Cold War. But if American policy-makers

70 were simply pawns in an economic game of expansionist capitalism, as the revisionists seem to think, why do the revisionists hold them responsible for not attempting to reach an accord with the Soviets? The policy-makers, swept up by

75 a tidal wave of capitalism, clearly had little control and little choice in the matter.

Even if American officials had been free and willing to make conciliatory gestures toward the Soviets, the Cold War would not have been

80 prevented. Overtures of friendship would not have been reciprocated (as far as we can judge, since information on the inner workings of the Kremlin during that time is scant). Soviet expert George F. Kennan concluded that Russian hostility could

85 not be dampened by any effort on the part of the United States. The political and ideological differences were too great, and the Soviets had

too long a history of distrust of foreigners—exacerbated at the time by Stalin's rampant paranoia, which infected his government—to embark on a process of establishing trust and peace with the United States, though it was in their interest to do so.

1. The author refers to Polish-Americans (line 32) chiefly to illustrate that:
    A. the president had an excellent rapport with ethnic minorities.
    B. immigrants had fled from Eastern European countries to escape Communism.
    C. giving up the idea of Eastern European self-determination would have been costly in political terms.
    D. the political landscape of the United States had changed considerably since the president had been elected.

hint ▶ Why did the author include information about Polish-Americans?

2. The purpose of the second paragraph (lines 19-33) in relation to the passage is mostly likely to:
    F. criticize the American post-war course of action in regard to the Soviet Union.
    G. show that the argument of revisionist historians described in the previous paragraph is simplistic.
    H. recognize that Roosevelt had already promised self-determination to Eastern European countries.
    J. point out that the president was stuck to his course because of the number of Polish-American voters.

hint ▶ How does the paragraph contribute to the whole passage?

3. The primary purpose of the passage is to:
    A. explore a popular myth about U.S. involvement in the Cold War.
    B. compare historical figures such as Roosevelt and Stalin.
    C. refute a point of view about U.S. involvement in the Cold War.
    D. analyze the choices made by U.S. and Soviet leaders during the Cold War.

hint ▶ Use Question the Author to identify the author's purpose.

B

4. The purpose of the last paragraph (lines 78-94) in relation to the passage as a whole is most likely to:

   F. show that any friendly actions by American officials would have been rebuffed by Soviet officials.
   G. argue that American policy-makers were pawns in an economic game of expansionist capitalism.
   H. discuss the conclusions of Soviet expert George F. Kennan.
   J. describe the reasons why the Soviets should have had an interest in establishing trust with the United States.

   hint *How does the part contribute to the whole?*

5. According to the passage, negotiations between the United States and the Soviets regarding a reconstruction loan broke down because:

   A. the vast majority of American voters opposed such a move.
   B. Roosevelt felt obligated to oppose any attempt to win votes in the next election.
   C. Congress put restrictions on the loan that were unacceptable to the Soviets.
   D. American officials were caught up in a wave of expansionist capitalism.

   hint *Use Track It Down to answer this detail question.*

6. The author mentions Stalin's "rampant paranoia" (lines 89–90) mainly as:

   F. a reason why the Soviets would not have responded well to overtures by American policy-makers.
   G. a comic reference to a leader that has been shown by history to have been truly despotic.
   H. a rationale for why the United States should have been more aggressive in containing the spread of Soviet influence in Eastern Europe.
   J. a rebuttal of the reasoning put forth by historians who believe that the United States could not have prevented the Cold War with the Soviet Union.

   hint *Find and reread the paragraph where Stalin is mentioned.*

7. The author discusses opinion polls regarding the American people's views on possession of atomic weapons (lines 44-49) in order to:

A. show that the number of people who believed the United States should keep atomic weapons was greater than the number of people who believed other countries would develop their own weapons.

B. highlight one reason why American elected officials were unable to give up the United States' monopoly on the atomic bomb.

C. indicate that the American public was well educated about nuclear technology and the prospects for its proliferation.

D. demonstrate the stubbornness of the Soviets in insisting that the United States reveal nuclear secrets.

hint Ask yourself why the author included this information, then make a prediction based on your conclusion.

8. The author uses the question "But if American … with the Soviets?" in lines 69–74, primarily to:

F. pose an unanswered question to the reader.

G. question the motivations of revisionist historians.

H. point out a flaw in the previously mentioned argument put forth by revisionist historians.

J. highlight a sense of uncertainty that is associated with the era during which the Cold War occurred.

hint How does this part of the passage contribute to the whole?

B

KAP Wrap

Imagine that you are writing about a specific event that occurred with your family or group of friends. What particular quotes might you include from the people involved in your description of the event? Why would you include these quotes? How would they contribute to the description of the event?

ReKAP

Review the strategies from Lessons A and B. Then fill in the blanks to show what you have learned.

1. I will use Track It Down and Predicting for all _____ questions.

2. Track It Down:

   • Track down and reread the part of the _____ that contains the _____.

   • Point out the _____.

3. I will use Think Like the Author and Predicting for all _____ questions.

4. Think Like the Author:

   • _____ and reread the part of the passage referenced in the questions.

   • Ask yourself _____ the author included this part of the text.

   • Consider how the _____ contributes to the _____.

Vocabulary-in-Context Questions

Vocabulary-in-context questions ask you to pick out the correct definition of a word or phrase as it is used in the passage. What makes these questions easy to answer is that you do not have to know the definitions beforehand because the words appear in context along with a line reference. What makes this type of question difficult to answer is that the words may be challenging, or they may have more than one potential meaning.

Vocabulary-in-context questions are one of the least frequently occurring question types on the ACT Reading Test. You should expect to see between 1 and 3 of them per test.

Identifying Vocabulary-in-Context Questions

Vocabulary-in-context questions provide a line reference. They ask for the meaning of a word or phrase. When a vocabulary-in-context question asks about a word, the word is italicized. The following are examples of vocabulary-in-context questions:

- As it is used in line 2, the word *xxxx* most nearly means:

- When the author writes, "xxxx" (lines 6–7), he most likely means that:

Using Context

You should never assume you know the right answer to a vocabulary-in-context question, even if the word is familiar to you. These questions can be tricky because they often ask about words that have several meanings. Depending on the context, a word may have different definitions.

Try It Out!

Discuss the question below.

1. How would the word *conductor* be used by a violinist? a train passenger? an electrician?

Answering Vocabulary-in-Context Questions

During Step 3 of the 3-Step Method for ACT Reading Comprehension, you will find the important information you need to answer the questions. For vocabulary-in-context questions, you will use both research and reasoning to examine the context clues.

Context Clues

- **Find** the word or phrase in the passage and **reread** the sentence around it.

- **Use the clues** to figure out the meaning of the word or phrase.

First you must find the word or phrase in the passage. Use the line number reference to locate it quickly. Next, you should reread the sentence containing the word or phrase and look for clues to the meaning of the word or phrase. Finally, use the clues to figure out its meaning.

keep in mind

Sometimes you will need to read more than just the sentence containing the word or phrase in order to understand the context.

Predicting with Vocabulary-in-Context Questions

After you use Context Clues, remember to make a prediction based on the conclusion you have made about the meaning of the word or phrase.

Try It Out!

Read the excerpted passage about a famous Spanish architect below. Then use Context Clues and Predicting to answer the vocabulary-in-context questions on the following page.

International reaction to the Spanish architect Antoni Gaudí has always been ambivalent. Architecture critic Nikolaus Pevsner ignored him altogether in the 1936 edition of his seminal *Pioneers of Modern Design.* It was only after 1962 that Gaudí was admitted to its pages. George Orwell,
5 in Barcelona during the Civil War, was more explicit, calling the Gaudí's Sagrada Familia church "one of the most hideous buildings in the world." However, many architects would say Orwell was talking through his hat. Le Corbusier described the school Gaudí designed as part of the Sagrada Familia project as "a masterpiece." Norman Foster has called Gaudí's
10 methods revolutionary. Modern Spain's best-known architect, Santiago Calatrava, shows Gaudí's influence in his use of *trencadís* (broken ceramic tiles) as decoration, his use of arches, and his primary source of inspiration— nature.

The ornate decoration of many Gaudí buildings can be seen as, at best,
15 superfluous, and at worst kitsch. In his excellent biography *Gaudí*, published by HarperCollins last year, U.K.-based Dutch architect Gijs van Hensbergen says of the Catalan's first private commission, a house in Barcelona for the wealthy tilemaker Manuel Vicens, "ornamentation is everywhere in riotous and tasteless profusion."

20 While Gaudí was unlucky in love and had poor health, he was enormously fortunate in those with whom he surrounded himself. He found patrons, particularly businessman Eusebi Guell, who rarely interfered with his vision. Given that Gaudí was given to changing his designs over and over during the building process, his patrons needed to have bottomless
25 pockets. Gaudí was also backed by superb Catalan craftsmen, particularly in stone and iron, and his studio included men both loyal and brilliant in their own right. One, the largely unrecognized Josep Jujol, is described by Van Hensbergen as one of architecture's "greatest creative geniuses."

Main Idea: _____

Author's Purpose: _____

1. As it is used in line 18, the word *riotous* most nearly means:

   Find the word or phrase in the passage and reread the sentence around it.

   Use the clues to figure out the meaning of the word or phrase.

   Prediction: _____

   A. humorous.
   B. disorderly.
   C. revolutionary.
   D. lawless.

2. As it is used in line 22, the word *patrons* most nearly means:

   Find the word or phrase in the passage and reread the sentence around it.

   Use the clues to figure out the meaning of the word or phrase.

   Prediction: _____

   F. patriots.
   G. clients.
   H. paternal individuals.
   J. condescending individuals.

keep in mind

If you can't predict an answer by looking at the context, plug each answer choice into the passage and eliminate your way to the correct answer.

3. The phrase "was talking through his hat" (line 7) means that some architects believe that Orwell's opinion of Gaudí was:

   Find the word or phrase in the passage and reread the sentence around it.

   Use the clues to figure out the meaning of the word or phrase.

   Prediction: _____

   A. unintelligible or garbled.
   B. credible but wrong.
   C. extremely inaccurate.
   D. spiteful and hurtful.

C

Test Practice Unit 3

When your teacher tells you, carefully tear out this page.

1. Ⓐ Ⓑ Ⓒ Ⓓ   15. Ⓐ Ⓑ Ⓒ Ⓓ

2. Ⓕ Ⓖ Ⓗ Ⓙ   16. Ⓕ Ⓖ Ⓗ Ⓙ

3. Ⓐ Ⓑ Ⓒ Ⓓ   17. Ⓐ Ⓑ Ⓒ Ⓓ

4. Ⓕ Ⓖ Ⓗ Ⓙ   18. Ⓕ Ⓖ Ⓗ Ⓙ

5. Ⓐ Ⓑ Ⓒ Ⓓ   19. Ⓐ Ⓑ Ⓒ Ⓓ

6. Ⓕ Ⓖ Ⓗ Ⓙ   20. Ⓕ Ⓖ Ⓗ Ⓙ

7. Ⓐ Ⓑ Ⓒ Ⓓ

8. Ⓕ Ⓖ Ⓗ Ⓙ

9. Ⓐ Ⓑ Ⓒ Ⓓ

10. Ⓕ Ⓖ Ⓗ Ⓙ

11. Ⓐ Ⓑ Ⓒ Ⓓ

12. Ⓕ Ⓖ Ⓗ Ⓙ

13. Ⓐ Ⓑ Ⓒ Ⓓ

14. Ⓕ Ⓖ Ⓗ Ⓙ

C

DO NOT TURN THE PAGE UNTIL TOLD TO DO SO.

READING TEST

18 Minutes—20 Questions

DIRECTIONS: There are two passages in this test. Each passage is followed by several questions. After reading a passage, choose the best answer to each question and fill in the corresponding oval on your answer document. You may refer to the passages as often as necessary.

Passage III

SOCIAL SCIENCE: The following passage is an adapted excerpt from "The Wolf at the Door" by Javier Iannuzzi. The passage discusses the history of the gray wolf and its controversial reintroduction into Yellowstone Park and other areas.

A man who goes by the name "Timber" was shooting a film in Yellowstone Park, the wilderness preserve that spans parts of Wyoming, Idaho, and Montana. It was just past dawn.
5   Timber and the rest of the crew were watching grizzly bears polish off a bison carcass. Then, as Timber describes it, "A lone wolf appeared out of the early morning mist. The hair on the back of my neck stands up even today when I think of it. Here
10 we are, miles from the road, nine or more grizzlies coming in to feed, along with about 200 ravens, bison, coyotes, elk and this one lone black wolf.... I've witnessed many unusual or interesting sights in Yellowstone, but this will always be a morning I
15 will never forget."

A gray wolf (*Canis lupus*) may be one of the most breathtaking sights in nature. It's a lean, leggy animal, with a head the size of a human chest and a body that's sometimes almost five feet
20 long. Whereas coyotes appear delicate, wolves are massive. Some are completely black.

Despite their reputation as loners, wolves are highly social creatures. They're often devoted to their mates and dedicated to their young. For
25 those who support reintroducing wolves into Yellowstone and other native habitats, the animals are symbols of a tight-knit family—symbols that the human race would do well to emulate.

For those against the reintroduction of
30 wolves, the animals are symbols of something else. They're predators, after all, and if they don't get their daily fill of meat from wild game, they're likely to turn to livestock. Indeed, two weeks after the federal government began releasing wolves
35 from Canada into Yellowstone and central Idaho,

a ranch calf was discovered dead. Next to it was the body of a wolf. Folks were fairly certain that the wolf had killed the calf. Who had shot the wolf remains a mystery.

40   "Concern for wildlife should not overshadow concern for people," notes the president of the American Farm Bureau, an organization that has filed a lawsuit against the federal government in response to the wolf-reintroduction program.
45 The Farm Bureau argues that since the gray wolf is not technically an endangered species (it wavers between endangered and threatened), special provisions for it violate the law. If the wolf population flourishes, farmers and ranchers may
50 experience a threat to their property and perhaps even to their lives.

Nature and civilization are often in conflict, but in the case of wolves, humans may have exacerbated things. As settlers moved west in
55 the early 1800s, they shot bison and left many of the carcasses to rot. Wolves, which had roamed western North America for two million years, took advantage of the easy and abundant food supply. The wolf population swelled. The herds of bison
60 thinned. By the end of the 1800s, there remained many wolves, few bison, an increasing number of people, and a new food supply for wolves in the form of domestic livestock. Ranchers killed wolves in droves to protect their sheep and cows. By the
65 20th century, the vast majority of the American wolf population was either driven north or eliminated.

People now seeking to restore wolf populations may be partly motivated by a desire to
70 make amends for humans' perceived abuses. They may also want to restore the reputation of wolves. Culturally, wolves are often considered evil man-eaters, although, as one advocacy group points out, more people are killed by lightning than
75 by wolves. Finally, advocates argue that wolves make a positive contribution to the ecosystem. Predators keep other animal populations in check. Without wolves, smaller game would become

GO ON TO THE NEXT PAGE.

more abundant than the food supply could
80 support, in which case they would starve to death.

Yellowstone Park officials and the federal
government appear to agree with those who
advocate for the reintroduction of wolves. In
1939, Yellowstone ended its policy of eliminating
85 all predators from the park. In 1973, with the
Endangered Species Act, Congress made it a
federal offense to kill a wolf. The crime would cost
a perpetrator up to $100,000 and a year in jail.

In recent years, many species of wolves have
90 outgrown their status as endangered animals,
although gray wolves remain on the Endangered
Species List. As the wolf population grows,
dissenters like the American Farm Bureau may
more effectively enforce their views. As advocates
95 and dissenters duke it out in the courts, wolves
that have already been reintroduced in the lower
48 states continue to prowl, hunt, meet, mate, and
roam in increasing numbers through national
parks and inhabited wilderness.

1. As it is used in the passage, *swelled* (line 59) most
    nearly means:
    A. grew.
    B. burst.
    C. floated upward.
    D. slimmed down.

2. According to the passage, one reason for the
    severe decrease in the American wolf population
    after the late 1800s was:
    F. an increase in the bison population.
    G. a decrease in food supply.
    H. an increase in the number of ranchers.
    J. a decrease in the amount of livestock.

3. Which of the following is NOT cited as a
    motivation for restoring the wolf population?
    A. Rebalancing the food chain
    B. Undoing human cruelty
    C. Protecting cattle populations
    D. Dispelling negative myths

4. The author most likely included Timber's story in
    order to:
    F. challenge the popular notion that wolves are
        man-eaters.
    G. illustrate the majestic presence that wolves
        possess.
    H. provide a picture of the immense size of a
        gray wolf.
    J. demonstrate that the wolf is a highly social
        creature.

5. According to the passage, which of the following
    strategies were implemented to protect the
    wolves?
    I.   Criminal punishments for hunting.
    II.   Removal of wolves from the list of
          endangered species.
    III. The establishment of advocacy groups.
    A. I and II only
    B. I and III only
    C. II and III only
    D. I, II, and III

6. The author's conclusion about the eventual
    outcome of the legal battle between wolf
    supporters and opponents is that:
    F. few people are even aware that this is an
        issue in American courts.
    G. it will eventually depend on the decisions of
        Congress and the Supreme Court.
    H. the opponents are likely to prevail.
    J. it is less significant because the wolf
        population has already been re-established.

7. The phrase "more people are killed by lightning"
    most nearly means that:
    A. wolves' evil reputation has been etched in
        American culture.
    B. there are many dangers inherent to living in
        the American West.
    C. wolves only attack when they are provoked.
    D. the odds of being killed by a wolf are very
        low.

8. This passage is primarily concerned with:
    F. calling for the restoration of the wolf
        population to its pre-1800s numbers.
    G. portraying wolves as an important and
        essential part of the Western American
        ecosystem.
    H. highlighting the weaknesses in the
        arguments made by the American Farm
        Bureau.
    J. discussing the historical background and
        current situation of the American gray wolf.

C

GO ON TO THE NEXT PAGE.

9. The author's intention in the fourth paragraph is most likely to:

    A. suggest what would happen if the wolf population were allowed to flourish.

    B. debunk myths about the evil nature of wolves.

    C. stress that wolves kill a very small amount of cattle.

    D. indicate that ranchers' concerns about wolves have some validity.

10. The author mentions wolves' dedication to their families (line 24) in order to:

    F. express that a social animal is less likely to kill maliciously.

    G. highlight the dangerous implications of killing off a family animal.

    H. challenge their reputation as mean, solitary animals.

    J. demonstrate wolves' superiority to humans with regard to familial structure.

Passage IV

NATURAL SCIENCE: The following passage is excerpted from "Can We Curb Global Warming," by Sandeep Khera ©Manhattan Beach Courier, June 2005, Vol. 23, Issue 6, p. 9).

Since the late 19th century, the temperature of Earth's atmosphere has risen by approximately one degree Fahrenheit. Earth's atmospheric temperature has remained relatively stable for the

5 last several thousand years, so many scientists identify global warming as a serious problem. One degree may sound like a very slight increase, but even this slight warming of our atmosphere may have dramatic consequences. Effects of

10 global warming could include melting glaciers, rising seas, and changing weather patterns. Those changes could in turn result in more natural disasters, such as floods, droughts, and severe storms. Not everyone agrees on how extreme

15 the effects of global warming could be, or even how likely they are to occur, but most people are concerned that global warming will threaten the complex balance of Earth's ecosystem.

The atmosphere is comprised primarily of

20 carbon dioxide, methane, and nitrous oxide. It naturally traps heat from the Sun, providing a protective layer of warmth that keeps Earth from freezing. This process is called the "greenhouse effect," because Earth's atmosphere acts like

25 the panes of glass on a greenhouse—letting in the radiation from the Sun and storing it to heat the life within. Increasingly, human activities are adding more and more "greenhouse gases" to the atmosphere—especially carbon dioxide.

30 The fuel we burn to provide gasoline for our cars, heat for our homes, and electricity for our factories also emits greenhouse gases and pollutants. In the United States, the energy for everyday human activities accounts for about 98

35 percent of carbon dioxide emissions, 24 percent of methane emissions, and 18 percent of nitrous oxide emissions. Eventually, these emissions and pollutants increase the heat trapped in the atmosphere.

40 Recognizing that global warming connects everyone, governments have proposed both domestic and international agreements to regulate harmful emissions. Agreements such as the Kyoto Protocol (1997) aim to reduce the

45 amount of greenhouse gases that industrialized countries add to the atmosphere. To reach this goal, the world's energy habits will have to change significantly. Consider that humans today use 130 times the amount of energy that they used in

GO ON TO THE NEXT PAGE.

50 pre-industrial times; that the cost of importing crude oil (which supplies over one-third of the world's energy) represents between one-third and two-thirds of most countries' budgets; and that many countries that are major exporters of crude
55 oil depend primarily on that revenue to maintain their economies. In short, changing the economic and social infrastructure that has developed around energy could entail as dramatic a shift as global warming might provoke in the ecosystem.

60 One increasingly popular solution to our environmental and energy problems is natural gas. Colorless, odorless, and shapeless, natural gas is trapped below the ground and produces energy when burned. Burned natural gas releases
65 significantly lower levels of carbon dioxide than fuel oil and releases hardly any ash at all. People consider it to be "clean burning." At the same time, natural gas generates a tremendous amount of energy and already accounts for 24 percent of
70 the energy consumed in the United States.

What's not to like? Those wary of natural gas as a long-term solution for our environmental and energy problems point out that natural gas is almost entirely comprised of methane—a
75 greenhouse gas around 20 times stronger than carbon dioxide! They also caution that the process of extracting, storing, and delivering natural gas presents environmental hazards that may offset the benefits of its relatively clean
80 burning properties. Natural gas, like crude oil, must be found, drilled, and piped to its users—a process that requires heavy machinery that emits greenhouse gases and disrupts the land, both at the point of excavation and over the area of
85 distribution. Natural gas is also subject to sudden fires and leaks.

In light of its low ratio of greenhouse gas to energy produced—as well as ongoing improvements to extraction and distribution
90 mechanisms—natural gas appears to be an appealing alternative to crude oil. The trouble remains that natural gas, like crude oil, is not a renewable resource. In fact, natural gas is often found in the same reservoirs as crude oil; no one
95 knows when these reservoirs will run out.

At the moment, consumers benefit from the popularity of natural gas: it has the potential to decrease the greenhouse gases we emit into the atmosphere, and it comes at a lower cost than
100 many other energy sources. Natural gas has developed as an energy source alongside crude oil, so many of the technical and commercial processes to extract and deliver natural gas are already in place. In addition to its improved—

105 although not perfect—effect on the atmosphere, advocates for natural gas make a "one bird in the hand is worth two in the bush" argument: natural gas is already a viable energy source that can meet our needs for the foreseeable future. The danger
110 is that if the world doesn't keep looking for better long-term solutions, we might be left empty-handed all the same.

11. As it is used in the passage, the phrase "in light of" (line 87) most nearly means:
   A. despite.
   B. luminous of.
   C. given.
   D. visible in.

12. According to the passage, the greenhouse gas being added to the atmosphere in the greatest quantity is:
   F. methane.
   G. carbon dioxide.
   H. nitrous oxide.
   J. crude oil.

13. According to the passage, all of the following are potential advantages of natural gas EXCEPT:
   A. it is clean burning.
   B. it has low carbon dioxide emissions.
   C. it has no risks during extraction.
   D. it has a low cost relative to many other energy sources.

14. The author's main intention in the third paragraph (lines 40–59) is to:
   F. condemn governments who refuse to address global warming.
   G. highlight the financial opportunities available to supporters of the Kyoto Protocol.
   H. emphasize the difficulties of fighting global warming.
   J. develop a historical context for world oil consumption.

15. The author's statement, "In the United States, the energy for everyday human activities accounts for about 98 percent of carbon dioxide emissions, 24 percent of methane emissions, and 18 percent of nitrous oxide emissions," (lines 33–37) is meant to demonstrate that greenhouse gases are:
   A. the inevitable byproduct of daily life.
   B. mainly produced to create energy in the United States.
   C. detrimental to the atmosphere.
   D. produced in greater amounts by the United States than by any other country.

GO ON TO THE NEXT PAGE.

16. According to the passage, the "greenhouse effect" is responsible for:
    F. feeding plant life.
    G. deflecting solar rays.
    H. warming Earth.
    J. releasing harmful gases.

17. According to the passage, which of the following does NOT represent a reason natural gas may be a viable long-term energy solution?
    A. It is already a popular energy source.
    B. It exists in much greater quantities than crude oil.
    C. It generates great amounts of energy.
    D. It produces fewer carbon dioxide emissions than does fuel oil.

18. As a greenhouse gas and in comparison to carbon dioxide, methane is about
    F. four times weaker.
    G. 20 times stronger.
    H. 24 times stronger.
    J. 130 times stronger.

19. The temperature information given in the first paragraph ("the temperature of Earth's… Fahrenheit.") is included primarily to:
    A. establish the fact that Earth has been warming over the last century.
    B. demonstrate how atmospheric warming has already devastated the environment.
    C. introduce scientific disagreement over the seriousness of global warming.
    D. show the broad range of atmospheric temperatures over the past thousand years.

20. The author's main conclusion about the threat of global warming is that:
    F. altering energy policies will prove impossible in the long run.
    G. natural gas will provide the most attractive energy source indefinitely.
    H. change must be immediate or the consequences will be disastrous.
    J. the world's current fuels are unsustainable in the long run.

END OF TEST.

STOP! DO NOT TURN THE PAGE UNTIL TOLD TO DO SO.

KAP Wrap

Think about a word or phrase you have recently heard or have recently used. Explain how that word or phrase could be interpreted differently based on the context.

Unit 4
ACT Reading III

Thinking KAP

Imagine that you are home alone on a Saturday afternoon. You are eating a sandwich at the kitchen table. Your dog is standing on his hind legs and begging for a bite. Suddenly, the phone rings. You have been waiting for a friend to call. You quickly set your sandwich down and get up from the table. You talk with your friend for several minutes. When you hang up and return to the table, your sandwich is nowhere to be found, but there are several crumbs on the floor. You call out, "Hello?!" but no one answers. Your dog has disappeared. When you find him, he is in another room licking his lips.

Circle the most likely explanation for the disappearance of your sandwich.

1. The sandwich got up and walked away.

2. Your father or mother came home hungry and ate the sandwich.

3. Space aliens snuck into your house and took the sandwich.

4. Your dog ate the sandwich.

Inference Questions

Inference questions require you to draw conclusions that are not stated by the author. The correct answer to an inference question is not stated directly in the text. When you make an inference, you do not state a fact or an opinion. You draw a conclusion based on the details in the passage.

Inference questions represent about 1/2 of all questions on the ACT Reading Test. You should expect to see between 17 and 20 of them per test.

Identifying Inference Questions

Like detail questions, inference questions refer to the passage. However, while detail questions make very concrete references to the passage, inference questions make non-concrete references to the passage. Inference questions often use the words *conclude*, *infer*, *suggest*, or *imply*. The following are common phrases indicating inference questions:

- The passage suggests …
- Xxxx implies …
- Xxxx's comments imply …
- Xxxx most directly supports the conclusion that …
- Xxxx would likely agree that …
- It can be inferred that …

Try It Out!

Read the question stems below. Circle the inference questions.

1. Information in the passage suggests that the author regards Wayland the Smith as:
2. According to the passage, art most likely began:
3. As it is used in line 4, *secure* most nearly means:
4. The author's comments in paragraph 4 (lines 8–9) suggest that Achilles:
5. In the second paragraph (lines 22–24), the author states that arms were decorated as a way of:
6. Based on information in the passage, the author would most likely agree with which of the following statements regarding arms-making?

Broad- and Narrow-Inference Questions

You may recall from Unit 2 that inference questions come in two varieties—narrow and broad. Narrow-inference questions require you to draw conclusions based on a limited part of the passage, such as a single detail or paragraph, while broad-inference questions require you to draw conclusions based on the entire passage, or a large portion of it.

Answering Narrow-Inference Questions

What makes narrow-inference questions difficult to answer is that the correct answers will not be explicitly stated in the passage. What makes this type of question easy to answer is that the answers will not stray far from the text. During Step 3 of the 3-Step Method for ACT Reading Comprehension, you will find the important information you need to answer the question. After you have read a passage and determined that a question is asking you to make an inference about a specific part of the passage, you will use **Getting Grounded in the Details** to research and reason your way to a conclusion.

With inference questions, it's not a "matter of opinion." There is only one right answer choice that is true based on the details in the passage.

Getting Grounded in the Details

- **Find** and **reread** the part of the passage that relates to the question.

- **Ground** yourself in the details.

When you use Getting Grounded in the Details, the conclusions you make should be drawn from the details stated in the passage. In the Thinking KAP activity, you circled the most likely explanation for the disappearance of your sandwich. Only the correct answer was related to the details of the situation. Similarly, the correct answer to a narrow-inference question, while not stated directly in the passage, will not be far removed. Take logical steps—not leaps—away from the details when you draw inferences.

Predicting and Eliminating with Narrow-Inference Questions

After you use Getting Grounded in the Details, remember to make a prediction. With narrow-inference questions, it is sometimes difficult to make a prediction. In these situations, or when you can't find a match for your prediction, use Eliminating. When you use Eliminating, look at each answer choice and ask yourself, "Does this *have* to be true based on the details I have grounded myself in?" Answer choices that are merely *likely* to be true can still be wrong. You want the one answer choice that *has* to be true based on the details in the passage.

Try It Out!

Read the excerpted passage from the short story "Graduation" by Jon Krupp below. Then use Getting Grounded in the Details and Predicting and Eliminating to answer the questions that follow.

Rosemary sat at her kitchen table, working at a crossword puzzle. Crosswords were nice; they filled the time and kept the mind active. She needed just one word to complete this morning's puzzle. The clue was "A Swiss river," and the first of its three letters was "A." Unfortunately, Rosemary
5   had no idea what the name of the river was and could not look it up. Her atlas was on the desk, and the desk was in the guest room, currently being occupied by her grandson Victor. Looking up over the tops of her bifocals, Rosemary glanced at the kitchen clock—it was almost 10 A.M. Land sakes! Did the boy intend to sleep all day? She noticed that the arthritis in her wrist
10 was throbbing, and she put down her pen. At 87 years of age, she was glad she could still write at all. She had decided long ago that growing old meant that you could not take anything for granted.

Something Victor had said last night over dinner had disturbed her. Now what was it? Oh yes, he had been talking about one of his college courses—a
15 "gut," he had called it. When she had asked him to explain the term, Victor said it was a course that you took simply because it was easy to pass. Rosemary, who had not even had a high school education, found the term repellent. If she had been allowed to continue her studies, she would never have taken a "gut."
20
The memory flooded back then, still as painful as an open wound all these years later. It was the first day of high school. She had graduated from grammar school the previous year, but her father had forbidden her to go on to high school that fall, saying that she was needed on the farm. After much tearful pleading, she had gotten him to promise that next year, she could start
25 high school. She had endured a whole year of chores instead of books, with animals and rough farmhands for company instead of people her own age. Now, at last, the glorious day was at hand. She had put on her best dress (she owned two), her heart racing in anticipation. But her father was waiting for her as she came downstairs.
30
"Where do you think you're going?" he asked.

"To high school, Papa."

"No, you're not. Take that thing off and get back to work."

"But Papa, you promised!"

"Do as I say!" he thundered.
35
There was no arguing with Papa when he spoke that way. Tearfully, she had trudged upstairs to change clothes. Rosemary still wondered what life would have been like if her father had not been waiting at the bottom of the stairs that day, or if somehow she had found the strength to defy him.

Main Idea: _____

Author's Purpose: _____

keep in mind

The correct answer to an inference question will usually be just a baby step away from the details in the passage.

A

1. The passage suggests that Rosemary's attitude toward the physical afflictions of old age is generally one of:

   Find and reread the part of the passage that relates to the question.

   Ground yourself in the details.

   Prediction: _____

   A. sadness.
   B. acceptance.
   C. resentment.
   D. optimism.

2. It can be inferred from the passage that Rosemary is disturbed by Victor's:

   Find and reread the part of the passage that relates to the question.

   Ground yourself in the details.

   Prediction: _____

   F. intention to drop out of college.
   G. disregard for her harsh upbringing.
   H. ability to sleep all day.
   J. willingness to take easy courses.

3. Information given in the passage suggests that Rosemary's father:

   Find and reread the part of the passage that relates to the question.

   Ground yourself in the details.

   Prediction: _(difficult to predict)_____

   Eliminate answer choices that don't *have* to be true based on the details you've grounded yourself in.

   A. did not love Rosemary.
       Does this *have* to be true based on the details? _____
   B. valued pursuing an education over working on the farm.
       Does this *have* to be true based on the details? _____
   C. frequently changed his mind once he had made a decision.
       Does this *have* to be true based on the details? _____
   D. intimidated Rosemary.
       Does this *have* to be true based on the details? _____

keep in mind

Stick to the material covered in the passage. The most common wrong answer choices for narrow-inference questions are out of scope or extreme.

A

The 3-Step Method for ACT Reading Comprehension

 STEP 1: Read actively.

- ▣ *Summarize each paragraph.*

- ▣ *Question the Author.*

 STEP 2: Examine the question stems.

- ▣ *Identify the question type.*

- ▣ *Determine the correct strategy.*

 STEP 3: Answer the questions.

- ▣ *Find the important information.*

- ▣ *Predict and eliminate.*

Getting Grounded in the Details

- **Find** and **reread** the part of the passage that relates to the question.
- **Ground** yourself in the details.

Read the text below and answer the following questions.

Passage I

NATURAL SCIENCE: This passage from a textbook about the solar system discusses research examining the possibility of life on Mars.

When the first of the two Viking Landers touched down on Martian soil on July 20, 1976, and began to send camera images back to Earth, the scientists at the Jet Propulsion Laboratory
5   could not suppress a certain nervous anticipation, like people who hold a ticket to a lottery they have a one-in-a-million chance of winning. The first photographs that arrived, however, did not contain any evidence of life. What was
10   revealed was merely a barren landscape littered with rocks and boulders. The view resembled nothing so much as a flat section of desert. In fact, the winning entry in a contest at J.P.L. for the photograph most accurately predicting what
15   Mars would look like was a snapshot taken from a particularly arid section of the Mojave Desert.

The scientists were soon ready to turn their attention from visible life to microorganisms. The twin Viking Landers carried experiments
20   designed to detect organic compounds. Researchers thought it possible that life had developed on early Mars just as it is thought to have developed on Earth, through the gradual chemical evolution of complex organic molecules.
25   To detect biological activity, Martian soil samples were treated with various nutrients that would produce characteristic by-products if life forms were active in the soil. The results from all three experiments were inconclusive. In the
30   fourth experiment, a soil sample was heated to look for signs of organic material, but none were found—an unexpected result because scientists thought organic compounds from the steady bombardment of the Martian surface by
35   meteorites would be present.

The absence of organic materials, some scientists speculated, was the result of intense ultraviolet radiation penetrating the atmosphere of Mars and destroying organic compounds in the
40   soil. Although Mars' atmosphere was at one time rich in carbon dioxide and thus thick enough to protect its surface from the harmful rays of the Sun, the carbon dioxide had gradually left the atmosphere and been converted into rocks. This
45   means that even if life had gotten a start on early Mars, it could not have survived the exposure to ultraviolet radiation when the atmosphere thinned. Mars never developed a protective layer of ozone as Earth did.

50   Despite the disappointing Viking results, there are those who still keep open the possibility of life on Mars. They point out that the Viking data cannot be considered the final word on Martian life because the two landers only sampled
55   limited—and uninteresting—sites. The Viking landing sites were not chosen for what they might tell of the planet's biology. They were chosen primarily because they appeared to be safe for landing a spacecraft. The landing sites were
60   on parts of the Martian plains that appeared relatively featureless from orbital photographs.

The type of terrain that these researchers suggest may be a possible hiding place for active life has an earthly parallel: the ice-free region of
65   southern Victoria Land, Antarctica, where the temperatures in some dry valleys average below zero. Organisms known as endoliths, a form of blue-green algae that has adapted to this harsh environment, were found living inside certain
70   translucent, porous rocks in these Antarctic valleys. The argument based on this discovery is that if life did exist on early Mars, it is possible that it escaped worsening conditions by similarly seeking refuge in rocks. Skeptics object, however,
75   that Mars in its present state is simply too dry, even compared with Antarctic valleys, to sustain any life whatsoever.

1. The researchers' argument that life may exist in Martian rocks rests on the idea that:

Find and reread the part of the passage that relates to the question.

Ground yourself in the details.

Prediction: _____

- **A.** life adapted to harsh conditions in a similar manner on two planets.
- **B.** organisms may adopt identical survival strategies in similar environments.
- **C.** life developed in the form of a blue-green algae on Mars.
- **D.** organisms that survived in Antarctica could survive on Mars.

ACT ADVANTAGE
ENGLISH & READING

2. The passage suggests that an important difference between Mars and Earth is that, unlike Earth, Mars:

Find and reread the part of the passage that relates to the question.

Ground yourself in the details.

Prediction: _____

    F.   accumulated organic compounds in its soil.
    G.   is exposed to more harmful rays of ultraviolet radiation.
    H.   once possessed an atmosphere rich in carbon dioxide.
    J.   is incapable of sustaining any form of life that may have developed.

A

Shared Practice

■ *Use the 3-Step Method for ACT Reading Comprehension—including Getting Grounded in the Details and Predicting and Eliminating—for the passage and questions below.*

Passage II

PROSE FICTION: This passage is adapted from Katherine Mansfield's short story "Miss Brill," which was originally published in *The Garden Party and Other Stories*. In the passage, Miss Brill wears an old fur for her weekly visit to the park.

Miss Brill was glad that she had decided on her fur. Dear little thing! It was nice to feel it again. She had taken it out of its box that afternoon, shaken out the moth-powder, given it a good

5 brush, and rubbed the life back into the dim little eyes. "What has been happening to me?" said the sad little eyes. Oh, how sweet it was to see them snap at her again.

There were a number of people out this

10 afternoon, far more than last Sunday. And the band sounded louder.

Only two people shared her "special" seat: a fine old man in a velvet coat, his hands clasped over a huge carved walking stick, and a big old

15 woman, sitting upright, with a roll of knitting on her embroidered apron. They did not speak. This was disappointing, for Miss Brill always looked forward to the conversation. She had become really quite expert, she thought, at listening as

20 though she didn't listen, at sitting in on other people's lives just for a minute while they talked round her.

To and fro, in front of the flower beds and the band rotunda, the couples and groups paraded,

25 stopped to talk, to greet, to buy a handful of flowers from the old beggar who had his tray fixed to the railings. Other people sat on the benches and green chairs, but they were nearly always the same, Sunday after Sunday, and—Miss Brill had

30 often noticed—there was something funny about nearly all of them. They were odd, silent, nearly all old, and from the way they stared they looked as though they'd just come from dark little rooms or even—even cupboards!

35 Two young girls in red came by and two young soldiers in blue met them, and they laughed and paired and went off arm-in-arm. A beautiful woman came along and dropped her bunch of violets, and a little boy ran after to hand them to

40 her, and she took them and threw them away as if they'd been poisoned. Dear me! Miss Brill didn't know whether to admire that or not.

Oh, how fascinating it was! How she enjoyed it! How she loved sitting here, watching it all! It

45 was like a play. It was exactly like a play. Who could believe the sky at the back wasn't painted? But it wasn't till a little brown dog trotted on solemnly and then slowly trotted off, like a little "theatre" dog, a little dog that had been drugged,

50 that Miss Brill discovered what it was that made it so exciting. They were all on the stage. They weren't only the audience, not only looking on; they were acting. Even she had a part and came every Sunday. No doubt somebody would have

55 noticed if she hadn't been there; she was part of the performance after all.

The band had been having a rest. Now they started again. And what they played was warm, sunny, yet there was just a faint chill—not

60 sadness—no, not sadness—a something that made you want to sing. The tune lifted, lifted, the light shone; and it seemed to Miss Brill that in another moment all of them, the whole company, would begin singing. The young ones, the laughing ones

65 who were moving together, they would begin, and the men's voices, very resolute and brave, would join them. And then she too, she too, and the others on the benches—they would come in with a kind of accompaniment—something low, that

70 scarcely rose or fell, something so beautiful, so moving....

Just at that moment a boy and girl came and sat down where the old couple had been. They were beautifully dressed; they were in love. The

75 hero and heroine, of course, just arrived from his father's yacht. And still soundlessly singing, still with that trembling smile, Miss Brill prepared to listen.

"No, not now," said the girl. "Not here, I can't."

80 "But why? Because of that stupid old thing at the end there?" asked the boy. "Why does she

come here at all—who wants her? Why doesn't she keep her silly old mug at home?"

85 "It's her fur which is so funny," giggled the girl.

On her way home, Miss Brill usually bought a slice of honey-cake at the baker's. It was her Sunday treat. Sometimes there was an almond in her slice, sometimes not. It made a great 90 difference. If there was an almond, it was like carrying home a tiny present—a surprise— something that might very well not have been there.

But today she passed the baker's by, climbed 95 the stairs, went into the little dark room—her room like a cupboard—and sat down. She sat there for a long time. The box that the fur came out of was on the bed. She unclasped the necklet quickly; quickly, without looking, laid it inside. 100 But when she put the lid on, she thought she heard something crying.

1. From Miss Brill's memory of taking her fur out of storage (lines 1-8), it is most reasonable to infer that she thought of the fur:

   A. as something like a pet.
   B. only as a fashion accessory.
   C. as part of her costume for the stage.
   D. as an accessory that others might think of as humorous.

hint *Use the line reference to find the part of the passage that relates to the question.*

2. According to the passage, Miss Brill observes which of the following?

   F. A woman throwing away poisoned violets
   G. Two young girls meeting two young soldiers
   H. An old man planting flowers
   J. The young lovers boarding a yacht

hint *Eliminate your way to the correct answer choice.*

3. According to the passage, Miss Brill changes her normal Sunday routine by:

   A. talking with the young boy and girl.
   B. becoming an actress on stage.
   C. watching the actions of others in the park.
   D. going home without stopping at the baker's for a slice of honey-cake.

hint *Use your summary statements to track down the part of the passage where Miss Brill changes her Sunday routine.*

4. From the last paragraph of the passage, it is most reasonable to infer that:
    F. Miss Brill will never return to the park.
    G. Miss Brill no longer cares about her fur.
    H. Miss Brill feels like crying about that day's experience in the park.
    J. Miss Brill will no longer eavesdrop on other people's conversations.

    hint ▷ *What has to be true based on the details in the last paragraph?*

5. It is most reasonable to infer from the description of the boy and girl as "The hero and heroine, of course, just arrived from his father's yacht" (lines 74-76) that Miss Brill:
    A. is well-acquainted with them.
    B. has heard from others in the park that they are in love.
    C. thinks of them as actors on the stage of the park.
    D. is overly concerned about their relationship.

    hint ▷ *The correct answer will be only a small logical step away from the details in the passage.*

6. As it is used in the passage, ***company*** (line 63) most closely means:
    F. gathering of guests.
    G. a group of friends and acquaintances.
    H. a group of actors or performers.
    J. a business organization.

    hint ▷ *Look for clues to the meaning of the word in the words and sentences surrounding it.*

Name_____   Date_____

7. From the passage, it is most reasonable to infer that after Miss Brill listens to the boy and girl's conversation (lines 79-85), she realizes that:

    A. her dream of acting on stage is unrealistic.
    B. she can no longer enjoy her Sundays in the park.
    C. she is a character in the "play" that takes place in the park.
    D. some people in the park think that she is odd.

hint *Your prediction should be grounded in the details of the passage.*

8. According to the passage, Miss Brill gets the idea that Sundays in the park are like an exciting play in which she participates when she:

    F. sees the old woman knitting.
    G. watches a dog slowly trot by.
    H. sings with the other people in the park.
    J. takes her fur out of storage.

hint *Point out the important information in the paragraph where Miss Brill decides that Sundays in the park are like a play.*

A

KAP Wrap

Write about a situation in which you jumped to the wrong conclusion about something. How did you go astray? What details of the situation did you miss or leap too far away from?

A

Thinking KAP

Read the three statements below.

- Aurora is 30 years old.
- Bill is younger than Aurora.
- Carlos is younger than Bill.

Based on the statements above, which of the following conclusions *has* to be true? Circle the conclusion that is true. Underline the information in the statements above that *makes* it true.

1. Aurora is the oldest person in her family.

2. Bill is younger than 25.

3. Carlos is younger than Aurora.

Broad-Inference Questions

You may remember from Lesson A that broad-inference questions ask you to draw conclusions based on the whole passage or a large portion of it. What makes broad-inference questions easy to answer is that they sometimes discuss a theme that is repeated in the text. What makes this type of question difficult to answer is that you sometimes cannot do any research or make any predictions.

Main-Idea and Author's-Purpose Questions

There are two particular subtypes of broad-inference questions. Questions that ask about the main idea of a paragraph or of the passage are broad-inference questions. Questions that ask about the author's purpose are also broad-inference questions. Look at the examples of these types of questions below.

Main-Idea Questions

- The main conclusion reached about the future of the relationship between the people and the jaguars in the Pantanal is that:

- The main point of the second paragraph (lines xx-xx) is that:

- The main idea of the passage is that:

- The primary purpose of the passage is to convey the idea that:

Author's-Purpose Questions

- The primary purpose of the passage is to …

- The main concern of the passage is to …

In Unit 2, you learned to use Question the Author to identify the main idea of the passage and the author's purpose. This strategy will help you answer these special kinds of broad-inference questions.

keep in mind

Of the 17-20 inference questions on the ACT Reading Test, about 4 of them will be main-idea or author's purpose questions, and 2 or 3 will be other broad-inference questions. The remainder will be narrow-inference questions.

Answering Broad-Inference Questions

During Step 3 of the 3-Step Method for ACT Reading Comprehension, you will find the important information you need to answer the question. For main idea and author's purpose broad-inference questions, you will use Question the Author to find the important information. For other questions that ask you to make an inference about the whole passage or a large portion of it, it is often difficult to find the important information. Line or paragraph references are not provided in the question stems, and there is no specific text to examine. Because many inferences can be made for broad-inference questions, it is difficult to make predictions. Instead, you will eliminate. Use **Eliminating for Truth** to answer broad-inference questions that do not ask about the main idea or the author's purpose.

Eliminating for Truth

- **Look** at each answer choice.

- **Point** to something in the passage that makes the answer choice true.

- If you can't point to something that makes the answer choice true, **eliminate** it.

---

keep in mind

Remember to read actively. With broad-inference questions, *why* is often more important than *what*.

Broad-inference questions are unique in that you will not start out by finding specific information in the text. Instead, after you read the question, you will use Eliminating. In the Thinking KAP activity, you circled the conclusion that *had* to be true, and you underlined the information in the statements that *made* it true. Similarly, you should look at each answer choice to a broad-inference question. Try to point to something in the passage that makes it true. When you come across the correct answer choice to a broad-inference question, you should be able to point to something—or several things—in the passage that makes it true. If you can't point to anything, the answer choice is probably incorrect.

In the Thinking KAP activity, the statements that you eliminated were extreme or out of scope. While 30 may seem old to you (even if your parents and teachers would disagree), it's extreme to conclude that Aurora is the oldest member of her family. The only actual age reference is tied to Aurora. Therefore, it is out of scope to conclude that anyone other than Aurora is older or younger than 25—there is simply no support for this in the information that you know. Similarly, for broad-inference questions, most of the answer choices you eliminate will be extreme or out of scope.

B

Read the excerpted passage about American houses below. Then use Eliminating for Truth to answer the questions that follow.

People carry in their minds a picture of what constitutes an "American house." For most of us, it is and has long been a freestanding dwelling that rises from its own piece of land. Whether that piece of land is a 40-foot-wide lot on a city street or an expanse of farmland stretching off toward the
5 horizon is almost irrelevant; what matters is that the house stands as an individual object, separate from its neighbors. This may not be the sort of dwelling in which every American actually lives—millions inhabit apartment buildings and blocks of row houses—yet the detached house holds such an allure for the imagination that it remains a national ideal, in good times and
10 bad, in periods both of dense urban development and of outward suburban dispersal. So deeply embedded in the country's consciousness is the ideal of a freestanding dwelling that even young children, when asked to draw a house, will unhesitatingly make a sketch of a family-sized dwelling with a pitched roof on top, a few windows in its facade, and a prominent front door.

15 Some of the details that embellish this notion of the American house have, of course, changed greatly with the passage of time. In the 1850s, when landscape architect Andrew Jackson Downing was exerting a major influence on residential design, the image of an American house would have included verandas and vestibules, parlors, and pantries. In the 1920s, a decade
20 enchanted by "Old English" architecture but also gripped by a concern for cleanliness, it often summoned up a picturesque, even quaint, exterior with arched doorways and a steeply pitched roof, yet with a shiny white-surfaced kitchen and bathroom within. In the 1960s, the prevailing vision was of a house that had substituted a back patio or deck for the front porch and
25 had added a "family room" as a casual, unceremonious alternative to the formality of the living room.

Despite such modifications, the governing ideal remained constant in its essentials—an individual residence enclosing a comfortable amount of space beneath the slopes of its roof and enjoying dominion over a certain amount of
30 land beyond its walls. Gradually, too, the American house was accompanied by a standard arrangement of its grounds. In the front grew a neatly kept lawn, setting a scene of dignity and repose. To the rear, a more informal yard provided a space for relaxation and outdoor recreation. Side yards acted as buffers against the noise and nosiness of neighbors, while at the same time
35 making each household feel more autonomous.

This was by no means a perfect or universal way to provide shelter, but it did satisfy many of the needs of millions of people. From East Coast to West, vast numbers of houses were built in accordance with the common image of the American house—dwellings set apart from one another in a pattern that
40 suited, above all, the interests of families.

Main Idea: _____

Author's Purpose: _____

keep in mind

Don't get bogged down in details. Focus on the "big picture" as you read.

B

1. The passage suggests that the ideal of living in a detached house:

    Look at each answer choice.

    Point to something in the passage that makes the answer choice true.

    If you can't point to something that makes the answer choice true, eliminate it.

    A. is not realized by many Americans.
    B. is only held by those living in farmland country.
    C. is less popular during periods of economic depression.
    D. appeals most of all to young children rather than to adults.

2. The passage suggests that the most essential characteristic of the ideal "American house" is that it must:

    Look at each answer choice.

    Point to something in the passage that makes the answer choice true.

    If you can't point to something that makes the answer choice true, eliminate it.

    F. have a neatly kept front lawn.
    G. combine traditional architecture with modern cleanliness.
    H. have a facade with windows and a prominent front door.
    J. be a freestanding dwelling.

When making inferences, limit yourself to what you know from the passage.

3. Based on the passage, it is most reasonable to conclude that the author believes that:

    Look at each answer choice.

    Point to something in the passage that makes the answer choice true.

    If you can't point to something that makes the answer choice true, eliminate it.

    A. builders of houses in America will continue to craft freestanding dwellings for centuries into the future.
    B. despite many changes over time, the American house has kept its overarching form intact.
    C. as the population of America grows, there will be fewer opportunities to build freestanding dwellings in the future.
    D. landscape architect Andrew Jackson Downing was the preeminent architect of the 19th century.

B

The 3-Step Method for ACT Reading Comprehension

 ## *STEP 1: Read actively.*

- ### *Summarize each paragraph.*

- ### *Question the Author.*

 ## *STEP 2: Examine the question stems.*

- ### *Identify the question type.*

- ### *Determine the correct strategy.*

 ## *STEP 3: Answer the questions.*

- ### *Find the important information.*

- ### *Predict and eliminate.*

Eliminating for Truth

- **Look** at each answer choice.
- **Point** to something in the passage that makes the answer choice true.
- If you can't point to something that makes the answer choice true, **eliminate** it.

Read the text below and answer the following questions.

Passage I

NATURAL SCIENCE: This passage from a textbook about the solar system discusses research examining the possibility of life on Mars.

When the first of the two Viking Landers touched down on Martian soil on July 20, 1976, and began to send camera images back to Earth, the scientists at the Jet Propulsion Laboratory
5 could not suppress a certain nervous anticipation, like people who hold a ticket to a lottery they have a one-in-a-million chance of winning. The first photographs that arrived, however, did not contain any evidence of life. What was
10 revealed was merely a barren landscape littered with rocks and boulders. The view resembled nothing so much as a flat section of desert. In fact, the winning entry in a contest at J.P.L. for the photograph most accurately predicting what
15 Mars would look like was a snapshot taken from a particularly arid section of the Mojave Desert.

The scientists were soon ready to turn their attention from visible life to microorganisms. The twin Viking Landers carried experiments
20 designed to detect organic compounds. Researchers thought it possible that life had developed on early Mars just as it is thought to have developed on Earth, through the gradual chemical evolution of complex organic molecules.
25 To detect biological activity, Martian soil samples were treated with various nutrients that would produce characteristic by-products if life forms were active in the soil. The results from all three experiments were inconclusive. In the
30 fourth experiment, a soil sample was heated to look for signs of organic material, but none were found—an unexpected result because scientists thought organic compounds from the steady bombardment of the Martian surface by
35 meteorites would be present.

The absence of organic materials, some scientists speculated, was the result of intense ultraviolet radiation penetrating the atmosphere of Mars and destroying organic compounds in the
40 soil. Although Mars' atmosphere was at one time rich in carbon dioxide and thus thick enough to protect its surface from the harmful rays of the Sun, the carbon dioxide had gradually left the atmosphere and been converted into rocks. This
45 means that even if life had gotten a start on early Mars, it could not have survived the exposure to ultraviolet radiation when the atmosphere thinned. Mars never developed a protective layer of ozone as Earth did.

50 Despite the disappointing Viking results, there are those who still keep open the possibility of life on Mars. They point out that the Viking data cannot be considered the final word on Martian life because the two landers only sampled
55 limited—and uninteresting—sites. The Viking landing sites were not chosen for what they might tell of the planet's biology. They were chosen primarily because they appeared to be safe for landing a spacecraft. The landing sites were
60 on parts of the Martian plains that appeared relatively featureless from orbital photographs.

The type of terrain that these researchers suggest may be a possible hiding place for active life has an Earthly parallel: the ice-free region of
65 southern Victoria Land, Antarctica, where the temperatures in some dry valleys average below zero. Organisms known as endoliths, a form of blue-green algae that has adapted to this harsh environment, were found living inside certain
70 translucent, porous rocks in these Antarctic valleys. The argument based on this discovery is that if life did exist on early Mars, it is possible that it escaped worsening conditions by similarly seeking refuge in rocks. Skeptics object, however,
75 that Mars in its present state is simply too dry, even compared with Antarctic valleys, to sustain any life whatsoever.

B

1. The passage supports which of the following statements about the possibility of life on Mars?

   Look at each answer choice.

   Point to something in the passage that makes the answer choice true.

   If you can't point to something that makes the answer choice true, eliminate it.

   A. The sole purpose of the Viking Landers' mission was to check for the existence of life on Mars.
   B. Mars was once much more hospitable for life than was Earth.
   C. Future experiments will show that life cannot exist on Mars due to its dryness.
   D. Some scientists and researchers believe that there is no life on Mars.

B

2. Information in the passage suggests that the majority of experts believe that:

Look at each answer choice.

Point to something in the passage that makes the answer choice true.

If you can't point to something that makes the answer choice true, eliminate it.

    F.   conditions on Mars are not conducive to the existence of life.

    G.   after Earth, Mars is the most likely candidate to contain life in this solar system.

    H.   Mars almost certainly contained life before it lost its carbon-dioxide-rich atmosphere.

    J.   other than lacking water, Mars has all the necessary building blocks for life.

B

Shared Practice

■ *Use the 3-Step Method for ACT Reading Comprehension—including Eliminating for Truth—for the passage and questions below.*

Passage II

HUMANITIES: The following passage is excerpted from "Europe's Renaissance" by Kristin Myers, Kelly L. Childs, and Kenneth McHale.

Like any historical period, there is plenty of argument about exactly when Europe's Renaissance began. But most historians agree that this period of remarkable economic, intellectual,
5   and artistic flowering started sometime in the late 14th century and came to an end in the 16th century. The more interesting question is how and why the Renaissance came about at all.

Renaissance is French for "rebirth." It would
10 be hard to find a more accurate word to describe what happened in Europe at the close of the Middle Ages. The Middle Ages were dominated by a rigid, top-down system called *feudalism*. In feudalism, a powerful lord would be given land by
15 his king. This lord in turn had vassals who worked the land for him and, in exchange for occasionally taking up arms in his or the king's defense, got to keep a share of their own work product and enjoy the protection of the lord's castle in times
20 of crisis. The other great power of this time was the Christian Church, to which the kings themselves were vassals. The medieval world was thus divided between two classes—masters and servants.

25 In the early 15th century, however, a new class began to emerge. Europe was recovering from a century-long plague, the Black Death, which had depopulated its cities and driven terrified people into the countryside. When the
30 plague finally lifted, people desperate for income surged back into the cities. Changes to banking systems and the opening of foreign markets through exploration had increased the money supply. As urban populations increased, so did the
35 opportunities for work and profit.

Great city-states like Florence, in northern Italy, flourished as traders and merchants demanded a greater role in their own government. As men and women who had forged their own
40 fortunes rose to positions of power and influence, other things changed as well. Art and philosophy

began to place a new emphasis on human achievement. Men like Leonardo da Vinci—the quintessential Renaissance man—created great
45 works of art for city-funded projects and, at the same time, invented war machines and other military innovations for the city's protection. Artists like Michelangelo celebrated his beloved republic with works like his statue of David and
50 his Tomb of the Medici, which glorified the city's leading family.

Another Florentine genius, Niccolò Machiavelli, wrote works of political philosophy that remain widely respected today. His words
55 express the mood of the times: "A return to first principles in a republic is sometimes caused by the simple virtues of one man. His good example has such an influence that the good men strive to imitate him, and the wicked are ashamed to
60 lead a life so contrary to his example." This sort of thinking took the emphasis off of piety and feudal obedience and put it on individual achievement.

The "simple virtues" celebrated by the Renaissance could range from statesmanship to
65 artistry in paint or stone to pure inventiveness. Many consider the artistic Renaissance to have begun with the painter Giotto. While medieval art had produced stiff and unnatural representations of the human figure, the frescoes
70 that Giotto painted for the Arena Chapel in Padua reached back to a classical artistic tradition that emphasized the power and beauty of the human form. Michelangelo's Sistine Chapel frescoes positively reveled in this new approach,
75 realistically rendering naked bodies with powerful artistry.

This tremendous outpouring of art and innovation was fueled by economic growth. While political power remained concentrated in
80 the hands of the rich, the ranks of the wealthy now included common people who had enriched themselves through trade. For the first time in history, there was a power to rival both the feudal kings of old and the previously omnipotent
85 Roman Catholic Church. This new group—the middle class—would eventually become Europe's true ruler.

And yet we continue to focus on the artists and thinkers of the era when we consider the
90 Renaissance or seek to understand it better. And why not? It was their works that best expressed the spirit of an age in which the human being was the measure of all things.

1. According to the passage, the Renaissance can be most fully described as a(n):

   A. primarily artistic movement that discarded prior feudalistic restrictions.
   B. time ruled by artistic and philosophical geniuses.
   C. economic revolution responsible for creating the middle class.
   D. period of innovation that focused on the power of the individual.

   hint *If you can't find a match for your prediction, eliminate your way to the correct answer.*

2. Based on information from the passage, which of the following would most likely have been created by Michelangelo?

   F. A new, more protective piece of armor
   G. The model for a city fortification
   H. A painting featuring nude bodies
   J. A pamphlet detailing his political views

   hint *For which answer choice can you point to something in the passage that makes it true?*

3. According to the passage, Machiavelli believed that "the simple virtues of one man" (line 57) are beneficial to society because:

   A. humans are naturally attracted to pious men.
   B. one admirable person could provide a model for all others.
   C. evil people could be prosecuted more easily.
   D. virtuous individuals create wealth for all.

   hint *Point to the important information and make a prediction based on the text.*

4. The passage most fully supports which of the following statements concerning the Black Death and the Renaissance?

   F. The Black Death caused a population shift that facilitated the Renaissance.
   G. The Black Death provided much of the inspiration for the artwork and philosophical ideas of the Renaissance.
   H. The Renaissance re-established the feudalistic system which had been destroyed by the Black Death.
   J. Renaissance thinkers looked to the Black Death as the prototype for a new economic model.

   hint *When a question requires you to draw a conclusion about a large part of the passage, use Eliminating for Truth.*

B

5. It can be inferred from the passage that Renaissance thinkers believed the individual was entitled to each of the following EXCEPT:

A. an opportunity to pursue his own personal sense of achievement.
B. protection provided by the city in which he lived.
C. the right to openly rebel against the Church.
D. the ability to acquire and accumulate wealth.

hint ▷ *Select the answer choice for which you cannot point to something in the passage that makes it true.*

6. As it is used in line 69 and line 74, *frescoes* most nearly means:

F. statues carved to celebrate the human form.
G. paintings completed on parts of buildings.
H. pictures of oddly proportioned people.
J. sculptures inspired by classical artistic tradition.

hint ▷ *How is the word used in the passage? Make a prediction based on the context.*

7. The primary concern of the passage is to:

A. contrast the Middle Ages with the Renaissance.
B. discuss the historical context and legacy of a famous period.
C. compare the various artistic, economic, and philosophical achievements of a historical group.
D. highlight Florence's preeminence throughout the Renaissance.

hint ▷ *Use Question the Author to answer main-idea and author's-purpose questions.*

8. The main function of the last paragraph (lines 88–93) in relation to the passage as a whole is to:

F. distinguish art and writing as the most well-known aspects of the Renaissance legacy.
G. argue that without the artists and thinkers of the period, economic change would have proven impossible.
H. illustrate that Leonardo da Vinci remains the most recognizable figure of the Renaissance.
J. demonstrate that individualism was the most important idea of the Renaissance.

hint ▷ *How does the paragraph contribute to the passage as a whole?*

ACT ADVANTAGE
ENGLISH & READING

B

KAP Wrap

Imagine that you go to a friend's house for dinner. Your friend's grandma serves you the most delicious meal you have ever eaten. Without directly telling your friend's grandma, "I loved the meal," how could you help her make the inference that you loved the meal? Write about three details of your behavior that would help her make this broad inference.

ReKAP

Review the strategies from Lessons A and B. Then fill in the blanks to show what you have learned.

1. I will use Getting Grounded in the Details for all _____-inference questions.

2. Getting Grounded in the Details:

   • _____ and reread the part of the passage that relates to the _____.

   • Ground yourself in the _____.

3. I will use Eliminating for Truth for all _____-inference questions.

4. Eliminating for Truth:

   • Look at each _____ _____.

   • _____ to something in the passage that makes the answer choice _____.

   • If you can't point to something that makes the answer choice true, _____ it.

Strategy Instruction

Writer's-View Questions

Writer's-view questions ask you to consider some aspect of the passage from the writer's perspective. They may mention the author's, narrator's, or writer's opinion or point of view. What makes writer's-view questions easy to answer is that you will think about the author's intentions as you read the text, so your notes will be very helpful. What makes this type of question difficult to answer is that they can be worded in a variety of ways. Writer's-view questions tend to appear most commonly after Prose Fiction passages.

Identifying Writer's-View Questions

Writer's-view questions can be worded in a variety of ways, which makes them harder than other question types to recognize. However, they all make a reference to what the author was thinking or feeling as she wrote—her opinion or point of view—or to how she did something. The following are examples of writer's-view questions:

- The passage is written from the point of view of:

- Which of the following best describes the author's approach to presenting ... the narrator's discovery about himself?

- The juxtaposition of [two anecdotes] seems to suggest the narrator's dismay with:

Try It Out!

Read the question stems below. Circle the writer's-view questions.

1. Based on her depiction of Miss Brill, the author seems to perceive this character as:
2. According to the passage, Miss Brill observes which of the following?
3. As it is used in the passage, *company* (line 63) most closely means:
4. Which of the following best describes the method by which the author reveals elements of Miss Brill's character?
5. From the last paragraph of the passage, it is most reasonable to infer that:
6. From the passage, it is most reasonable to infer that after Miss Brill listens to the boy and girl's conversation (lines 79-85), she realizes that:

Answering Writer's-View Questions

During Step 1 of the 3-Step Method for ACT Reading Comprehension, you summarized each paragraph. Most writer's-view questions follow Prose Fiction passages. When reading Prose Fiction passages, your summary statements should concentrate on the *feelings* and *attributes* of the main characters as well as the author's approach toward them.

During Step 3, you will find the important information you need to answer the question. For writer's-view questions, you will use **Analyzing the Author's Approach** to research and reason your way to the correct answer.

Analyzing the Author's Approach

- **Review** your summary statements.

- **Analyze** the author's approach toward characters or topics mentioned in the question stem.

- **Find** the answer choice that is consistent with the author's approach.

keep in mind

Writer's-view questions ask *how* the author feels about something or *how* the author wrote the passage. Author's-purpose and function questions ask *why* the author wrote the passage or some part of it.

With writer's-view questions, there are rarely specific parts of the passage that you can find and reread. Instead, when answering a writer's-view question, review your summary statements.

As you review your summary statements, analyze the author's approach toward the characters or topics mentioned in the question stem. How does the author feel about the characters or topics? How does she portray them? How do you know?

With writer's-view questions, making a prediction is usually difficult. Instead, look at the answer choices and find the one that is consistent with the author's approach.

Eliminating with Writer's-View Questions

Use Eliminating to find the answer choice that is consistent with the author's approach. In particular, watch for tempting wrong answer choices where just one portion is untrue. Also look out for wrong answer choices that distort the details of the passage.

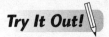

Try It Out!

Read the excerpt below adapted from Willa Cather's novel, *O Pioneers!*, which is set in the Nebraska prairie. Then use Analyzing the Author's Approach and Eliminating to answer the questions that follow.

"I want you to see Emil, Carl. He is so different from the rest of us!"

"How different?"

"Oh, you'll see! I'm sure it was to have children like Emil, to give them a chance, that Father left Sweden."

5   "Is he going to farm here with you?"

"He shall do whatever he wants to," Alexandra declared. "He is going to have a real chance; that's what I've worked for!"

Alexandra looked at Carl with her calm, deliberate eyes. "Why are you dissatisfied with yourself?" she asked earnestly.

10   Her visitor winced and paused. "You see," he said, "measured by your standards here, I'm a failure. I couldn't buy even one of your cornfields. I've enjoyed many things in New York, but I've got nothing to show for it."

"But you show for it yourself, Carl. I'd rather have had your freedom than my land."

15   Carl shook his head mournfully. "Freedom so often means that one isn't needed anywhere. Here you have a background of your own; you would be missed. But in the cities there are thousands of rolling stones like me. We're all alike, paying exorbitant rent for a few square feet of space near the heart of things; we have no ties, we know nobody, we own nothing. When people die, 20   they scarcely know where to bury them."

Alexandra was silent. He knew that she understood what he meant. At last she said slowly, "And yet I would rather have Emil grow up like that than like his other brothers. We pay a high rent, too, though we pay differently. We grow hard and heavy. We don't move lightly and easily as you do, and our 25   minds get stiff. If the world were no wider than my cornfields, I wouldn't feel that it was worthwhile to work. No, I would rather have Emil like you. I felt that as soon as you came."

Main Idea: _____

Author's Purpose: _____

When reading Prose Fiction, it's important to keep track of who said what and to distinguish between the thoughts of who said and felt what.

1. Her depiction of the conversation between Carl and Alexandra suggests that the author sympathizes with:

    Review your summary statements.

    Analyze the author's approach toward characters or topics mentioned in the question stem.

    Use Eliminating to find the answer choice that is consistent with the author's approach.

    A. Carl's longing for the simple life.
    B. Alexandra's idea of "freedom."
    C. Emil's opinion of Alexandra.
    D. Alexandra's disdain for the "city man."

2. Which of the following statements made by Alexandra in the passage best captures the author's characterization of her?

    Review your summary statements.

    Analyze the author's approach toward characters or topics mentioned in the question stem.

    Use Eliminating to find the answer choice that is consistent with the author's approach.

    F. "He is going to have a real chance; that's what I've worked for!" (lines 6–7).
    G. "Why are you dissatisfied with yourself?" (lines 8–9).
    H. "We pay a high rent, too, though we pay differently." (line 23).
    J. "I want you to see Emil, Carl. He is so different from the rest of us!" (line 1).

keep in mind

Writer's-view questions may pull from different parts of the passage or from the passage as a whole.

Test Practice Unit 4

When your teacher tells you, carefully tear out this page.

1. Ⓐ Ⓑ Ⓒ Ⓓ   15. Ⓐ Ⓑ Ⓒ Ⓓ

2. Ⓕ Ⓖ Ⓗ Ⓙ   16. Ⓕ Ⓖ Ⓗ Ⓙ

3. Ⓐ Ⓑ Ⓒ Ⓓ   17. Ⓐ Ⓑ Ⓒ Ⓓ

4. Ⓕ Ⓖ Ⓗ Ⓙ   18. Ⓕ Ⓖ Ⓗ Ⓙ

5. Ⓐ Ⓑ Ⓒ Ⓓ   19. Ⓐ Ⓑ Ⓒ Ⓓ

6. Ⓕ Ⓖ Ⓗ Ⓙ   20. Ⓕ Ⓖ Ⓗ Ⓙ

7. Ⓐ Ⓑ Ⓒ Ⓓ

8. Ⓕ Ⓖ Ⓗ Ⓙ

9. Ⓐ Ⓑ Ⓒ Ⓓ

10. Ⓕ Ⓖ Ⓗ Ⓙ

11. Ⓐ Ⓑ Ⓒ Ⓓ

12. Ⓕ Ⓖ Ⓗ Ⓙ

13. Ⓐ Ⓑ Ⓒ Ⓓ

14. Ⓕ Ⓖ Ⓗ Ⓙ

C

DO NOT TURN THE PAGE UNTIL TOLD TO DO SO.

DIRECTIONS: There are two passages in this test. Each passage is followed by several questions. After reading a passage, choose the best answer to each question and fill in the corresponding oval on your answer document. You may refer to the passages as often as necessary.

Passage III

PROSE FICTION: The passage below is an adapted excerpt from *Bleak House*, by Charles Dickens. In this passage, Esther recounts some of her childhood experiences.

I can remember, when I was a very little girl indeed, I used to say to my doll when we were alone together, "Now, Dolly, I am not clever, you know very well, and you must be patient with me,
5 like a dear!"

My dear old doll! I was such a shy little thing that I seldom dared to open my lips, and never dared to open my heart, to anybody else. It almost makes me cry to think what a relief it used to be
10 to me when I came home from school of a day to run upstairs to my room and say, "Oh, you dear faithful Dolly, I knew you would be expecting me!" and then to sit down on the floor, leaning on the elbow of her great chair, and tell her all I had
15 noticed since we parted.

I was brought up, from my earliest remembrance—like some of the princesses in the fairy stories, only I was not charming—by my godmother. At least, I only knew her as such.
20 She was a good, good woman! She went to church three times every Sunday, and to morning prayers on Wednesdays and Fridays, and to lectures whenever there were lectures; and never missed. She was handsome; and if she had ever smiled,
25 would have been (I used to think) like an angel—but she never smiled. She was always grave and strict. She was so very good herself, I thought, that the badness of other people made her frown all her life. It made me very sorry to consider how
30 good she was and how unworthy of her I was, and I used ardently to hope that I might have a better heart; and I talked it over very often with the dear old doll, but I never loved my godmother as I ought to have loved her and as I felt I must have loved her
35 if I had been a better girl.

I had never heard my mama spoken of. I had never been shown my mama's grave. I had never

been told where it was.

Although there were seven girls at the
40 neighboring school where I was a day boarder, and although they called me little Esther Summerson, I knew none of them at home. All of them were older than I, to be sure (I was the youngest there by a good deal), but there seemed
45 to be some other separation between us besides that, and besides their being far more clever than I was and knowing much more than I did. One of them in the first week of my going to the school (I remember it very well) invited me home to a little
50 party, to my great joy. But my godmother wrote a stiff letter declining for me, and I never went. I never went out at all.

It was my birthday. There were holidays at school on other birthdays—none on mine. There
55 were rejoicings at home on other birthdays, as I knew from what I heard the girls relate to one another—there were none on mine. My birthday was the most melancholy day at home in the whole year.

60 Dinner was over, and my godmother and I were sitting at the table before the fire. The clock ticked, the fire clicked; not another sound had been heard in the room or in the house for I don't know how long. I happened to look timidly
65 up from my stitching, across the table at my godmother, and I saw in her face, looking gloomily at me, "It would have been far better, little Esther, that you had had no birthday, that you had never been born!"

70 I broke out crying and sobbing, and I said, "Oh, dear godmother, tell me, pray do tell me, did Mama die on my birthday?"

"No," she returned. "Ask me no more, child!"

75 I put up my trembling little hand to clasp hers or to beg her pardon with what earnestness I might, but withdrew it as she looked at me, and laid it on my fluttering heart. She said slowly in

GO ON TO THE NEXT PAGE.

a cold, low voice—I see her knitted brow and
80 pointed finger—"The time will come—and soon
enough—when you will understand this better
and will feel it too. I have forgiven her"—but her
face did not relent—"the wrong she did to me, and
I say no more of it, though it was greater than you
85 will ever know. Forget your mother and leave all
other people to forget her. Now, go!"

I went up to my room, and crept to bed,
and laid my doll's cheek against mine wet with
tears, and holding that solitary friend upon my
90 bosom, cried myself to sleep. Imperfect as my
understanding of my sorrow was, I knew that I had
brought no joy at any time to anybody's heart and
that I was to no one upon earth what Dolly was to
me.

95 Dear, dear, to think how much time we
passed alone together afterwards, and how often
I repeated to the doll the story of my birthday and
confided to her that I would try as hard as ever I
could to repair the fault I had been born with. I
100 hope it is not self-indulgent to shed these tears as I
think of it.

1. According to the passage, Esther only remembers:
    A. being brought up by her parents.
    B. being brought up by her mother for a short time.
    C. being brought up by her godmother for a short time.
    D. being brought up by her godmother.

2. It is most likely that Esther thinks of her doll as:
    F. her only friend and confidante.
    G. only an amusing plaything.
    H. like a sister to her.
    J. a beautiful toy that is too fragile to touch.

3. As it is used in the passage, *stiff* (line 51) most closely means:
    A. difficult to bend.
    B. overly formal.
    C. unchanging.
    D. lifeless.

4. Which of the following most likely contributes to Esther's belief that she has been born with a fault (line 99)?
    F. Her birthday is never celebrated.
    G. She has never heard anyone talk about her father.
    H. Her godmother told her that she should never have been born.
    J. Her godmother does not let her attend birthday parties.

5. Esther's godmother's words, actions, and facial expression as described in paragraph 10 (lines 75–86) suggest that she:
    A. wishes to scold Esther for pestering her about her birthday.
    B. does not know what happened to Esther's mother.
    C. continues to resent Esther's mother.
    D. has forgotten Esther's mother.

6. Based on information in the passage, it can be inferred that Esther considers her childhood as:
    F. an adventure.
    G. a time of loneliness and confusion.
    H. a period of dedication to education and self-improvement.
    J. a period of attempting to become more like her godmother.

7. From Esther's statement, "I was to no one upon earth what Dolly was to me" (lines 93–94), it is reasonable to infer that Esther:
    A. believes that no one loves her.
    B. believes that she will never become friends with the girls at school.
    C. believes that her godmother doesn't love her.
    D. transferred her love for her mother to Dolly.

8. In the passage, it is implied that all of the following contribute to separating Esther from the other girls at her school EXCEPT that:
    F. the other girls are older than Esther.
    G. Esther's godmother does not allow Esther to socialize with the other girls outside of school.
    H. Esther believes that the other girls are much smarter.
    J. Esther's self-indulgence makes the other girls not want to be around her.

9. According to the passage, one reason that Esther thinks of her godmother as a "good, good woman" (line 20) is:
    A. that her smile is like that of an angel.
    B. that she forgave Esther's mother.
    C. that she frequently attends church services.
    D. that she gave Esther a doll.

10. In the passage, Esther describes herself as a child as:
    F. self-indulgent and not very clever.
    G. shy and not very clever.
    H   shy and faithful.
    J. self-indulgent and faithful.

GO ON TO THE NEXT PAGE.

Passage IV

HUMANITIES: This passage is an excerpt from the concluding chapter of Emily Post's *Etiquette*, a 1922 guide to proper manners and behavior.

Whether we Americans are drifting toward or from finer perceptions, both mental and spiritual, is too profound a subject to be taken up except on a broader scope than that of the present volume.
5 Yet it is a commonplace remark that older people invariably feel that the younger generation is speeding swiftly on the road to perdition. But whether the present younger generation is really any nearer to that frightful end than any previous
10 one, is a question that we, of the present older generation, are scarcely qualified to answer. To be sure, manners seem to have grown lax, and many of the amenities apparently have vanished. But do these things merely seem so to us because young
15 men of fashion do not pay party calls nowadays and the young woman of fashion is informal? It is difficult to maintain that youth today is so very different from what it has been in other periods of the country's history, especially as "the
20 capriciousness of beauty," the "heartlessness" and "carelessness" of youth, are charges of a too suspiciously bromidic flavor to carry conviction.

The present generation is at least ahead of some of its "very proper" predecessors in that
25 weddings do not have to be set for noon because a bridegroom's sobriety is not to be counted on later in the day! That young people of today prefer games to conversation scarcely proves degeneration. That they wear very few clothes is
30 not a symptom of decline. There have always been recurring cycles of undress, followed by muffling from shoe-soles to chin. We have not yet reached the undress of Pauline Bonaparte, so the muffling period may not be due!

35 However, leaving out the mooted question of whether etiquette may not soon be a subject for an obituary rather than a guide-book, one thing is certain: we have advanced prodigiously in aesthetic taste.

40 Never in the recollection of anyone now living has it been so easy to surround oneself with lovely belongings. Each year's achievement seems to stride away from that of the year before in producing woodwork, ironwork, glass, stone,
45 print, paint, and textile that is lovelier and lovelier. One cannot go into the shops or pass their windows on the streets without being impressed with the ever-growing taste of their display. Nor can one look into the magazines devoted to
50 gardens and houses and house-furnishings and fail to appreciate the increasing wealth of the beautiful in environment.

That such exquisite "best" as America possessed in her Colonial houses and gardens and
55 furnishings should ever have been discarded for the atrocities of the period after the Civil War, is comparable to nothing but Titania's *Midsummer Night's Dream* madness that made her believe a donkey's features more beautiful than those of the
60 ancient Greek god Apollo!

Happily, however, since we never do things by halves, we are studying and cultivating and buying and making, and trying to forget and overcome that terrible marriage of our beautiful
65 Colonial ancestress with the dark-wooded, plush-draped, jig-sawed upstart of vulgarity and ignorance. In another country her type would be lost in his, forever! But in a country that sent a million soldiers across three thousand miles
70 of ocean, in spite of every obstacle and in the twinkling of an eye, why even comment that good taste is pouring over our land as fast as periodicals, books, and manufacturers can take it?

Three thousand miles east and west, two
75 thousand miles north and south, white tiled bathrooms have sprung like mushrooms seemingly in a single night, charming houses, enchanting gardens, beautiful cities, cultivated people, created in thousands upon thousands
80 of instances in the short span of one generation. Certain great houses abroad have consummate quality, it is true, but for every one of these, there are a thousand that are mediocre, even offensive. In our own country, beautiful houses
85 and appointments flourish like field flowers in summer; not merely in the occasional gardens of the very rich, but everywhere.

And all this means? Merely one more incident added to the many great facts that prove us a
90 wonderful nation. (But this is an aside merely, and not to be talked about to anyone except just ourselves!) At the same time it is no idle boast that the world is at present looking toward America; and whatever we become is bound to lower or
95 raise the standards of life. The other countries are old; we are youth personified! We have all youth's glorious beauty and strength and vitality and courage. If we can keep these attributes and add finish and understanding and perfect taste
100 in living and thinking, we need not dwell on the Golden Age that is past, but believe in the Golden Age that is sure to be.

GO ON TO THE NEXT PAGE.

11. The main purpose of the passage can most closely be described as an effort to:

    A. encourage optimism about America's future.
    B. describe various trends in American fashion.
    C. compare the younger generation to earlier ones.
    D. deplore the decline of America's youth.

12. The author's attitude toward the subject of the passage can best be characterized as:

    F. cautious ambivalence.
    G. strong disapproval.
    H. hopeful positivism.
    J. rational objectivism.

13. It can be reasonably inferred that the author believes that the Golden Age:

    A. occurred in Europe.
    B. occurred during the Colonial period.
    C. occurred during the post-Civil War period.
    D. lies in the future.

14. According to the first and second paragraphs, the author describes the younger generation, as compared to earlier generations, as:

    F. opposed to earlier standards.
    G. opposed to strong moral foundations.
    H. in favor of more rigid rules of etiquette.
    J. exhibiting the same basic level of decorum.

15. As described in the passage, the effect of post-Civil War aesthetics on earlier styles is best summarized by which of the following?

    A. Post-Civil War aesthetics had a powerful impact on initial post-war generations but no impact on more recent ones.
    B. Post-Civil War aesthetics impacted popular style temporarily but subsequently waned in influence.
    C. Post-Civil War aesthetics impacted American style by challenging its definition of beauty.
    D. Post-Civil War aesthetics' impact was limited by the traditions of craftsmen and America's preference for conventional styles.

16. When the author states, "the muffling period may not be due!" (lines 33–34), she most likely is implying that:

    F. youthful tastes have not reached an extreme.
    G. trends are inevitably cyclical.
    H. Americans are more modest than Europeans.
    J. fashion is subject to whim.

17. The passage indicates that the primary purpose for setting a wedding at noon was to:

    A. follow the rules of previous generations.
    B. prevent the groom from doubting his commitment to get married.
    C. work around the typical behavior of bridegrooms.
    D. allow for conversation only after the wedding.

18. It can be inferred from the passage that the author most likely thinks the basis of the older generation's complaints about the younger generation are grounded in:

    F. the disappearance of familiar manners and styles.
    G. the decline of empathy in interpersonal relationships.
    H. the growing informality of social ritual.
    J. the perception of rapid change.

19. The author describes the quality of certain great houses as "consummate" (line 81) because their quality:

    A. challenges community standards.
    B. is excellent compared to most other houses.
    C. overpowers the designs of neighboring houses.
    D. typifies architectural trends.

20. The comparison in the fifth paragraph (lines 53–60) between America's change in style and "Titania's *Midsummer Night's Dream* madness" most directly refers to the similar confusion between:

    F. past and present.
    G. dream and reality.
    H. ugliness and beauty.
    J. inaccuracy and accuracy.

END OF TEST.

STOP! DO NOT TURN THE PAGE UNTIL TOLD TO DO SO.

KAP Wrap

Think about something you wrote recently in which you expressed your view about a topic. How did you let your view be known in your writing?

Unit 5
ACT English I

The 3-Step Method for ACT English Success

Thinking KAP

Describe what you do when you are shopping for a CD or DVD.

1. How do you decide which CD or DVD to consider purchasing?

2. Do you look only at ones in a particular category?

3. What do you do to narrow your choices?

The 3-Step Method for ACT English Success

In the Thinking KAP activity, you described how you make choices when purchasing CDs or DVDs. Similarly, the ACT English test asks you to make choices about the correct answer to a large number of questions in a relatively short period of time. So, you will need an approach to help you respond efficiently and accurately to the questions.

In Unit 2, you learned a method for answering questions on the ACT Reading Test. For the ACT English Test, you will use a different method—i.e., the 3-Step Method for ACT English Success. In this lesson, you will learn each step of the method.

Every question on the ACT English Test refers to: a sentence in a selection, a paragraph in a selection, or the selection as a whole. Although being sure about English conventions (pronoun use, punctuation, etc.) will certainly help you, you will also need to use context clues to determine the correct answers.

keep in mind

The ACT English Test asks you to think as an editor thinks: What's the clearest way to convey the information?

Try It Out!

Look closely at the underlined portion of the sentence below.

When he began the <u>test Anthony</u> was certain that he would do well.

Is the underlined portion correct? _____

What are the clues that help you decide? _____

_____

Step 1: Read Efficiently

Step 1 of the 3-Step Method for ACT English Success is to read efficiently. The ACT English Test consists of 75 multiple-choice questions. You will have 45 minutes to complete this portion of the test, so you will need to stay focused and work quickly.

Pause at Each Underlined Portion

The first part of Step 1 is to pause at the end of each sentence that has an underlined section. You will most likely address each question only once, so pausing will help you to absorb the context of the sentence and the question being asked.

Identify the Issue

The second part of Step 1 is to identify the issue. You will need to decide whether the question is asking you to apply a grammatical rule, determine the best stylistic choice, or choose the most appropriate organization. Deciding in advance what issue the question is addressing helps you eliminate wrong choices.

keep in mind

Read only the amount of text necessary to answer the question.

Try It Out!

Use Step 1 for the selection below.

Mrs. Fletcher

People often complain <u>that are</u> generation is politically apathetic and
1
depressed. Just 25 years ago, it was common for students to join strikes and anti-war protests.

Identify the issue: _____

Step 2: Predict and Eliminate

In earlier units, you learned how to use Predicting and Eliminating to answer questions on the reading portion of the ACT. On the ACT English test, you will use Predicting in the same manner—i.e., to think of an answer to a question before reading the choices. You will use Eliminating to confirm that the answer you have chosen is correct or to increase your odds of selecting the correct answer. Eliminating is helpful when you are unable to make a prediction or when your prediction does not match any of the answer choices.

Read the Answer Choices and Any Question Stems

Read each answer choice and look for a match to your prediction. It is important to read all four choices. Frequently, more than one answer choice is grammatically correct. Since you are looking for the *best* answer, if you choose the first *correct* answer, it may not be the best answer to the question.

Rule Out Choices that Don't Address the Issue

If an answer choice does not address the issue you have identified in Step 1, eliminate it. You should also eliminate answer choices that introduce additional issues, such as wordiness or grammatical errors.

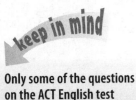

Only some of the questions on the ACT English test will have question stems. All of the questions will have four answer choices.

Try It Out!

Use Step 2 for the question below.

     Many <u>students think</u> that choosing (C) when in doubt was a good test-taking
                  1
strategy, but Ms. Chang taught them more reliable strategies.

Identify the issue: *verb tense doesn't match*

Prediction: _____

1.   **A.**   NO CHANGE
       Eliminate? _____*Yes*_____
     B.   student thinks
       Eliminate? _____
     C.   students thinks
       Eliminate? _____
     D.   students thought
       Eliminate? _____

Step 3: Plug In

This step helps make the context work to your advantage. To make a reasonable decision about the best answer, you must take context into consideration.

Substitute Remaining Choices

Once you have eliminated any choices that don't address the issue, systematically plug in the remaining answers to determine the choice that works best in the context.

Select the Best Choice

On the ACT, more than one answer choice may be grammatically correct. Choose the one that is also clearest and most relevant to the given context.

You should use Eliminating for every question on the ACT English test.

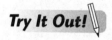

Use Steps 1, 2, and 3 to answer Question 2 below.

Mrs. Fletcher

People often complain <u>that are</u> generation is politically <u>apathetic and</u> ₁ ₂
<u>depressed</u>. Just 25 years ago, it was common for students to join strikes and anti- ₂
war protests. These days, though, most young people are more likely to be found watching MTV or shopping at the mall than rallying to support a treasured belief.

Identify the issue: _____

Prediction: _____

2. **F.**   NO CHANGE
    Eliminate? _____
    G.   apathetic, uninterested, and ignorant of politics.
    Eliminate? _____
    H.   apathetic and unhappy.
    Eliminate? _____
    J.   apathetic.
    Eliminate? _____

    (   ) **is the best choice because** _____.

The 3-Step Method for ACT English Success

 STEP 1: Read efficiently.

- *Pause at each underlined portion.*

- *Identify the issue.*

 STEP 2: Predict and eliminate.

- *Read the answer choices and any question stems.*

- *Rule out choices that don't address the issue.*

 STEP 3: Plug in.

- *Substitute remaining choices.*

- *Select the best choice.*

Robin Hood Stories

Many stories about noble heroes have been handed down to us from the Middle Ages. Robin Hood is among the most well-known. Although there is no conclusive evidence that a man named Robin Hood ever actually existed, the story of Robin Hood and his band of merry men <u>has became</u> one of the most popular traditional
1
tales in English literature. He is the hero in a series of ballads dating back to at least the 14th century. Life was very difficult for most of England's citizens during that era, so it is not surprising that these ballads tell of discontent and unhappiness among the lower classes in northern England. In fact, this turbulent time eventually led to the Peasant's Revolt of 1381.

Identify the issue: _____

Prediction: _____

1.   **A.**   NO CHANGE
   Eliminate? _____
   B.   has been becoming
   Eliminate? _____
   C.   has become
   Eliminate? _____
   D.   becomes
   Eliminate? _____

   ( ) is the best choice

   because _____.

A good deal of the peasants' rebellion against the ruling class <u>stemmed by</u> the restriction of hunting
₂
rights. Without access to hunting, peasants—who owned very little—often faced lean winters. The stories in these early ballads reveal the cruelty that was a part of medieval life. According to these ballads, Robin Hood was a rebel. Many of the most striking episodes depict him and his companions robbing and killing representatives of authority, then giving the gains to the poor. These tales generally blame the greed of officials and privileged nobles, who often trampled the rights of less powerful citizens. Robin Hood, however, is usually presented as righting wrongs—a peasant's hero.

Identify the issue: _____

Prediction: _____

2. **F.**   NO CHANGE
Eliminate? _____
G.   stemmed from _____
Eliminate? _____
H.   stemmed of _____
Eliminate? _____
J.   stemmed with _____
Eliminate? _____

(   ) **is the best choice**

because _____.

Robin Hood and his men found their greatest enemy in the Sheriff of Nottingham—a local agent of the central government. While Robin could be ruthless with <u>those persons who were known to have</u> abused
3
their powers, he was kind to the oppressed. He was truly revered by the common people.

In the 18th century, storytellers distorted Robin Hood's tale by suggesting that he was a fallen nobleman. They also gave him a love interest—Maid Marian. Over 100 years later, Robin Hood's tale has reappeared in various films. Like other legends with strong central characters and a basic plot about good and evil, Robin Hood's story is timeless; every generation can relate to this tale of struggle, love, life, and death.

Identify the issue: _____

Prediction: _____

3. **A.**   NO CHANGE
    Eliminate? _____
    B.   those persons who
    Eliminate? _____
    C.   those who
    Eliminate? _____
    D.   those
    Eliminate? _____

    (   ) is the best choice

    because _____.

Shared Practice

■ *Use the 3-Step Method for ACT English Success to answer the questions below.*

PASSAGE II

The History of Marbles

Taws, alleys, and flints are the names of particular kinds of marbles. The names of marbles may originate <u>from its</u> appearances, as in "cloudies;" uses, as in
₁
shooters; or make-ups. "Alleys," for example, were once made of alabaster. Marbles may be made from many different materials. In the 18th century, marbles were actually made from marble chips. Nowadays, marbles may consist of glass, baked clay, steel, onyx, plastic, or agate. Perhaps the key word regarding <u>marbles are</u>
₂
<u>"variety."</u>
₂

1. A. NO CHANGE
    B. by its
    C. from there
    D. from their

hint ▷ *What issue is the question addressing?*

2. F. NO CHANGE
    G. marbles is "variety."
    H. marbles being "variety."
    J. marbles were "variety."

hint ▷ *Look at the tense of each answer choice in context to determine the most appropriate choice.*

Marbles can be <u>manipulated by</u> a variety of ways:
3
"Knuckling" is a technique in which the bottom of the

hand is balanced against the ground, while a marble

placed against the forefinger is shot outward with the

thumb. Marbles <u>can also be thrown, rolling, dropped,</u>
4
<u>or kicked.</u>
4

3.   A.   NO CHANGE
      B.   manipulated with
      C.   manipulated within
      D.   manipulated in

hint ▸ *Plug in each answer choice.*

4.   F.   NO CHANGE
      G.   are used for throwing, rolling, dropping, and
            kicking.
      H.   can also be thrown, rolled, dropped, or
            kicked.
      J.   can also throw, roll, drop, or kick.

hint ▸ *Rule out choices that introduce new issues.*

There were also many varieties of marble games.
5

The most common American version involves winning

opponents' marbles by knocking them out of a

designated area with one's own marbles. This is similar

to a popular marble game called "Taw," also known as

Ringtaw or Ringer. Marbles in a game of Taw are

arranged in a cross shape, bound by a large ring. The

object of Taw is to shoot these marbles out of the ring.

Other marble games are called "pot games." Players in a

pot game, such as Moshie, try to knock one another's

marbles into a hole. Some people prefer to play Nine

Holes or Bridgeboard, in which players shoot his or her
6

marbles through numbered arches on a board.
6

5. **A.** NO CHANGE.
  B. Many varieties also being
  C. There are also many varieties
  D. There was also many varieties

hint ▶ *Read the sentence before or after the verb to place the verb tense in context.*

6. **F.** NO CHANGE
  G. your marbles
  H. their marbles
  J. our marbles

hint ▶ *Identify the word to which the pronoun refers.*

The popularity of marbles <u>spans centuries</u> and has
affected people of all cultures. The first marble games
took place in antiquity.

7.   **A.**   NO CHANGE
      B.   span centuries
      C.   spanning centuries
      D.   spans hundreds of years

hint   *An answer choice that is longer than the underlined portion may not be the most concise response.*

<u>It was played with</u> nuts, fruit pits, or pebbles. Even
the great Augustus Caesar, along with his Roman peers,
was known to have played marble games as a child.
Marbles have come a long way since those days.

8.   **F.**   NO CHANGE
      G.   They were played with
      H.   They were playing with
      J.   It plays with

hint   *Rule out answer choices that don't address the issue.*

A

KAP Wrap

Think about the 3-Step Method for ACT English Success. What parts of the method do you already use, consciously or unconsciously? What parts of the method do you find easiest to use? Which parts do you need to know more about or to practice more?

lesson B *Grammar Questions*

Thinking KAP

Think about sending email or text messages: Do you use abbreviations or emoticons? Describe how you use words or symbols in different ways than you would if you were speaking.

B

Identifying Issues in Grammar Conventions

In the Thinking KAP activity, you wrote about using abbreviations and symbols when you use text messaging or email. The rules that help us make sense of text are called **conventions**. For example, when you write ":)" in an email, your friend understands that as a smiley face. A reader who is unfamiliar with the conventions of electronic communications might wonder what "colon, right parenthesis" means.

Grammar questions on the ACT focus on the conventions of standard English grammar. You may notice that the underlined word may not be the best choice or that the verb tense is wrong. You may also see a poorly chosen idiom. In Lesson A, you learned to identify the issue in a sentence in Step 1 of the 3-Step Method for English Success. In this lesson, you will focus on learning to recognize issues in conventions of English grammar.

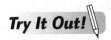

Try It Out!

In the sentences below, underline the parts that do not conform to English grammar.

1. Scott is the older of the whole class.

2. Abdul and Anthony hasn't called me back.

3. The bike was stolen off of the bike rack.

You do not have to recognize grammar *terms* on the ACT English Test, but you do have to recognize the proper *use* of conventions.

Questions about Word Choice

Word-choice questions ask you to find the correct subject-verb agreement, pronoun agreement, or use of words in context. Take a look at the examples below.

Incorrect	Correct
The train <u>whistle</u> in the station.	The train whistles in the station.
The players and <u>his or her</u> coaches celebrated the end of the season at a banquet.	The players and their coaches celebrated the end of the season at a banquet.
The students could hand in no <u>less</u> than ten assignments.	The students could hand in no fewer than ten assignments.

Word-choice questions will often ask you to choose among answer choices that, taken alone, are correct. You have to determine if they fit within the context. As you read the questions, use the 3-Step Method for ACT English Success to decide first if the issue is word choice and then which word fits best.

keep in mind

Word-choice questions represent about 1/10 of all questions on the ACT English Test. You should expect to see 7 or 8 of them per test.

Try It Out!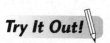

Use the 3-Step Method for ACT English Success to answer the word-choice question below.

We have had <u>little</u> luck finding someone to drive us to the track meet, so
₁
instead we are going to ride on the team bus.

Identify the issue: _____

Prediction: _____

1. **A.** NO CHANGE
    B. less
    C. few
    D. no

B

Questions about Verb Tenses

Verb-tenses questions ask you to decide whether the tense of the verb matches the context or whether the sequence of verbs is correct. Take a look at the examples below.

Incorrect	Correct
At the zoo, Minh watched the otters. They <u>are</u> playing, swimming, and eating.	At the zoo, Minh watched the otters. They were playing, swimming, and eating.
While the boy <u>has been</u> at school, his little sister colored on his desk.	While the boy was at school, his little sister colored on his desk.

keep in mind

Verb-tenses questions represent about 1/10 of all questions on the ACT English Test. You should expect to see about 7 of them per test.

Like word-choice questions, verb-tenses questions will often ask you to choose among answer choices that, taken alone, are correct. You have to determine if they fit within the context. Generally on the ACT, the simplest tense that works in the given context is the correct answer. As you read the questions, use the 3-Step Method for ACT English Success to decide first if the issue is verb tense and then which word or phrase fits best.

Try It Out!

Use the 3-Step Method for ACT English Success to answer the verb-tenses question below.

In the 1920s, Duke Ellington <u>pays</u> more than rent in New York; he paid his dues
₁
on the bandstand.

Identify the issue: _____

Prediction: _____

1.   F.   NO CHANGE
     G.   paid
     H.   has to pay
     J.   pay

Questions About Idioms

Idiom questions ask you to determine if a phrase is used correctly in context. Issues for idiom questions will be whether or not the idiom fits into the passage context or uses the correct preposition. Take a look at the examples below.

Incorrect	Correct
Our senior economics seminar is <u>much like</u> a debating club than a high-school class.	Our senior economics seminar is more like a debating club than a high-school class.
Everyone regarded him <u>to be</u> a genius.	Everyone regarded him as a genius.

An idiom may be correctly constructed, but may not fit in with the context of the passage. The most common error will be a misused preposition. As you read the questions, use the 3-Step Method for ACT English Success to decide first if the issue is incorrect use of an idiom and then which choice fits best.

You may be able to use your ear to "hear" which preposition sounds right.

Try It Out!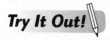

Use the 3-Step Method for ACT English Success to answer the idiom question below.

The space shuttle program, <u>administered from</u> the National Aeronautics and
1
Space Administration (NASA), started before today's high-school students were

born.

Identify the issue: _____

Prediction: _____

1. **F.**   NO CHANGE
    G.   administered for
    H.   administered by
    J.   administered with

B

The 3-Step Method for ACT English Success

 STEP 1: Read efficiently.

- *Pause at each underlined portion.*

- *Identify the issue.*

 STEP 2: Predict and eliminate.

- *Read the answer choices and any question stems.*

- *Rule out choices that don't address the issue.*

 STEP 3: Plug in.

- *Substitute remaining choices.*

- *Select the best choice.*

The Owl and The Bicycle

I grew up in Maine, where everything seems to fade when autumn arrives. Nature becomes paler. The sky seems less blue, and the trees seem less green. When you stand on the banks of the Penobscot River after most of the leaves have fallen, you can look across a wide open space. The cold gray-brown of the ground rushes up and <u>collided</u> with an endless pale sky. Dark
₁
comes early and stays late. It's not unusual to see a pale sliver of moon at four o'clock. When I think about those fall afternoons, I can still feel the chill.

Back then, I had a racing bike. I also had a driver's license, and I loved driving my mother's two-toned Buick Skylark on those long, open country roads, which was fun and fast, but riding the bicycle made me feel as if I were wearing a pair of wings. That year, I rode almost every day, until the snow began to stick to the ground.

Identify the issue: _____

Prediction: _____

1.   **A.**   NO CHANGE
     B.   has collided
     C.   collides
     D.   feels like it is colliding

B

I could have ridden to the lake or along the banks of the river, but I usually rode the bike path that wandered through the woods to the university in the next town. It was serene and often empty. The thin asphalt riding strip meandered through stands of tall firs, spruces, and birches; it passed along the back of some open fields and the backyards of tiny wood frame houses. I rode slowly through the wooded sections, but upon reaching the flat, open areas, I rode <u>more fastly</u>.
2

As I rode, I often watched the migrating birds flying high overhead: Sometimes I saw Canadian geese in their neat bands of organized Vs; other times, I saw flocks of little black birds. They looked like a great swarm of dots moving across the sky.

Identify the issue: _____

Prediction: _____

2. **F.** NO CHANGE
   G. much faster
   H. more fast
   J. much fastest

B

On one afternoon, when it was cold enough to make me regret not wearing gloves, I saw something that stunned me. I stood as still as a figure caught in a painting. From a corner of the icy sky, an enormous white streak whooshed down into the thick meadow grasses; it was the biggest bird I had ever seen. It had a huge head. Its wingspan was astounding. When it flew back from its momentary landing, its talons were clutching some unlucky creature. It sailed past me, <u>as a</u>
3
big clipper ship speeding across the open ocean. I was an intruder in the middle of its hunting grounds; I felt privileged to have seen such a rare bird.

"Perhaps it was a great snowy owl," my father said, when I described it at dinner.

"Maybe. I'm no ornithologist, so I can't say for certain. Whatever it was, it was unforgettable," I said.

I live in the city now, so I don't have a bike. The only birds I see are the little brown sparrows that pop around my kitchen window, searching for crumbs. I take a train to art class every week, because someday I want to be able to paint that owl.

Identify the issue: _____

Prediction: _____

3.   A.   NO CHANGE
     B.   just as if it was
     C.   more like
     D.   like

B

Shared Practice

■ *Use the 3-Step Method for ACT English Success to answer the questions below.*

PASSAGE II

Maria Merian

At a time when it was considered daring, even shocking, to be a female painter, Maria Sibylla Merian <u>were</u> not only a painter, but also a zoologist and
₁
botanist. Merian was born in Frankfort, in 1647. Although her father died when she was three years old, he had a lasting influence on her. A publisher and

1. A. NO CHANGE
    B. are
    C. is
    D. was

hint ▷ *Identify the issue so that you can easily eliminate incorrect answer choices.*

engraver, Merian's father was <u>known for</u> his production
₂
of a volume of scientific flower engravings. Her

2. F. NO CHANGE
    G. known of
    H. known about
    J. known by

hint ▷ *Remember that an idiom can be correct but still inappropriate to the context. Keeping in mind the main idea may help you to decide the idiom's appropriateness.*

B

stepfather, a flower painter, <u>also shares similar</u>

<u>interests.</u>
  3

    At the age of 18, Merian married Johann Andreas,

yet another artist. He specialized in still-life paintings

of flowers. Marriage, however, did not diminish her

desire to succeed. In 1679, Merian advanced in the

science community; she published her first of a three-

volume study of 186 insects <u>at Europe.</u>
                             4

3. **A.** NO CHANGE
      B. shares similar interests as well.
      C. also shared similar interests.
      D. had similar interests that he shared with her.

hint *In Step 2, you should eliminate any answer choice giving a verb tense that won't work in the context.*

4. **F.** NO CHANGE
      G. of Europe.
      H. through Europe.
      J. to Europe.

hint *Some prepositions almost always indicate motion. In Step 3, think about the basic meaning of the preposition as you plug in answer choices.*

B

Some of her observations were revolutionary. While her contemporaries believed that insects somehow sprang from the mud, Merian found that <u>there is</u> a
₅
distinct life cycle. She also discovered that each kind of insect has a predilection for a particular plant. Her

second volume followed in 1684, the same year that

<u>her and her husband</u> separated.
₆

5. **A.** NO CHANGE
   B. it had
   C. they are
   D. they have

hint *Remember that answer choices may be correct, but one part of the choice may be inappropriate in the context.*

6. **F.** NO CHANGE
   G. her along with her husband
   H. both she and her husband
   J. she and her husband

hint *Be careful not to choose an answer that introduces another error.*

B

Sometime in the 1690s, <u>they were eventually divorced</u>
₇

<u>and ended their marriage.</u>
₇

    Merian was one of the first people to travel to the

New World for biological research. In 1699, the city of

7.   **A.**   NO CHANGE
       B.   they divorced.
       C.   they ended their marriage and were divorced.
       D.   they put an end to their marriage: divorce.

hint ▷ *Even if you encounter an issue you haven't studied, the 3-Step Method for ACT English Success will still help you to answer the question.*

Amsterdam <u>funded and financed</u> her trip to the Dutch
₈

colony of Surinam, on the South American coast.

8.   **F.**   NO CHANGE
       G.   funded
       H.   monetarily funded
       J.   monetarily funded and financed

hint ▷ *Remember to choose the simplest, most appropriate tense.*

KAP Wrap

The ACT tests your ability to recognize the best choice. Where and how could you practice this skill during the school day? In science? In English? In the library? Develop a brief action plan for reading analytically to find the best choice.

B

Style Questions

ReKAP

Review the strategies from Lessons A and B. Then fill in the blanks with what you have learned.

The 3-Step Method for ACT English Success:

Step 1: Read efficiently.

- _____
- _____

Step 2: Predict and eliminate.

- _____
- _____

Step 3: Plug In.

- _____
- _____

Style Questions: Connections and Wordiness

Style questions ask about connections and wordiness. As with grammar-convention questions, you must look for the best choice for the given context.

Connections Questions

Three kinds of connections questions —i.e., sentence transitions, clause linkage, and paragraph transitions—ask about how ideas connect to each other. The fourth type of connection question—conjunctions—asks you to decide if the underlined word is appropriate.

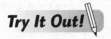

Try It Out!

Underline the connections errors in the examples below.

1. She is allergic to flowers, she always buys bouquets for presents.

2. Liliana studied diligently, yet she wanted to become a physician.

3. First, you sift the flour, sugar, salt, and baking powder together. You crack the eggs and whisk them with milk. Third, you pour the egg mixture into the dry ingredients.

4. He stopped on the side of the road and changing the tire.

In connections questions, decide if the connection should express the continuation of an idea or a disagreement with it. Then, choose the most appropriate transition. In Step 1, decide the purpose—continuation or disagreement—of the transition word and then whether or not the selection works. In Step 2, look for the relationship between the clauses, sentences, or paragraphs to eliminate implausible answers quickly.

Wordiness Questions

ACT wordiness questions test your ability to choose the most concise way to express an idea. What makes a sentence wordy often varies: There may be too many words; there may be redundant words; or there may be words that are irrelevant. Look at the examples below.

Incorrect	Correct
Regardless of the fact that it is two below zero, the mail has to be delivered.	Although it is two below zero, the mail has to be delivered.
The baby fussed and cried and sobbed and made a lot of noise.	The baby cried loudly.
Tessa was quite happy to be at her grandparents' again, and it was very cloudy.	Tessa was quite happy to be at her grandparents' again.

Use the 3-Step Method for ACT English Success with wordiness questions. As you identify the issue or eliminate answer choices, ask, "Do these words mean the same thing?" Choose the response that is more concise but expresses the same idea.

Wordiness questions represent about 1/10 of all questions on the ACT English Test. You should expect to see 7 or 8 of them per test.

Try It Out!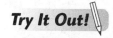

Use the 3-Step Method for ACT English Success to answer the wordiness question below.

   When Cortez returned to Spain, his ship's cargo <u>included and held</u> three chests
                                                          1
of cacao beans.

Identify the issue: _____

Prediction: _____

1. A.   NO CHANGE
    B.   included, held
    C.   included
    D.   including and holding

Test Practice Unit 5

When your teacher tells you, carefully tear out this page.

1. Ⓐ Ⓑ Ⓒ Ⓓ   15. Ⓐ Ⓑ Ⓒ Ⓓ   29. Ⓐ Ⓑ Ⓒ Ⓓ

2. Ⓕ Ⓖ Ⓗ Ⓙ   16. Ⓕ Ⓖ Ⓗ Ⓙ   30. Ⓕ Ⓖ Ⓗ Ⓙ

3. Ⓐ Ⓑ Ⓒ Ⓓ   17. Ⓐ Ⓑ Ⓒ Ⓓ

4. Ⓕ Ⓖ Ⓗ Ⓙ   18. Ⓕ Ⓖ Ⓗ Ⓙ

5. Ⓐ Ⓑ Ⓒ Ⓓ   19. Ⓐ Ⓑ Ⓒ Ⓓ

6. Ⓕ Ⓖ Ⓗ Ⓙ   20. Ⓕ Ⓖ Ⓗ Ⓙ

7. Ⓐ Ⓑ Ⓒ Ⓓ   21. Ⓐ Ⓑ Ⓒ Ⓓ

8. Ⓕ Ⓖ Ⓗ Ⓙ   22. Ⓕ Ⓖ Ⓗ Ⓙ

9. Ⓐ Ⓑ Ⓒ Ⓓ   23. Ⓐ Ⓑ Ⓒ Ⓓ

10. Ⓕ Ⓖ Ⓗ Ⓙ   24. Ⓕ Ⓖ Ⓗ Ⓙ

11. Ⓐ Ⓑ Ⓒ Ⓓ   25. Ⓐ Ⓑ Ⓒ Ⓓ

12. Ⓕ Ⓖ Ⓗ Ⓙ   26. Ⓕ Ⓖ Ⓗ Ⓙ

13. Ⓐ Ⓑ Ⓒ Ⓓ   27. Ⓐ Ⓑ Ⓒ Ⓓ

14. Ⓕ Ⓖ Ⓗ Ⓙ   28. Ⓕ Ⓖ Ⓗ Ⓙ

DO NOT TURN THE PAGE UNTIL TOLD TO DO SO.

C

DIRECTIONS: In the two passages that follow, certain words and phrases are underlined and numbered. In the right-hand column, you will find alternatives for the underlined part. In most cases, you are to choose the one that best expresses the idea, makes the statement appropriate for standard written English, or is worded most consistently with the style and tone of the passage as a whole. If you think the original version is best, choose "NO CHANGE." In some cases, you will find in the right-hand column a question about the underlined part. You are to choose the best answer to the question. For each question, choose the alternative you consider best and fill in the corresponding oval on your answer document. Read each passage through once before you begin to answer the questions that accompany it. For many of the questions, you must read several sentences beyond the question to determine the answer. Be sure that you have read far enough ahead each time you choose an alternative.

PASSAGE I

Sherlock Holmes

Sherlock Holmes—the <u>ingenious and extremely clever</u> detective with the deer-stalker hat, pipe, and
[1]

magnifying glass—is a universally recognizable character. Everyone knows of Holmes's ability to solve even the <u>most bizarrest</u> mysteries, through the
[2]

application of cold logic. <u>Therefore, everyone</u> is also
[3]
familiar with the phrase, "Elementary, my dear Watson;" this was Holmes's perennial response to the requests of his baffled sidekick, Dr. Watson, for <u>explanation on</u> Holmes' amazing deductions.
[4]

<u>Strictly speaking, Holmes' "deductions" were not</u>
[5]
<u>deductions at all, but inductive inferences.</u>
[5]

Everyone does not know, however, about the creator of Sherlock Holmes—Sir Arthur Conan Doyle. Fans of Holmes might be surprised to discover that Conan

1. **A.** NO CHANGE
   B. ingenious
   C. ingenious, extremely clever
   D. cleverly ingenious

2. **F.** NO CHANGE
   G. bizarrest
   H. most bizarre
   J. more bizarre

3. **A.** NO CHANGE
   B. Although everyone
   C. For this reason, everyone
   D. Everyone

4. **F.** NO CHANGE
   G. explanations on or about
   H. explanations of
   J. explaining

5. **A.** NO CHANGE
   B. (Strictly speaking, of course, Holmes's "deductions" were not deductions at all, but inductive inferences.)
   C. Holmes's "deductions" were, strictly speaking, not deductions at all, but inductive inferences.
   D. OMIT the underlined portion.

GO ON TO THE NEXT PAGE.

Doyle did not want to be engraved forever in the memory of the people as the author of the Sherlock Holmes stories.

In fact, Conan Doyle killed Holmes at the end of the second book of short stories and subsequently felt a great sense of relief. Conan Doyle promised himself that Sherlock Holmes won't ever again divert him from more serious writing. It took eight years, along with the offer of a princely sum of money, before Conan Doyle could be persuaded to revive the detective.

Conan Doyle was also knighted by the Queen of England, although not for his literary works. Admirers of Holmes' coldly scientific approach to his detective work may also be taken aback and very surprised when they learn that Conan Doyle was deeply immersed in spiritualism. For example, him and his family attempted to communicate with the dead through automatic writing—a ridiculous, absurd, laughable process, it is writing thought to be directed by a channelled spirit. Conan Doyle claimed to have grasped materialized hands and watched heavy objects swimming through the air, during sessions led by the medium. Convinced by these experiences of the validity of paranormal phenomena, he lectures on spiritualism in towns and villages throughout Britain.

6. F. NO CHANGE
   G. to go down in the annals of history
   H. to be permanently thought of forever
   J. to be remembered

7. A. NO CHANGE
   B. Despite this,
   C. Regardless,
   D. Yet,

8. F. NO CHANGE
   G. would never
   H. might never
   J. would not likely ever

9. A. NO CHANGE
   B. as well as
   C. and
   D. and including

10. F. NO CHANGE
    G. Although not for his literary works, Conan Doyle was also knighted by the Queen of England.
    H. Knighted by the Queen of England, although not for his literary works, Conan Doyle was also.
    J. OMIT the underlined portion.

11. A. NO CHANGE
    B. stunned and amazed
    C. taken aback
    D. taken aback and most surprised

12. F. NO CHANGE
    G. he and his family
    H. they and his family
    J. his family and he

13. A. NO CHANGE
    B. something we no longer believe in,
    C. a silly process, it is
    D. OMIT the underlined portion.

14. F. NO CHANGE
    G. phenomena, he lectured
    H. phenomena was that he lectured
    J. phenomena. He lectured

GO ON TO THE NEXT PAGE.

Conan Doyle seemed never to have asked himself why spirits would manifest themselves in such curious ways or to have reflected on the fact that many of these effects are the standard trappings of cheating mediums. One wonders <u>what will Sherlock Holmes have to</u> <u>believe?</u>
15

15. A. NO CHANGE
    B. what Sherlock Holmes would have said.
    C. What is Sherlock Holmes going to say?
    D. , What had Sherlock Holmes said?

PASSAGE II

My Rafting Adventure

White water rafting <u>being</u> a favorite pastime of
16
mine for several years. I have drifted down many challenging North American rivers—including the Snake, the Green, and the Salmon. I have spent some of my best moments in dangerous rapids, yet nothing <u>have</u>
17
<u>ever</u> matched the thrills I experienced when facing my
17
first rapids, on the Deschutes River.

<u>My father and me</u> spent the morning floating down
18
a calm and peaceful stretch of the Deschutes in his wooden MacKenzie river boat. This trip was the wooden boat's first time down rapids, as well as <u>my.</u> I could hear
19
the water roar <u>as we were getting close and approaching</u>
20
Whitehorse Rapids. I felt much like a novice skier peering down her first steep slope; I was scared but excited.

The water <u>churned about,</u> covering me with a
21
refreshing spray. My father, positioned toward the stern, controlled the oars. The carefree expression he usually

16. F. NO CHANGE
    G. have been
    H. has been
    J. was

17. A. NO CHANGE
    B. has ever
    C. having ever
    D. ever

18. F. NO CHANGE
    G. My father and I
    H. I and my father
    J. Me and my father

19. A. NO CHANGE
    B. mine.
    C. my very first trip.
    D. as well.

20. F. NO CHANGE
    G. as we were approaching
    H. as we got close at
    J. as we approached

21 A. NO CHANGE
    B. was churning about,
    C. churned up,
    D. churning all over the place,

GO ON TO THE NEXT PAGE.

wore on the river had been replaced <u>from a look</u> of
₂₂
intense concentration, as he maneuvered around the
boulders that dotted our path. To release tension, we
began to holler <u>as if we had been</u> kids on a roller coaster;
₂₃
our voices echoed across the water as we lurched about
violently.

Suddenly we came to a jarring halt <u>and stop</u>; the left
₂₄
side of the bow was wedged on a large rock. A whirlpool
twirled around us; if we capsized, we would be sucked
into the undertow. Instinctively, I threw all of my weight
toward the right side <u>of the tilting boat.</u>
₂₅
Luckily, it was just enough force to dislodge us,

<u>while</u> we continued on down for about 10 minutes of
₂₆
spectacular rapids.

Later that day, we <u>will go through</u> Buckskin Mary
₂₇
Rapids and Boxcar Rapids. When we pulled up on the
bank that evening, we saw <u>how it was</u> that the boat had
₂₈
received its first scar: <u>that scar was</u> a small hole on the
₂₉
upper bow, made from the boulder with which we had
wrestled. In the years to come, the two of us went down
many rapids, and the boat <u>receiving</u> many bruises.
₃₀
However, the trip through Whitehorse was the most
memorable one of all.

22. F. NO CHANGE
    G. of a look
    H. by a look
    J. for a look

23. A. NO CHANGE
    B. sort of like
    C. like
    D. as if we had been trying to be like

24. F. NO CHANGE
    G. or stop
    H. and stopped
    J. OMIT the underlined portion.

25. A. NO CHANGE
    B. on the tilting boat.
    C. that tilted the boat.
    D. that the boat tilted.

26. F. NO CHANGE
    G. in spite of the fact that
    H. and
    J. finally

27. A. NO CHANGE
    B. would have gone through
    C. go through
    D. went through

28. F. NO CHANGE
    G. the way
    H. the shocking fact
    J. OMIT the underlined portion.

29. A. NO CHANGE
    B. The scar was
    C. A scar which was
    D. OMIT the underlined portion.

30. F. NO CHANGE
    G. was receiving
    H. received
    J. receive

END OF TEST.

STOP! DO NOT TURN THE PAGE UNTIL TOLD TO DO SO.

KAP Wrap

Find a paragraph from a book you are reading or from one that you have read. Identify at least three connections as best choices, or suggest better ones, using the criteria you thought about in Lesson C. If you find evidence of wordiness, suggest better options.

Unit 6
ACT English II

Thinking KAP

Describe how you put batteries into a radio, camera, or cell phone.

A

Strategy Instruction

Sentence Sense

In Unit 5, you learned the 3-Step Method for ACT English Success. You will use this method for every question on the ACT English Test. In this unit, you will refine your ability to read efficiently, eliminate, and plug in the remaining responses. This lesson will focus on sentence sense.

In the Thinking KAP activity, you probably wrote something like, "the cell phone won't work correctly when the batteries aren't in right." Sentences also don't "work correctly" if they're not put together properly. They may not make sense to the reader or may communicate something different than the author's intent.

Sentence-sense questions on the ACT test your composition skills by asking you to decide whether the selection includes a sentence fragment, an incorrect clause structure, an unnecessary use of the passive voice, or an incorrect modifier construction.

Identifying the issue in a sentence-sense question helps rule out irrelevant answer choices.

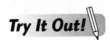

Briefly explain to a partner why the sentence structures below are incorrect.

1. Losing the game.

2. Kevin decided to help out with the laundry, he needed his favorite shirt.

3. Only the dog chased squirrels; he had no interest in birds or mice.

Questions about Sentence Fragments

Sentence-fragment questions ask you to recognize when one of the sentence components—i.e., subject, verb, or independent clause expressing a complete thought—is missing. Take a look at the examples below.

Incorrect	Correct
<u>Because he left his shoes at the beach</u>	Milena was angry at her brother because he left his shoes at the beach.
He ran down the beach <u>and stepping on a sea urchin.</u>	He ran down the beach and stepped on a sea urchin.
<u>Built sand castles until going home</u>	The boy built sand castles until he had to go home.

keep in mind

The subject and verb of every clause should match.

As you identify the issue in Step 1 of the 3-Step Method for ACT English Success, verify that the sentence has all its components. Any missing component indicates a fragment. On the ACT, sentence-sense questions will often include a verb used in such a fashion that it does not complete a thought in the independent clause.

Try It Out!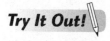

Use the 3-Step Method for ACT English Success to answer the sentence-sense question about fragments below.

<u>Keeping the discovery</u> quiet for a while, but then he couldn't resist bragging
       1
about it.

Identify the issue: _____

1. **A.** NO CHANGE
   B. The discovery he was keeping
   C. He kept the discovery
   D. Keeps the discovery

Questions About Clause Structure

Clause-structure questions will ask you to decide if two clauses are properly connected. To fix a clause-structure issue either insert a semicolon, add a conjunction, make one clause subordinate, or split the sentence in two sentences. The ACT will also ask about run-on sentences. To fix a run-on sentence issue either add a semicolon, change a verb form to –ing, or make two separate sentences. Take a look at the examples below.

For, and, not, but, or, yet, and so are the only words that can connect independent clauses with just a comma. Use the acronym FANBOYS to remember these coordinating conjunctions.

Incorrect	Correct
The kayaker survived through his knowledge and skill <u>having recognized the onset of hypothermia and keeping himself warm.</u>	The kayaker survived through his knowledge and skill; he recognized the onset of hypothermia and kept warm.
Swimming is excellent <u>exercise, many</u> people dislike having contact with pool-cleaning chemicals.	Swimming is excellent exercise, but many people dislike having contact with pool-cleaning chemicals.
The children were <u>excited, the holiday was approaching.</u>	The children were excited because the holiday was approaching.
The little duck fell into the Blue River <u>and kept swimming and he arrived at the mouth of the river and saw an enormous city.</u>	The little duck fell into the Blue River and kept swimming. Then, he arrived at the mouth of the river and saw an enormous city.

Try It Out!

Use the 3-Step Method for ACT English Success to answer the sentence-sense question about clauses below.

Thoreau used his writing to spread his message of resistance and <u>activism, he published</u> an essay entitled "Civil Disobedience" (also known as "Resistance to Civil Government").

Identify the issue: _____

1. **F.** NO CHANGE
   G. activism; he published
   H. activism; which he is why he published
   J. activism; to publish

Modifier- and Passive-Voice Questions

In active constructions, the subject does or is something. In passive constructions, the subject has something done to it. Good writers use the active voice whenever possible. When a passive structure is underlined on the ACT, it is most likely the issue. The best choice will be the one that expresses the same idea and uses an active construction.

Modifier questions will generally concern placement. A modifying word or phrase should be as close as possible to the word that it is modifying. Plugging in the answer in Step 3 will help you determine the best placement. Take a look at the examples below.

Incorrect	Correct
More fish were caught by experienced fishermen than by the weekend crowd.	Experienced fishermen caught more fish than the weekend crowd caught.
Handling the salt dough, the child created carefully a village of figurines.	Carefully handling the salt dough, the child created a village of figurines.
A well-known rendezvous spot in New York City, we arranged to meet Grandma and Grandpa by the clock in Grand Central Terminal.	We arranged to meet Grandma and Grandpa by the clock in Grand Central Terminal, a well-known rendezvous spot in New York City.

keep in mind

Keeping an eye out for sentence-sense errors in your own writing and reading will help you recognize them on the test.

Try It Out!

Use the 3-Step Method for ACT English Success to answer the sentence-sense question about modifiers below.

Following the instructions carefully, our teacher was pleased with how well we did on the ACT.
[1]

Identify the issue: _____

1. **A.** NO CHANGE
    B. Following the instructions carefully, we did well on the ACT, which pleased our teacher.
    C. Following the instructions carefully, the ACT was something we did well on, pleasing our teacher.
    D. Following the instructions carefully, doing well on the ACT was something that pleased our teacher.

The 3-Step Method for ACT English Success

 ### STEP 1: Read efficiently.

- *Pause at each underlined portion.*
- *Identify the issue.*

 ### STEP 2: Predict and eliminate.

- *Read the answer choices and any question stems.*
- *Rule out choices that don't address the issue.*

 ### STEP 3: Plug in.

- *Substitute remaining choices.*
- *Select the best choice.*

The History of Telecommunications

Few of the people who use cellular phones today know the history of telecommunications over the past two centuries. Until the early 19th century, the fastest way to send a message was by horseback. That changed dramatically <u>in 1844, Samuel Morse demonstrated his</u> <u>electric telegraph system.</u> (You may recognize Samuel
[1]
Morse as the inventor of the Morse Code.) Soon America was linked coast to coast by telegraph wires.

Identify the issue: _____

1. **A.** NO CHANGE
   B. in 1844, when Samuel Morse demonstrated his electric telegraph system.
   C. in 1844. When Samuel Morse demonstrated his electric telegraph system.
   D. in 1844; when Samuel Morse demonstrated his electric telegraph system.

Three decades later, Alexander Graham Bell invented the telephone. The modern era of telecommunications had begun. While the cellular phone may be new, wireless communication almost dates back a hundred years. By the late 1800s, inventor Guglielmo Marconi was already experimenting with radio waves. He developed a tower that could transmit a radio signal over several miles. By the end of the 19th century, ships at sea were transmitting radio communications, sending messages to the shore, and communicating with other ships.

Identify the issue: _____

2. **F.** NO CHANGE
   G. dates back a hundred (almost) years.
   H. dates back a hundred years almost.
   J. dates back almost a hundred years.

During the last five decades, there have been tremendous advances in communication. In 1956, Europe and America <u>linked by underwater telephone cables</u>. Since the 1960s, hundreds of communication satellites have been sent into Earth's orbit. Over the last few years, cellular phones and pagers have become as commonplace as portable radios. The Internet, the most recent innovation in this area, will eventually advance communication in ways we cannot even imagine today.

Identify the issue: _____

3. **A.** NO CHANGE
   B. were linked by underwater telephone cables.
   C. having been linked by underwater telephone cables.
   D. linked with underwater telephone cables.

Shared Practice

■ *Use the 3-Step Method for ACT English Success to answer the questions below.*

PASSAGE II

Basketry

Basketry may be the world's earliest <u>handicraft, the</u>

<u>oldest</u> examples of basketry are 10,000 years old.
¹

1. **A.** NO CHANGE
    B. handicraft—the oldest
    C. handicraft the
    D. handicraft. The

hint *Look for the answer choice that will fix the issue but doesn't include new errors.*

These ancient <u>fragments. Which have been</u> preserved
²
well in the dry environment of Danger Cave, Utah, show

that early Native Americans knew the art of weaving

semi-rigid materials into useful objects. The remains of

baskets are found on every continent.

2. **F.** NO CHANGE
    G. fragments which have been
    H. fragments, which have been
    J. fragments, which, have been

hint *Consider the punctuation as you look for the best choice.*

Material, rather than technique or decoration, <u>is
usually in identifying a baskets' origin most useful.</u>
Willow, just pliant enough to be either woven or plaited,
is the favored basket-making material of northern
Europe. In other areas, basket makers use relatively
rigid materials, such as bamboo and rattan. Africa has

yielded the widest variety of basket-making <u>materials
including</u> palm leaves, tree roots, and grasses.

3. **A.** NO CHANGE
   B. is usually most useful in identifying a basket's origin
   C. is most useful usually in identifying a baskets origin
   D. most useful is usually in identifying a basket origin's

hint ▶ *The best choice for a modifier's position is closest to the word or phrase it's modifying.*

4. **F.** NO CHANGE
   G. materials. Including
   H. materials, which include
   J. materials; including

hint ▶ *Check all verb forms in the sentence to ensure that they work together correctly.*

Watching a craftsperson weave a basket can be a marvelous experience. The craftsperson, who works quick and gracefully, passes the weft over and under the foundation element, or warp. Such ancient techniques are a tangible link to the distant past.

Because each culture has its own unique basket-making patterns, the most common and most beautiful patterns worldwide are twillings and twinings.

5. A. NO CHANGE
    B. who works quickly
    C. which works quickly
    D. was working quickly

> **hint** Independent clauses have identifiable subjects and verbs; look for them as you identify the issue.

6. F. NO CHANGE
    G. And simply because
    H. After all,
    J. Although

> **hint** To choose the best structure, think about the way one clause relates to the others.

Unfortunately, the traditional art of basket making has been eroded by the pressures of commercialism. Many modern craftspeople <u>choosing</u> between
⁷
traditional artistry and financial security. Sadly, few factory-made baskets today show the delicate, geometric designs of the solitary artisan. Indeed, the handmade basket has become an "artwork." Now, collectors who prize the work of the traditional basket maker may fly thousands of miles in order to purchase genuine <u>designs and under such</u> financial pressure,
⁸
how long will the individual basket maker be able to preserve a high standard of craft?

7. **A.** NO CHANGE
   B. choosing and deciding
   C. must choose
   D. chose

hint *Look for the components of a complete sentence as you identify the issue.*

8. **F.** NO CHANGE
   G. designs; under such
   H. designs. Under such
   J. designs, since under such

hint *Run-on sentences that contain two ideas that are not closely connected should be fixed by creating separate sentences.*

KAP Wrap

Review the four categories of sentence errors. Write a sample correct-incorrect chart like the one in the text, using your own examples.

A

Thinking KAP

Identify at least five traffic signals and explain the meaning of each.

Strategy Instruction

Punctuation Questions

In the Thinking KAP activity, you listed common traffic signals along with their meanings. Just as traffic signals provide a shared language for drivers on the road, punctuation serves as a shared language for readers. When a traffic signal is placed incorrectly, drivers or pedestrians may misunderstand the situation; when punctuation is used incorrectly, the author's intentions may be misunderstood.

Punctuation questions on the ACT address five usage issues: commas, semicolons, colons, apostrophes, and dashes. Take a look at the examples below.

Punctuation questions represent approximately 1/7 of all questions on the ACT English Test. You should expect to see about 10 or 11 of them per test.

Incorrect	Correct
I bought sticky notes gel pens a binder, and some stickers for my little brother.	I bought sticky notes, gel pens, a binder, and some stickers for my little brother.
Aunt Louise fed us very well. She served croissants, jam and honey in the morning, quiche and salad at lunch, and roast chicken, baked potatoes and apple tart for dinner.	Aunt Louise fed us very well. She served croissants, jam, and honey in the morning; quiche and salad at lunch; and roast chicken, baked potatoes, and apple tart for dinner.
F. Scott Fitzgerald wrote several well-known novels, *The Great Gatsby, This Side of Paradise, Tender is the Night* and *The Beautiful and Damned.*	F. Scott Fitzgerald wrote several well-known novels: *The Great Gatsby, This Side of Paradise, Tender is the Night*, and *The Beautiful and Damned.*
Michaels brother is a policeman in Omaha.	Michael's brother is a policeman in Omaha.
The variety of urban fauna—crows seagulls rats racoons possum and even the occasional coyote is quite astounding.	The variety of urban fauna—crows, seagulls, rats, racoons, possum, and even the occasional coyote—is quite astounding.

B

Commas

There are a limited number of comma rules that are tested on the ACT. You will use the 3-Step Method for ACT English Success to answer all comma questions. Take a look at the examples below.

Rule	Correct Example
Use commas correctly in a list.	I bought sticky notes, gel pens, a binder, and some stickers for my little brother.
Use a comma after an independent clause beginning with a conjunction (FANBOYS).	Helen wanted to go home, but Paris wouldn't let her.
Use commas to set off an introductory phrase.	Taking one step at a time, the toddler worked to climb the stairs successfully.
Use commas to separate an appositive or a nonessential element.	The rules, as you well know, do not allow late admittance.

keep in mind

On the ACT English Test, a comma should follow every item in a list— even the second to last item (before the "and").

Try It Out!

Use the 3-Step Method for ACT English Success to answer the comma questions below.

The tree <u>frog for example blends</u> perfectly into its surroundings.

Identify the issue: ^{1} _comma—"for example" is nonessential_

1. **A.** NO CHANGE
   B. frog, for example blends
   C. frog, for example, blends
   D. frog for example, blends

Tree frogs are adept <u>at camouflage but</u> some types of tree frogs are
^{2}
nevertheless endangered.

Identify the issue: _____

2. **F.** NO CHANGE
   G. at camouflage, but
   H. at camouflage; but
   J. at camouflage. But

B

Semicolons and Colons

There are a limited number of rules for the use of semicolons and colons on the ACT. You will use the 3-Step Method for ACT English Success to answer all semicolon and colon questions. Take a look at the examples below.

Rule	Correct Example
Use a semicolon to combine two independent clauses.	The snow fell heavily during the night; by five o'clock the next morning, Peter was plowing the city streets.
Use a semicolon to separate items in a list when the items themselves contain commas.	Aunt Louise fed us very well. She served croissants, jam, and honey in the morning; quiche and salad at lunch; and roast chicken, baked potatoes, and apple tart for dinner.
Use a colon to introduce or emphasize a short phrase, quotation, explanation, or example.	One animal in particular uses its distinctive white stripe as a way of standing out from its surroundings: the skunk.
Use a colon to introduce a list.	F. Scott Fitzgerald wrote several well-known novels: *The Great Gatsby*, *This Side of Paradise*, *Tender is the Night*, and *The Beautiful and Damned*.

Use your knowledge of punctuation and conjunctions to help eliminate incorrect answers.

Try It Out!

Use the 3-Step Method for ACT English Success to answer the punctuation question below.

Chocolate ants have yet to catch on <u>in this country, Americans</u> enjoy eating
₁
chocolate, but they are not fond of eating insects.

Identify the issue: _____

1. A. NO CHANGE
    B. in this country: Americans
    C. in this country; Americans
    D. in this country. Americans

Apostrophes and Dashes

There are a limited number of rules for the use of apostrophes and dashes that are tested on the ACT. You will use the 3-Step Method for ACT English Success to answer all questions about apostrophes and dashes. Take a look at the examples below.

Rule	Correct Example
Use an apostrophe with a possessive noun.	Alda's small dog, Frantic, amused everyone in the neighborhood.
Use an apostrophe to signal a contraction.	It's never going to stop snowing!
Use a dash to indicate hesitation or an interruption in the main thought.	Lou rushed down the street, bought the paper, raced toward the subway and—Oh, no!—his lunch was on the counter at home.
Use a dash to enclose explanations (where you could use parentheses).	Cross-stitching—a form of embroidery—seems very simple, but is quite difficult to master.

keep in mind

If unsure, write out the missing letters in a contraction.

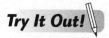
Try It Out!

Use the 3-Step Method for ACT English Success to answer the punctuation question below.

Uncle Harvey—he was my father's older brother taught me everything I know
₁
about chess.

Identify the issue: _____

1. **A.**   NO CHANGE
    B.   Uncle Harvey, he was my fathers older brother taught
    C.   Uncle Harvey—he was my fathers older brother, taught
    D.   Uncle Harvey—he was my father's older brother—taught

The 3-Step Method for ACT English Success

 ## STEP 1: Read efficiently.

- *Pause at each underlined portion.*

- *Identify the issue.*

 ## STEP 2: Predict and eliminate.

- *Read the answer choices and any question stems.*

- *Rule out choices that don't address the issue.*

 ## STEP 3: Plug in.

- *Substitute remaining choices.*

- *Select the best choice.*

B

Success

What does it mean to be successful? Does one measure success by money? If I told you about a man working as a teacher, a land surveyor, and a factory worker <u>and never holding any of these jobs for more</u> [1] <u>than a few years—would</u> [1] that man sound like a success to you? If I told you that he spent two years living alone in a small cabin that he built for himself, and that he spent those years looking at plants and writing in a diary, would you think of him as a celebrity or an important figure? What if I told you that he rarely ventured far from the town where he was born, that he was thrown in jail for refusing to pay his taxes, and that he died at the age of 45? Do any of these facts seem to point to a man whose life should be studied and emulated?

Identify the issue: _____

1. **A.** NO CHANGE
   B. worker, and never holding any of these jobs for more than a few years, would
   C. worker—and never holding any of these jobs for more than a few years—would
   D. worker and never holding any of these jobs for more than a few years: would

You may already know about this <u>man, you</u> may
even have read some of his writings. His name was
Henry David Thoreau, and he was, in addition to the
jobs listed above, a poet, an essayist, a naturalist, and a
social critic. Although the facts listed about him may
not seem to add up to much, he was a tremendously
influential person. Along with a few other writers—
Ralph Waldo Emerson, Mark Twain, and Walt
Whitman—Thoreau helped create the first literature
and philosophy that most people identify as uniquely
American.

Identify the issue: _____

2. **F.**   NO CHANGE
    G.   man you
    H.   man; you
    J.   man, You

B

In 1845, Thoreau built a cabin <u>near Walden Pond,</u> ₃ <u>and remained</u> there for more than two years: living ₃ alone, fending for himself, and observing the nature around him. He kept scrupulous notes in his diary, which he later distilled into his most famous work, *Walden*. Today, many visitors come to Walden Pond in Concord, Massachusetts to see where this noted philosopher lived and worked.

Identify the issue: _____

3.   **A.**   NO CHANGE
       B.   near Walden Pond; and
       C.   near Walden Pond and
       D.   near Walden Pond. And

B

Shared Practice

■ *Use the 3-Step Method for ACT English Success to answer the questions below.*

PASSAGE II

The Fires at Yellowstone

<u>During the summer of 1988 I</u> watched Yellowstone
₁
National Park go up in flames. In June, fires ignited by
lightning had been allowed to burn unsuppressed
because park officials expected that the usual summer
rains would douse the flames. However, the rains never
came. A plentiful fuel supply of fallen logs and pine

needles was <u>available, and winds</u> of up to 100 mph
₂
whipped the spreading fires along and carried red-hot
embers to other areas, creating new fires.

1. **A.** NO CHANGE
    B. During the summer of 1988, I
    C. During the summer of 1988; I
    D. During the summer of 1988: I

hint ▷ *The placement of the clause in the sentence helps you activate your prior knowledge about punctuation rules.*

2. **F.** NO CHANGE
    G. available and winds
    H. available. And winds
    J. available—and winds

hint ▷ *Think about the rules for FANBOYS.*

By the time park officials succumbed to the pressure of public opinion and decided to try to <u>extinguish the flames; it was too late.</u> The situation
₃
remained out of control in spite of the efforts of 9,000 fire fighters who were using state-of-the-art equipment. By September, a

large segment of <u>Yellowstone—more than 720,000</u>
₄
<u>acres—had been affected</u> by fire. Only nature was able
₄
to curb the destruction; the smoke did not begin to clear until the first snow arrived.

3. **A.** NO CHANGE
    B. extinguished the flames. It was too late.
    C. extinguished the flames, it was too late.
    D. extinguished the flames it was too late.

hint *Knowledge of punctuation rules helps you predict the correct choice.*

4. **F.** NO CHANGE
    G. Yellowstone: more than 720,000 acres had been affected
    H. Yellowstone, more than 720,000 acres had been affected
    J. Yellowstone. More than 720,000 acres had been affected

hint *Is the underlined portion parenthetical to the rest of the sentence? If so, what punctuation is acceptable?*

Name_____ Date_____

As an ecologist <u>whose studied</u> forests for 20 years, I
                         5
knew that this was not nearly the tragedy it

seemed to be. <u>Large fires are, after all, necessary</u> in
                                  6
order that the continued health of the forest ecosystem

be maintained. Fires thin out overcrowded areas and

allow the sun to reach species of plants stunted by

shade. Ash fertilizes the soil, and fire smoke kills forest

bacteria.

5. A. NO CHANGE
    B. who's studied
    C. whos' studied
    D. whose's studied

hint *Decide whether the apostrophe indicates possession or a contraction.*

6. F. NO CHANGE
    G. Large fires are, after all necessary
    H. Large fires are after all, necessary
    J. Large fires are after all necessary

hint *Decide whether the portion marked by a comma is necessary to understand the meaning of the sentence.*

In the case of the lodgepole pine,

fire is essential to <u>reproduction: the</u>
                              7

<u>pines' cones</u> only open when exposed to temperatures
        8
greater than 112 degrees. The fires in Yellowstone did

result in some loss of wildlife, but overall, the region's

animals proved to be fire-tolerant and fire-adaptive.

Large animals such as bison were often seen grazing

and bedding down in meadows near burning forests.

Also, the fire posed little threat to the members of any

endangered animal species in the park.

7. A. NO CHANGE
    B. reproduction the
    C. reproduction—the
    D. reproduction; the

hint *What are the most likely uses of a colon on the ACT?*

8. F. NO CHANGE
    G. pine's cones
    H. pines's cones
    J. pines cone's

hint *To decide if the apostrophe indicates possession, look for something to be possessed.*

B

KAP Wrap

Editors and writers often use "style guides" so that everyone working on a project is following the same set of signals. Using what you've learned in this lesson, write a quick punctuation chart, modeled on the charts in this lesson, that will be your own "style guide." Include examples of each of the five usage issues.

lesson C

Writing-Strategy and Organization Questions

ReKAP

Review the strategies from Lessons A and B. Then fill in the blanks to show what you have learned.

1. Sentence-sense question issues include

_____

_____

_____

2. Punctuation question issues include

_____

_____

_____

_____

_____

Writing-Strategy and Organization Questions

In previous lessons, you've looked at the passages at the sentence level. To answer questions about writing strategy and organization, you will consider either the whole passage or a specific paragraph.

Organization Questions

Organization questions ask you to find the most logical order for a certain portion of the passage. Look for the answer choice that causes the selection to flow the best. Also look for connections between sentences or paragraphs that signal that one must come before or after the other.

There are two types of organization questions—paragraph level and passage level. When you see a paragraph that seems to be jumbled and has numbers in brackets before every sentence, one of the questions that follows will ask about the proper order of the sentences. Paragraph three of "The Other Side of Chocolate" is an example of a paragraph with numbered sentences.

If there are numbers in brackets before each paragraph, expect a question that asks about the most logical order for the paragraphs within the passage. "The Other Side of Chocolate" has these bracketed numbers before each paragraph.

Organization questions are comparatively rare on the ACT English Test. Expect to see about two per test.

Try It Out!

Use the 3-Step Method for ACT English Success to answer the organization questions on the opposite page.

The Other Side of Chocolate

[1]

Since its move from Mexico to Europe, chocolate has become very popular across the world. People in most countries enjoy chocolate in one form or another. In fact, in Asia, chocolate-covered ants are a delicacy.

[2]

New research shows that moderate consumption of chocolate may actually be good for you. Researchers say chocolate contains a chemical that could prevent cancer and heart disease. Chocolate is very high in catechins, a chemical thought to be behind the benefits.

[3]

[1] Over the next century, cafes specializing in chocolate drinks began to appear throughout Europe. [2] It was from these beans that Europe experienced its first taste of what seemed to be a very unusual beverage. [3] Cortez came to the New World in search of gold, but his interest was also fired by the Aztecs' strange drink. [4] When Cortez returned to Spain, his ship's cargo held three chests of cacao beans. [5] The drink soon became popular among those people wealthy enough to afford it. 1

keep in mind

Look for the numbers in brackets that indicate organization questions.

[4]

The first people known to have made chocolate were the Aztecs, who used cacao seeds to make a bitter but tasty drink. However, it was not until Hernan Cortez's exploration of Mexico in 1519 that Europeans first learned of chocolate.

1. What would be the most logical order of sentences in the third paragraph?
   A. NO CHANGE
   B. 3, 2, 1, 4, 5
   C. 5, 2, 3, 4, 1
   D. 3, 4, 2, 5, 1

   Question 2 asks about the passage as a whole.

2. What would be the most logical order of paragraphs for this essay?
   F. NO CHANGE
   G. 4, 3, 1, 2
   H. 3, 1, 2, 4
   J. 4, 2, 1, 3

Writing-Strategy Questions

Writing-strategy questions ask you to think about the tone and topic of the passage. These questions may ask you to select the best sentence to include at a certain point in the passage; to describe the purpose of a detail, sentence, paragraph, or the whole passage; to decide where a certain sentence should be inserted (or if it does not belong anywhere); or to determine if the passage has fulfilled a certain assignment. Some of these questions will be marked within the passage by a number with a box around it. Others will come at the end of the question set and be denoted as questions that deal with the whole essay.

In Unit 2, you learned to use Question the Author to identify the main idea and author's purpose of a passage. You will use Question the Author to answer writing-strategy questions on the ACT English Test as well.

Writing-strategy questions represent about 1/6 of the test. You should expect to see about 12 of them per test.

Question the Author	
Main Idea:	What does the author want me to know?
Author's Purpose:	Why does the author want me to know this?

As you read the passage, think about what the author wants you to know and why the author wants you to know this. By using Question the Author, you will be able to tell what topic the author has discussed and also the tone with which the author has discussed the topic. For writing-strategy questions, look for the answer choice that is consistent with the topic and tone of the passage.

Try It Out!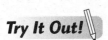

Use the 3-Step Method for ACT English Success to answer the writing-strategy questions on the opposite page.

The Other Side of Chocolate

[1] The first people known to have made chocolate were the Aztecs, who used cacao seeds to make a bitter but tasty drink. However, it was not until Hernan Cortez's exploration of Mexico in 1519 that Europeans first learned of chocolate.

Cortez came to the New World in search of gold, but his interest was also fired by the Aztecs' strange drink. When Cortez returned to Spain, his ship's cargo held three chests of cacao beans. It was from these beans that Europe experienced its first taste of what seemed to be a very unusual beverage. The drink soon became popular among those people wealthy enough to afford it. Over the next century, cafes specializing in chocolate drinks began to appear throughout Europe.

Since its move from Mexico to Europe, chocolate has become very popular across the world. People in most countries enjoy chocolate in one form or another. In fact, in Asia, chocolate-covered ants are a delicacy.

New research shows that moderate consumption of chocolate may actually be good for you. Researchers say chocolate contains a chemical that could prevent cancer and heart disease. Chocolate is very high in catechins, a chemical thought to be behind the benefits.

Main Idea: _____

Author's Purpose: _____

If you are asked to insert a new sentence into the passage, find the choice that is consistent with the author's main idea and tone.

1. The author wants to add a sentence to introduce the essay. Which of the following sentences would best serve this purpose?
   A. Europeans and Aztecs were among the first people to make chocolate.
   B. European history hasn't been the same since chocolate was discovered.
   C. Cacao beans were first brought to Europe from Mexico in the 16th century.
   D. The word "chocolate" is used to describe a variety of foods made from the beans of the cacao tree.

> Question 2 asks about the passage as a whole.

2. Suppose the author had been given the assignment of writing about culinary trends in history. Would this essay satisfy the requirement?
   F. Yes, because the essay discusses many culinary trends in history.
   G. Yes, because the essay shows how chocolate has been used over time.
   H. No, because the essay focuses too much on chocolate in present times.
   J. No, because the essay only covers chocolate and not other foods.

Test Practice Unit 6

When your teacher tells you, carefully tear out this page.

1. Ⓐ Ⓑ Ⓒ Ⓓ   15. Ⓐ Ⓑ Ⓒ Ⓓ   29. Ⓐ Ⓑ Ⓒ Ⓓ

2. Ⓕ Ⓖ Ⓗ Ⓙ   16. Ⓕ Ⓖ Ⓗ Ⓙ   30. Ⓕ Ⓖ Ⓗ Ⓙ

3. Ⓐ Ⓑ Ⓒ Ⓓ   17. Ⓐ Ⓑ Ⓒ Ⓓ

4. Ⓕ Ⓖ Ⓗ Ⓙ   18. Ⓕ Ⓖ Ⓗ Ⓙ

5. Ⓐ Ⓑ Ⓒ Ⓓ   19. Ⓐ Ⓑ Ⓒ Ⓓ

6. Ⓕ Ⓖ Ⓗ Ⓙ   20. Ⓕ Ⓖ Ⓗ Ⓙ

7. Ⓐ Ⓑ Ⓒ Ⓓ   21. Ⓐ Ⓑ Ⓒ Ⓓ

8. Ⓕ Ⓖ Ⓗ Ⓙ   22. Ⓕ Ⓖ Ⓗ Ⓙ

9. Ⓐ Ⓑ Ⓒ Ⓓ   23. Ⓐ Ⓑ Ⓒ Ⓓ

10. Ⓕ Ⓖ Ⓗ Ⓙ   24. Ⓕ Ⓖ Ⓗ Ⓙ

11. Ⓐ Ⓑ Ⓒ Ⓓ   25. Ⓐ Ⓑ Ⓒ Ⓓ

12. Ⓕ Ⓖ Ⓗ Ⓙ   26. Ⓕ Ⓖ Ⓗ Ⓙ

13. Ⓐ Ⓑ Ⓒ Ⓓ   27. Ⓐ Ⓑ Ⓒ Ⓓ

14. Ⓕ Ⓖ Ⓗ Ⓙ   28. Ⓕ Ⓖ Ⓗ Ⓙ

C

DO NOT TURN THE PAGE UNTIL TOLD TO DO SO.

DIRECTIONS: In the three passages that follow, certain words and phrases are underlined and numbered. In the right-hand column, you will find alternatives for the underlined part. In most cases, you are to choose the one that best expresses the idea, makes the statement appropriate for standard written English, or is worded most consistently with the style and tone of the passage as a whole. If you think the original version is best, choose "NO CHANGE." In some cases, you will find in the right-hand column a question about the underlined part. You are to choose the best answer to the question. For each question, choose the alternative you consider best and fill in the corresponding oval on your answer document. Read each passage through once before you begin to answer the questions that accompany it. For many of the questions, you must read several sentences beyond the question to determine the answer. Be sure that you have read far enough ahead each time you choose an alternative.

PASSAGE I

Liberal Arts Education

Although the concept of liberal arts has existed since the time of ancient Greece, the parameters <u>over the centuries have remained relatively unchanged of liberal arts study.</u> Liberal arts are defined as "any
₁

study given to reflection and free inquiry." <u>This not always being the case, however.</u> In medieval times, the
₂

seven liberal arts were divided into two parts: the Trivium ("the three roads") and the Quadrivium ("the four roads"). The Trivium consisted of grammar, rhetoric, and <u>logic, the Quadrivium consisted of arithmetic, geometry,</u> astronomy, and harmonics.
₃

However, the description of a liberal arts college is more limiting. A liberal arts college generally awards a Bachelor of Arts degree, primarily enrolls full-time students, typically has between 800 and 1,800 students, and does not provide professional or vocational

1. A. NO CHANGE
    B. over the centuries of liberal arts study have remained relatively unchanged.
    C. of liberal arts study have remained relatively unchanged over the centuries.
    D. of liberal arts study remaining relatively unchanged over the centuries.

2. F. NO CHANGE
    G. However, this has not always been the case.
    H. Although this has not always been the case.
    J. OMIT the underlined selection.

3. A. NO CHANGE
    B. logic; while the Quadrivium consisted of arithmetic, geometry,
    C. logic, so the Quadrivium consisted of arithmetic, geometry,
    D. logic; the Quadrivium consisted of arithmetic, geometry,

GO ON TO THE NEXT PAGE.

preparation. The liberal arts have been the primary
4
focus of undergraduate education in the United States

since it was a British colony. The number of liberal arts

colleges in the United States steady increased
5
throughout the 20th century, as private universities,

state universities, and community colleges all sought to

give their undergraduates a broad education.
6

The content of liberal arts study still focuses on the

arts, humanities, and sciences, and the basic notion of
7
forming well-rounded students in these areas is still the
7
concept behind liberal arts education today. There is

some concern, however, that the philosophy behind

liberal arts education is out of step with the times in

which today's students are living. Responding to this
8
concern, courses in computer science and information
8
technology have been added to the curriculum of many
8
colleges and universities. Does this mean the end of
8
liberal arts education as it has been practiced since the

days of Martianus Capella? I don't believe so. Most
9
liberal arts colleges award Master's and doctoral
9
degrees as well.
9

The study of liberal arts may have to evolve with the

times, but its basic premise—that well-rounded

students are well-educated students—remain as valid
10
today as it was in medieval times.

4. **F.** NO CHANGE
   G. The liberal arts has been
   H. The liberal arts having been
   J. The liberal arts being

5. **A.** NO CHANGE
   B. steadily increased
   C. increased in a steady fashion
   D. increased in a steadily fashion

6. **F.** NO CHANGE
   G. give its
   H. giving their
   J. gave its

7. **A.** NO CHANGE
   B. sciences; and the basic notion of forming well-rounded students
   C. sciences. And the basic notion of forming well-rounded students
   D. sciences: and the basic notion of forming well-rounded students

8. **F.** NO CHANGE
   G. Responding to this concern, computer science and information technology courses have been added to the curriculum of many colleges and universities.
   H. Responding to this concern, computer science and information technology are the subject of courses that have been added to the curriculum of many colleges and universities.
   J. Responding to this concern, many colleges and universities have added courses in computer science and information technology to the curriculum.

9. **A.** NO CHANGE
   B. Master's and doctoral degrees are awarded by most liberal arts colleges as well.
   C. Most degrees awarded by liberal arts colleges are Master's and doctoral ones.
   D. OMIT the underlined portion.

10. **F.** NO CHANGE
    G. remaining as valid today
    H. remains as valid today
    J. remained as valid today

C

The Library System

In the past 10 years, library systems have become

increasingly computerized, this has led to speculation
                    11

about the future of libraries. Some people believe that

not only the card catalogue, but also the library stacks

themselves, will eventually be rendered obsolete. It is

quite likely, they say, that in the next decade or so,

books as we know them will be replaced by electronic
                    12

data.
12

    This thought presents an interesting picture of the

future. Instead of spending an evening reading, curling
                    13

up with a laptop computer. With all the intriguing
                    13

possibilities the future holds, we are inclined to ignore

the past. While the future state may be interesting to
                    14

predict of the library system, it has a rich history as well.
          14

Libraries may have originated as early as the third

millennium B.C. in Babylonia. There, clay tablets were

used and utilized for record-keeping purposes and
      15

stored in a temple.

11. **A.** NO CHANGE
    B. increasingly computerized: this has led to speculation
    C. increasingly computerized, which has led to speculation
    D. increasingly computerized. Leading to speculation

12. **F.** NO CHANGE
    G. electronic data will replace books as we know them.
    H. books as we know them being replaced by electronic data.
    J. books as we know them are replaced by electronic data.

13. **A.** NO CHANGE
    B. Instead of spending an evening reading, curling up with a laptop computer instead.
    C. Curling up with a laptop computer instead of spending an evening reading.
    D. Instead of spending an evening reading, we may be curling up with a laptop computer.

14. **F.** NO CHANGE
    G. While predicting the future state may be interesting of the library system,
    H. While predicting the future state of the library system may be interesting,
    J. While the future of the library system may be an interesting state to predict,

15. **A.** NO CHANGE
    B. used—and utilized—
    C. used
    D. used, and therefore utilized,

GO ON TO THE NEXT PAGE.

In the seventh century B.C., approximately 20,000
                                         16
tablets organized by the King of Assyria have been
                 16
recovered for an enormous collection of fragments. The
               16
first libraries to store books were fourth century B.C.

Greek temples established in conjunction with the

various schools of philosophy. In the second century

A.D., libraries were founded in monasteries. Not until

the 13th century was university libraries created.
                              17
     During the Renaissance, library systems in the

form we have today emerged due to social changes: the

emergence of a middle class, a growth in literacy, and

the invention of the printing press. Although wars and
                                     18
revolutions hindered the development of the library

system in England. For example, Henry VIII ordered the

destruction of countless manuscripts and disbanded

some monastic libraries. Henry VIII was married six
                              19
times.
19
     Long ago, many English citizens were pondering

the fate of the nascent library system. Today's changes

are likewise causing some of us to consider the same
                                    20
thing, although in ways that medieval readers could
              20
never have imagined.
      20

16. **F.** NO CHANGE
    G. having organized an enormous collection, approximately 20,000 tablets and fragments have been recovered by the King of Assyria.
    H. an enormous collection of records organized by the King of Assyria: approximately 20,000 tablets and fragments recovered.
    J. the King of Assyria organized an enormous collection of records; approximately 20,000 tablets and fragments have been recovered.

17. **A.** NO CHANGE
    B. were university libraries created.
    C. was the creation of university libraries.
    D. were libraries created at any universities.

18. **F.** NO CHANGE
    G. Despite
    H. However,
    J. Even though

19. **A.** NO CHANGE
    B. Henry VIII, having been married six times.
    C. Six times, Henry VIII was married.
    D. OMIT the underlined portion.

20. **F.** NO CHANGE
    G. to consider the same thing, it is in ways that medieval readers could never have imagined.
    H. to have consideration of the same thing, although it is in ways that medieval readers could never have imagined.
    J. to consider the same thing, although in ways that medieval readers will never be able to imagine.

C

Nature's Disguises

[1]

Some animals <u>change its</u> coloring with the seasons.
21
The stoat, a member of the weasel family, is known as

the ermine in winter, because its brown fur changes to

white.

Chameleons are perhaps the most versatile of all

<u>animals that changes</u> their protective coloration. The
22
chameleon changes its color in just a few minutes

to whatever surface it happens to be <u>sitting over</u>.
23

[2]

<u>While animals like the chameleon have been using</u>
24
<u>their coloring</u> as a way of hiding from predators, the
24
skunk uses its distinctive white stripe as a way of

standing out from its surroundings. Far from placing <u>it</u>

<u>in danger; the skunk's</u> visibility actually protects it.
25

Unlike other <u>animals. The skunk</u> warns its
26

predators to avoid its infamous stink. <u>Think about it: the</u>
27
<u>question is</u> would your appetite be whetted by the
27
skunk's odor?

[3]

Researchers have been investigating how animal

species have come to use coloring as a means of

protecting themselves. One study has shown that

certain animals have glands which release special

21. A. NO CHANGE
     B. change up its
     C. change his
     D. change their

22. F. NO CHANGE
     G. animals who change
     H. animals which change
     J. animal that changes

23. A. NO CHANGE
     B. sitting on
     C. sitting within
     D. sitting about

24. F. NO CHANGE
     G. While animals like the chameleon using
         their coloring
     H. While animals like the chameleon used their
         coloring
     J. While animals like the chameleon use their
         coloring

25. A. NO CHANGE
     B. it in danger the skunk's
     C. it in danger, the skunk's
     D. it in danger, the skunks

26. F. NO CHANGE
     G. other animals, the skunk
     H. other animals: the skunk
     J. other animals; the skunk

27. A. NO CHANGE
     B. Think about it; the question is
     C. The question is
     D. OMIT this portion

GO ON TO THE NEXT PAGE.

hormones, resulting in the change of skin or fur color.

However, not all the animals that use camouflage have

these glands. You can bet that these folks will keep
                                                28
researching to see what they can find out about this
                                              28
really interesting subject.
            28

[4]

[1] The tree frog, for example, blends perfectly into

its surroundings. [2] This camouflage enables the tree

frog to hide from other animals that would be interested

in eating the tree frog. [3] Animals have a variety of

ways of protecting themselves from enemies. [4] Some

animals alter their shape or color to blend in with their

environment. [5] When it sits motionless, a background

of leaves completely hides the tree frog. 29

28. **F.** NO CHANGE
    G. The natural world is a vast and enormous treasury of mysterious phenomena.
    H. Scientists just cannot seem to figure out why this is.
    J. The topic remains as one of the many mysteries of the natural world.

29. What would be the most logical order of sentences in paragraph 4?
    A. NO CHANGE
    B. 3, 1, 4, 2, 5
    C. 4, 1, 5, 2, 3
    D. 3, 4, 1, 5, 2

Question 30 asks about the passage as a whole.

30. What would be the most logical order of paragraphs for this essay?
    F. NO CHANGE
    G. 1, 2, 4, 3
    H. 3, 1, 4, 2
    J. 4, 1, 2, 3

END OF TEST.

STOP! DO NOT TURN THE PAGE UNTIL TOLD TO DO SO.

KAP Wrap

Identify the main idea and author's purpose of a nonfiction paragraph that you've read or written recently. Consider how it is organized.

Unit 7
ACT Writing

Thinking KAP

Some have described the United States as a melting pot, in which many cultures come together to form one unique American culture. Others say that a salad-bowl metaphor is more accurate, in which cultures coexist while still maintaining their customs and traditions. Do you think the melting-pot metaphor or salad-bowl metaphor is more accurate?

What are the two sides of this argument?

_____

_____

Pick a stance.

_____

_____

List three reasons to support your position.

1. _____

   _____

2. _____

   _____

3. _____

   _____

A

Understanding the Assignment

As part of the Writing portion of the ACT, you will have 30 minutes to write an essay. You will be given a prompt that presents two sides of a particular debate or issue. You will be asked to take and defend a position on this issue. For example, consider the sample prompt below.

> Some schools are removing physical education from their curricula to make space for additional academic courses. Supporters of this decision believe that it is more important to develop the academic foundation that will help students succeed in the professional world. Others feel that physical education is a necessary means to train the next generation to care for their health, without which they will not succeed at all. In your opinion, should physical education be removed from school curricula?

Issues selected for topics on the ACT writing test are designed to be relevant to high-school students. If the topic seems unfamiliar to you, try to relate it to something in your life or experience.

Understanding the Directions

One of the easiest things you can do to help you on the essay section of the ACT is to get to know the directions, since they will always be the same. This paragraph will appear after every prompt.

> *In your essay, take a position on this question. You may write about either one of the two points of view given, or you may present a different point of view on this question. Use specific reasons and examples to support your position.*

On the ACT, you must identify a clear opinion and support it with facts and observations. You will not be graded on which position you take on the issue, but rather how you defend it.

Understanding the Rubric

The essay section of the ACT is scored differently from any other section. Graders use what is called a *holistic rubric*, which means that they have a set of guidelines with which to evaluate the essay.

Score	Competence	Organization	Language
6	clear and consistent competence, though it may have errors	is well organized and fully developed with supporting examples	displays consistent language facility, varied sentence structure, and range of vocabulary
5	reasonable competence, with occasional errors or lapses in quality	is generally organized and well developed with appropriate examples	displays language facility, syntactic variety, and range of vocabulary
4	adequate competence, with occasional lapses in quality	is well organized and adequately developed with examples	displays adequate but inconsistent language facility
3	developing competence, with weaknesses	inadequate organization or development	many errors in grammar or diction; little variety
2	some incompetence, with one or more weaknesses	poor organization or development	many errors in grammar and diction; no variety
1	incompetence, with serious flaws	no organization or development	severe grammar and diction errors obscure meaning

keep in mind

An off-topic essay will receive a score of 0; an essay that does not answer the question cannot receive a score higher than 3.

A

What other elements equal a high-scoring essay?

In addition to the requirements above, graders will be looking for the following things:

- Neatness: Your essay must be readable. If you edit what you've written, do it neatly. If you add a word, change a phrase, or cross out a sentence, do it carefully.

- Length: Although length isn't listed as one of the scoring criteria in the rubric, be sure to write enough to make and support a well-developed argument. Graders are likely to view a very short essay negatively.

Strategy for Essay Writing

You only have 30 minutes to plan and write your essay. The Strategy for Essay Writing below can help you make the most of every minute.

Strategy for Essay Writing
• Prompt
• Plan
• Produce
• Proofread

You can think of the Strategy for Essay Writing as the Four *P*s.

Here is a minute-by-minute plan of action for attacking the essay:

Minute 1: Prompt—Know it and understand it.

Minutes 2–6: Plan—Collect your ideas.

Minutes 7–26: Produce—Write your essay.

Minutes 27–30: Proofread—Read for consistency and errors.

Prompt

The first step of the Strategy for Essay Writing is Prompt. You have already learned that the directions will always be the same. The difference is the topic. As you read the essay assignment, first restate it in your own words. Then ask yourself, "What question do I need to answer in my essay?"

Try It Out!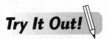

Read the prompt below.

> The principal of Elmwood High School set a rule that students will be punished if they are late to school. When one student was reprimanded for tardiness, his mother took responsibility, as she had been running late that morning. Should the principal hold the student accountable for this situation or does the fault lie with the mother?

In your own words, write the question you need to answer in your essay.

_____

_____

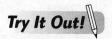

Read each prompt below. In your own words, write the questions you need to answer in your essays.

> The means by which young employees acquire jobs is changing rapidly. Some companies now welcome video resumes instead of traditional written applications. Others feel that such materials are inappropriate for the workplace. Do you feel that companies should consider non-traditional applications, including multimedia, when hiring new employees?

Restate the question in your own words.

_____

_____

_____

_____

keep in mind

If you have trouble understanding the issue presented in the prompt, focus on the question that comes at the end of the paragraph.

> There are an increasing number of online encyclopedias that allow for user-submitted content. Some teachers feel that these do not constitute scholarly sources and are not acceptable in research bibliographies. Others feel that they are refined by many different users and are therefore peer-reviewed, as in scholarly journals. Do you think that teachers should allow content from user-submitted encyclopedias in research papers?

Restate the question in your own words.

_____

_____

_____

_____

The Strategy for Essay Writing

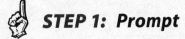 **STEP 1:** Prompt

STEP 2: Plan

STEP 3: Produce

STEP 4: Proofread

Read the prompt below. Then restate each of the two perspectives in your own words. This will help you decide which stance you would like to take.

> Recently, there has been a substantial debate regarding the presence of cell phones in public schools. Many people want to ban the presence or use of cell phones on school grounds because they can be distracting or targets of theft, and can enable cheating through messaging. Many parents and students, however, feel that having cell phones is an important safety precaution, allowing for contact in case of an emergency. Do you think that cell phones should be permitted on school grounds?

In your essay, take a position on this question. You may write about either one of the two points of view given, or you may present a different point of view on this question. Use specific reasons and examples to support your position.

Explain one side of this issue in your own words.

_____

_____

_____

_____

Now explain the other side of the issue in your own words.

_____

_____

_____

_____

A

Shared Practice

Think carefully about the issue presented in the following statement and the assignment below.

> Approaching the end of high school, it seems that everyone has advice to offer on how to succeed. Some feel that it is important to follow the advice of others and learn from their experiences. Others believe that the only way to learn is to try things on your own and find your own path. Do you believe that listening to advice is important in making decisions?

In your essay, take a position on this question. You may write about either one of the two points of view given, or you may present a different point of view on this question. Use specific reasons and examples to support your position.

Explain one side of this issue in your own words.

_____

_____

_____

_____

Now explain the other side of the issue in your own words.

_____

_____

_____

 If you have trouble identifying a different perspective, think about what someone different from you would think. How would your parents respond to the prompt? How would your teachers respond to the prompt?

KAP Wrap

Read the following sample student essay.

I think the melting pot metaphor can be updated to describe what has happened to American culture over the years. Each immigrant group that has come to the United States has added a new ingredeint to the melting pot so the recipe is always different. The changes in the melting pot are clear when you look at popular music and the English language itself.

Other cultures have influenced popular music tremendously. For example, a new genre called reggeaton has imerged on hip-hop stations. Latino artists use musical influences from salsa to hip-hop, and mix the English and Spanish languages to create unique songs. Other cultures have influenced popular music as well. Pop music also mixes Arabic melodies and Bhangra music with tradition American rhythms. Shifts in mainstream music show that there has been a fusion between musical tastes, but this also represents changes in the larger culture.

The English language has also experienced changes as different immigrant groups have mixed their own languages with American English. English itself has undergone many changes. For example, many food words from other languages are common knowledge in English. Almost everyone knows the words taco, dim-sum, gyro, and antipasto. There are other phrases that have made their way into mainstream English, such as "adios amigo" and "hasta la vista" that many people who don't speak Spanish still use.

In conclusion, America has changed drastically as new immigrants arrive in this country. Although many different subcultures exist, there has been a fusion taking place. Different cultures have melted together to create a new America that incorporates the diversity of the country.

Using the holistic rubric on page 299, score this student's essay and explain your reasoning.

(check one)   ☐ 1   ☐ 2   ☐ 3   ☐ 4   ☐ 5   ☐ 6

_____

_____

Thinking KAP

As the saying goes, "Don't judge a book by its cover." Judging something based on a first impression may be dangerous, but people make snap judgments all the time. Is it ever appropriate to make a judgment based on a first impression? How much information can a first impression or a book's cover really give us?

What are the two sides of this argument?

_____

_____

Pick a stance.

_____

_____

List three reasons to support your position.

1. _____

   _____

2. _____

   _____

3. _____

   _____

Strategy Instruction

Plan

The second step of the Strategy for Essay Writing is Plan. After you read the prompt carefully, spend just a few minutes planning what you will write in your essay. When planning, it is important to do three things:

1. Pick a stance.

2. Write a thesis.

3. Create an outline.

Picking a Stance

The essay that you will write on the ACT is a persuasive essay. This means that you need to pick a stance—or take one side of the argument—and prove your point.

Try It Out!

Examine the sides and pick a stance for the assignment below.

> Some schools function on a year-round schedule where students spend three months in class and then have one month off. Some educators feel that these students maintain continuity in their studies better than those who have a traditional summer vacation. Others feel that summer vacation is an important part of school culture. Do you think your school should go to a year-round schedule?

What are the two sides of this argument?

_____

_____

Which side do you think would be easier to support? Why?

_____

_____

It does not matter which stance you choose. The graders will only be looking at whether you have supported your position. If you are unsure which side of the argument to take, pick the side that you think you can write about more easily.

B

Writing a Thesis

A thesis statement establishes your viewpoint on a particular topic. Depending on the subject matter and your writing style, it may also hint at your ideas for support. You can think of this technique as signposting— posting signs as to what you are going to talk about. As long as you actually have time to address those topics, this is a great way to begin. After all, it shows the grader that you have thought and planned out how you will respond to the assignment.

- **Sample assignment:** Name someone who has influenced you in some way.

- **Sample thesis statement:** My first math teacher was a great influence on me because of her intellect, passion for teaching, and empathy for her students.

Try It Out!

Write your own thesis statement for the sample assignment above.

_____

_____

_____

_____

_____

_____

_____

keep in mind

One of the first things a grader will look for is your thesis statement. A good thesis statement will make your opinion clear and identify what support items you intend to use.

B

Creating an Outline

When creating your outline, you are planning what needs to be in each part of your essay. There are many situations where you don't want your writing to be formulaic. On the ACT, however, a formula is the safest way to create a reliable essay in a short amount of time. Your essay should be roughly structured into a five-paragraph format.

Formula for a Five-Paragraph Essay
• Introduction
• Body Paragraph: first point of support
• Body Paragraph: second point of support
• Body Paragraph: third point of support
• Conclusion

You cannot earn a high score on the essay with only one point of support. Include three to be safe.

Throughout your essay, use your thesis statement as a focus to keep your writing on the task.

- In your introduction, you will present your thesis statement. In general, the thesis statement should be the last sentence of your introduction.

- In each body paragraph, you will offer one point of support (with details and examples) to back up your thesis statement.

- In your conclusion, you will sum up your ideas. You may choose to restate your thesis at the beginning of the conclusion.

Try It Out!

Is public transportation a necessity? Imagine both sides of this issue, take a stance, and list three points of support.

Thesis statement: _____

_____

Three points of support: _____

_____

_____

_____

B

Points of Support

Identifying Specific Statements

When you support your thesis, it is important to be specific. Read the sentences below for examples of specific and nonspecific writing.

> Specific: My favorite city is Chicago, because it blends big-city culture with small-town neighborhoods and midwestern hospitality.

> Not specific: For a long time, I have known that Chicago is one of the best cities in the country.

The first sentence presents a clear stance and concrete ideas. The second sentence hints at a vague feeling.

Identifying Relevant Statements

It is also important that your supporting details be relevant, or directly related, to the thesis. It is easy to write a whole essay and then realize that you used examples that don't relate directly to the topic. In your planning stage, make sure you select supporting details that stick to the topic.

keep in mind

Not only are specific examples better for graders, but they also make your essay easier to write.

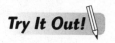

Try It Out!

Determine whether the supporting details below are specific and relevant to the thesis, "You shouldn't follow all the advice people give you."

EXAMPLE	SPECIFIC	NOT SPECIFIC
1. When I started my first job, my father had some good advice for me.		
2. Most advice is wrong.		

EXAMPLE	RELEVANT	NOT RELEVANT
3. I didn't need anyone's advice when I auditioned—and was chosen—for district chorus last fall.		
4. Had NASA officials listened to the advice of engineer Roger Boisjoly, who worked for the company that developed the space shuttle's O-rings, the *Challenger* disaster could have been averted.		

The Strategy for Essay Writing

 STEP 1: Prompt

 STEP 2: Plan

 STEP 3: Produce

 STEP 4: Proofread

B

Read the prompt below. Create a thesis statement and outline that responds to the prompt.

> Montefiore Middle School is considering whether or not to make its music program mandatory for all students. Some people believe that learning musical skills helps students develop their creative sides while reinforcing good study habits in other disciplines. Others feel that students should spend more time being exposed to math, science, history, and English. Do you feel that Montefiore Middle School should implement a mandatory music program?

Thesis statement

_____

_____

_____

First item of support

_____

_____

_____

Second item of support

_____

_____

_____

Third item of support

_____

_____

_____

B

Shared Practice

Think carefully about the issue presented in the following quotation and the assignment below.

> Due to the obesity crisis in America, many schools are removing soda and candy machines from cafeterias and replacing them with healthier snack options. Some people feel that this is a necessary step in helping students grow up healthy. Others think that it is better to instruct students to moderate intake and make healthy decisions for themselves. Do you agree that soda and candy machines should be removed from schools?

In your essay, take a position on this question. You may write about either one of the two points of view given, or you may present a different point of view on this question. Use specific reasons and examples to support your position.

Thesis statement

_____

_____

First item of support

_____

_____

Second item of support

_____

_____

Third item of support

_____

B

_____

hint ▷ *Remember that your thesis statement should clearly assert your position on the issue at hand. If possible, it should also signpost how you will support your stance.*

KAP Wrap

Read the following sample student essay.

People say you shouldn't judge a book by it's cover, and I disagree. I think there are times when you need to judge a book by it's cover like when you are interviewing someone for a job. Its important to dress well to go to a job interview because the person who is interviewing you is going to judge you based on your apearance. You need to be ready to show the best of yourself because you will be judged. A employer doesn't have the time to hire lots of people and then only choose one person for the job, so they need to make a decision based on your interview. Also sometimes you really have to judge a book by it's cover because you need to chose a book to read. When I go to the library I don't have time to read the entire book so I look at it's cover to decide if it looks intresting or not. Judging the cover of a book is a good idea because it saves you time and money.

Using the holistic rubric on page 299, score this student's essay and explain your reasoning.

(check one)   ☐ 1   ☐ 2   ☐ 3   ☐ 4   ☐ 5   ☐ 6

_____

_____

lesson C *Writing and Reviewing Your Essay*

ReKAP

Review your work in Lessons A and B. Then fill in the blanks to show what you have learned.

1. Write the four steps in the Strategy for Essay Writing below.

    _____

    _____

    _____

    _____

2. The three important steps in planning are:

    _____

    _____

    _____

Strategy Instruction

Writing a Strong Introduction

Now that you know all about reading a prompt, identifying a thesis, and establishing a support, you can complete Step 3 of the Strategy for Essay Writing—Produce. You already know the basic structure of the five-paragraph essay, and have developed specific and relevant items of support. It is time now to think about how to write an introduction and a conclusion.

The analogy that is most commonly used to describe an introduction is a funnel. It starts with a wide idea and slowly becomes more and more narrow, finally arriving at a thesis statement. Beginning with a brief anecdote or reference can be a very effective way to grab the reader's attention. Read the two sentences below.

A great introduction refers back to the prompt while asserting a clear position and support.

> When the door handle came off in my hand, I knew there were going to be problems.

> I think it is bad when things do not work right.

Which of these sentences grabs your attention more?

_____

_____

A clear and engaging writing style often makes the difference between a solid essay and a great one. For example, notice how the introduction below begins with a short story and leads into a strong thesis statement.

When the door handle came off in my hand, I knew there were going to be problems. I spent two hours trying to get out of my room before giving up and calling my mother at work. She was able to come home and open the door from the other side. We talked about how to deal with difficult situations, and how important it is not to panic when things don't go as expected. This clearly relates to the current political climate in Sudan. As the statement above says, it is just as important to keep a cool head as it is to take action. Rationality even in adversity is crucial to dealing with political situations, educational situations, and even social situations.

Writing a Strong Conclusion

When writing a conclusion, you can work backward from your introduction. Start with a sentence that reiterates the thesis statement you have developed. Then broaden it to the bigger picture once again. If you like, you can refer back to the anecdote or reference you made in the introduction to tie the entire essay together.

Restating Your Thesis

Look back at the thesis statement you wrote for your introduction. In your conclusion, restate your thesis, or put it in other words.

Sum Up Your Essay

Restate the basic points of support in your conclusion. This will help to sum up your essay.

keep in mind

Avoid introducing a new topic or idea in your conclusion. You will not have time or room to expand your ideas.

Try It Out!

Think carefully about the issue presented in the following prompt.

> Belmont High School is considering implementing a uniform requirement for all students. Some students feel that this will infringe on their freedom of speech through their clothing. Others think it will reduce distractions in the classroom on campus. Do you think Belmont High School should require all students to wear a uniform?

Write a thesis statement.

_____

_____

_____

How could you restate this thesis in your conclusion?

_____

_____

_____

Writing Strong Body Paragraphs

The key to writing strong body paragraphs is to develop each of your points of support completely, providing clear examples and using specific evidence.

Say it! Support it! Explain it!

- Start each body paragraph with a clear topic sentence.

- Support each idea with an example from history or books you have read. You could also use an example from your own life.

- Explain each idea with one or two additional sentences that tie your ideas together.

keep in mind

Use transitions in your essays to help your writing sound clear and logical. Words like *first*, *next*, *then*, *as a result*, *therefore*, and *consequently* can help link your body paragraphs together.

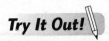

Try It Out!

Think carefully about the issue presented in the following prompt and the assignment below.

> Lakeside High School is considering implementing a new community service requirement for graduation. Students would have to complete 100 hours of community service over the course of their four years of study. Some people think that this is an excellent way to give back to the community and to train students to be socially conscious. Others feel that it might distract from studies or take away time that the students need to work at paying jobs. Do you think Lakeside High School should implement the community service program?

Imagine you have already written the introduction of this essay. Now write one of the body paragraphs.

_____

_____

_____

_____

Proofreading and Writing Tips

Step 4 of the Strategy for Essay Writing is Proofread. This can be a difficult task on a timed essay. Hopefully you'll have a few minutes after writing your essay to make sure that you have been successful. Read through it to make sure that the thoughts flow well together and there are no spelling or punctuation errors. If you do find errors, there are a couple of tricks you can use so you don't have to rewrite your essay. The grader will understand these editing marks.

If you want to cross something out, draw a single line through it.	~~my error~~
If you want to add something, use a caret.	I left out a word^right here.
You can also use an asterisk to add something.	I * something. *forgot
If you want to indicate the beginning of a new paragraph, use the paragraph (¶) symbol.	This ends one thought. ¶This begins a new idea.

keep in mind

While the essay is timed, don't rush your writing. Most people write messier and make more errors when rushing. It is better to work at a steady pace and produce good work.

There are a number of other tips to review before drafting your essay. Use these hints to create a solid essay and earn a good score every time.

- Use correct standard English; avoid slang and abbreviations.

- All common rules of grammar apply to the essay. While minor errors won't hurt a strong essay, strive to make as few as possible.

- Stick to your plan. Even if you change your mind midway through, complete the essay you planned to write. Remember, organization counts.

- Start a new paragraph for each new topic or idea.

- Use transition words like *then, next, after, for example,* and *on the other hand* generously. They'll help the graders follow your argument and thought process.

- Do not double-space your essay; you won't have enough room.

- Avoid wide margins. You'll be graded only on what's written in your essay booklet, so you don't want to run out of room.

- Consider printing if your handwriting is hard to read. Graders can't score what they can't decipher.

- If you find yourself running out of time, calmly wrap up your essay. It's better to clearly complete what you've started than to rush to get everything in.

Test Practice Unit 7

A new rule was added to the Official Code of Conduct of Malanga High School this year. It states that the school has the right to discipline students for actions that occur on or off campus, as well as during or outside of school hours. Some people feel that the school is exceeding its boundaries if it punishes students for behavior outside of school. Others feel that off-campus behavior affects on-campus behavior and student relations, so it is relevant. Do you believe that Malanga High School should discipline students for actions that occur outside of school?

In your essay, take a position on this question. You may write about either one of the two points of view given, or you may present a different point of view on this question. Use specific reasons and examples to support your position.

_____

_____

_____

_____

_____

_____

_____

_____

_____

_____

_____

_____

_____

_____

C

Name_____ Date_____

KAP Wrap

Now that you have completed a full-length essay, try to score it based on the holistic rubric on page 299. Be as objective as you can in analyzing your own work.

(check one) ☐1 ☐2 ☐3 ☐4 ☐5 ☐6

On the lines below, identify some weaknesses in your essay that you can practice before Test Day. Don't be discouraged if your essay has flaws; see them as opportunities for growth and development. Refer back to these notes as you write more essays in the future.

_____

_____

_____

_____

_____

_____

_____

_____

_____

_____

_____

_____

C

English Practice Test 2

English Practice Test 2

This is not the actual test, so don't worry! This is simply a chance to practice skills that will be on the real test. It will also give you and your teacher a sense of your strengths and weaknesses so that you can better prepare for Test Day.

This test is designed to resemble the ACT English Test and therefore has the range of topics and difficulty levels that you will see on Test Day. To best accustom yourself to test-like conditions, your teacher will administer the test using the same timing rules as the ACT English Test: all 75 questions to be completed in a total of 45 minutes.

All of the questions are multiple choice. Use the Answer Sheet to mark each answer so you can become accustomed to doing so on Test Day.

If you finish all 75 problems before time is called, review your work.

English Practice Test 2

When your teacher tells you, carefully tear out this page.

1. Ⓐ Ⓑ Ⓒ Ⓓ   15. Ⓐ Ⓑ Ⓒ Ⓓ   29. Ⓐ Ⓑ Ⓒ Ⓓ

2. Ⓕ Ⓖ Ⓗ Ⓙ   16. Ⓕ Ⓖ Ⓗ Ⓙ   30. Ⓕ Ⓖ Ⓗ Ⓙ

3. Ⓐ Ⓑ Ⓒ Ⓓ   17. Ⓐ Ⓑ Ⓒ Ⓓ   31. Ⓐ Ⓑ Ⓒ Ⓓ

4. Ⓕ Ⓖ Ⓗ Ⓙ   18. Ⓕ Ⓖ Ⓗ Ⓙ   32. Ⓕ Ⓖ Ⓗ Ⓙ

5. Ⓐ Ⓑ Ⓒ Ⓓ   19. Ⓐ Ⓑ Ⓒ Ⓓ   33. Ⓐ Ⓑ Ⓒ Ⓓ

6. Ⓕ Ⓖ Ⓗ Ⓙ   20. Ⓕ Ⓖ Ⓗ Ⓙ   34. Ⓕ Ⓖ Ⓗ Ⓙ

7. Ⓐ Ⓑ Ⓒ Ⓓ   21. Ⓐ Ⓑ Ⓒ Ⓓ   35. Ⓐ Ⓑ Ⓒ Ⓓ

8. Ⓕ Ⓖ Ⓗ Ⓙ   22. Ⓕ Ⓖ Ⓗ Ⓙ   36. Ⓕ Ⓖ Ⓗ Ⓙ

9. Ⓐ Ⓑ Ⓒ Ⓓ   23. Ⓐ Ⓑ Ⓒ Ⓓ   37. Ⓐ Ⓑ Ⓒ Ⓓ

10. Ⓕ Ⓖ Ⓗ Ⓙ   24. Ⓕ Ⓖ Ⓗ Ⓙ   38. Ⓕ Ⓖ Ⓗ Ⓙ

11. Ⓐ Ⓑ Ⓒ Ⓓ   25. Ⓐ Ⓑ Ⓒ Ⓓ   39. Ⓐ Ⓑ Ⓒ Ⓓ

12. Ⓕ Ⓖ Ⓗ Ⓙ   26. Ⓕ Ⓖ Ⓗ Ⓙ   40. Ⓕ Ⓖ Ⓗ Ⓙ

13. Ⓐ Ⓑ Ⓒ Ⓓ   27. Ⓐ Ⓑ Ⓒ Ⓓ   41. Ⓐ Ⓑ Ⓒ Ⓓ

14. Ⓕ Ⓖ Ⓗ Ⓙ   28. Ⓕ Ⓖ Ⓗ Ⓙ   42. Ⓕ Ⓖ Ⓗ Ⓙ

43. (A) (B) (C) (D)   60. (F) (G) (H) (J)

44. (F) (G) (H) (J)   61. (A) (B) (C) (D)

45. (A) (B) (C) (D)   62. (F) (G) (H) (J)

46. (F) (G) (H) (J)   63. (A) (B) (C) (D)

47. (A) (B) (C) (D)   64. (F) (G) (H) (J)

48. (F) (G) (H) (J)   65. (A) (B) (C) (D)

49. (A) (B) (C) (D)   66. (F) (G) (H) (J)

50. (F) (G) (H) (J)   67. (A) (B) (C) (D)

51. (A) (B) (C) (D)   68. (F) (G) (H) (J)

52. (F) (G) (H) (J)   69. (A) (B) (C) (D)

53. (A) (B) (C) (D)   70. (F) (G) (H) (J)

54. (F) (G) (H) (J)   71. (A) (B) (C) (D)

55. (A) (B) (C) (D)   72. (F) (G) (H) (J)

56. (F) (G) (H) (J)   73. (A) (B) (C) (D)

57. (A) (B) (C) (D)   74. (F) (G) (H) (J)

58. (F) (G) (H) (J)   75. (A) (B) (C) (D)

59. (A) (B) (C) (D)

ENGLISH TEST
45 Minutes—75 Questions

DIRECTIONS: In the following five passages, certain words and phrases are underlined and numbered. In the right-hand column are alternatives for each underlined portion. Select the one that best conveys the idea, creates the most grammatically correct sentence, or is most consistent with the style and tone of the passage. If you decide that the original version is best, select NO CHANGE. You may also find questions that ask about the entire passage or a section of the passage. These questions will correspond to small, numbered boxes in the test. For these questions, decide which choice best accomplishes the purpose set out in the question stem. After you've selected the best choice, fill in the corresponding oval on your Answer Grid. For some questions, you'll need to read the context in order to answer correctly. Be sure to read until you have enough information to determine the correct answer choice.

PASSAGE I

My Old-Fashioned Father

My father, though he is only in his early 50s, is stuck in his old-fashioned ways. He has a general mistrust of any innovation or technology that he can't immediately

grasp and he always tells us, that if something isn't broken, then you shouldn't fix it.

He has run a small grocery store in town, and if you were to look at a snapshot of his back office taken when

he opened the store in 1975, you would see that not much has changed since. He is the most disorganized person I know and still uses a pencil and paper to keep

track of his inventory. His small office is about to burst with all the various documents, notes, and receipts he

1. **A.** NO CHANGE
    B. ways he has a
    C. ways having a
    D. ways, and still has a

2. **F.** NO CHANGE
    G. tells us, that,
    H. tells us that,
    J. tells us that

3. **A.** NO CHANGE
    B. was running
    C. runs
    D. ran

4. **F.** NO CHANGE
    G. not be likely to see very much that has changed since.
    H. be able to see right away that not very much has changed since.
    J. not change very much.

5. Assuming that all are true, which of the following replacements for "inventory" would be most appropriate in context?
    A. inventory of canned and dry goods.
    B. inventory, refusing to consider a more current method.
    C. inventory, which he writes down by hand.
    D. inventory of goods on the shelves and in the storeroom.

has accumulated over the years, his filing cabinets have

long since been filled up. The centerpiece of all the

clutter is his ancient typewriter, which isn't even

electric. In the past few years, Father's search for

replacement typewriter ribbons has become an

increasingly more difficult task, because they are no

longer being produced. He is perpetually tracking down

the few remaining places that still have these

antiquated ribbons in their dusty inventories. When

people ask him why he doesn't upgrade his equipment,

he tells them, "Electric typewriters won't work in a

blackout. All I need is a candle and some paper, and I'm

fine." Little does Father know, however, is that the

"upgrade" people are speaking of is not to an electric

typewriter but to a computer.

[1] Hoping to bring Father out of the dark ages, my

sister, and I bought him a brand new computer for his

50th birthday. [2] We offered to help him transfer all of

his records onto it and to teach him how to use it. [3]

Eagerly, we told him about all the new spreadsheet

programs that would help simplify his recordkeeping

and organize his accounts; and emphasized the

advantage of not having to completely retype any

document when he found a typo. [4] Rather than

offering us a look of joy for the life-changing gift we

had presented him, however, he again brought up

the blackout scenario. [5] To Father, this is a concrete

argument, never mind the fact that our town hasn't

had a blackout in five years, and that one only lasted

6.
  F. NO CHANGE
  G. years; his filing cabinets
  H. years, and besides that, his filing cabinets
  J. years and since his filing cabinets

7.
  A. NO CHANGE
  B. know, besides, that
  C. know, however, that
  D. know, beyond that,

8.
  F. NO CHANGE
  G. me and my sister
  H. my sister and I
  J. my sister and I,

9.
  A. NO CHANGE
  B. On the other hand,
  C. In addition,
  D. Rather,

10.
  F. NO CHANGE
  G. accounts, and
  H. accounts and,
  J. accounts, we

11.
  A. NO CHANGE
  B. although,
  C. although
  D. despite the fact that

GO ON TO THE NEXT PAGE.

an hour or two. 12

12. The author wants to include the following statement in this paragraph:

> We expected it to save him a lot of time and effort.

The most logical placement for this sentence would be:
- **F.** before Sentence 1.
- **G.** after Sentence 1.
- **H.** after Sentence 4.
- **J.** after Sentence 5.

My father's state-of-the-art computer now serves as a very expensive bulletin board for the hundreds of adhesive notes he uses to keep himself organized. Sooner than later, we fully expect it will completely disappear under the mounting files and papers of the back office. In the depths of that disorganized office, the computer will join the cell phone my mom gave him a few years ago. Interestingly enough, every once in a while, that completely forgotten cell phone will ring from under the heavy clutter of the past. 15

13.
- **A.** NO CHANGE
- **B.** Sooner rather than later,
- **C.** Sooner or later,
- **D.** As soon as later,

14.
- **F.** NO CHANGE
- **G.** Deep in the disorganization of that office's, the computer will join the cell phone my mom gave him a few years back.
- **H.** In the disorganized depths of the office, the computer will soon be joined by the cell phone my mom gave him a few years ago.
- **J.** The computer will join the cell phone my mom gave him a few years back in the disorganized depths of that office.

15. Which of the following would provide the most appropriate conclusion for the passage?
- **A.** It's hard to say what else might be lost in there.
- **B.** We tell my father it's a reminder that he can't hide from the future forever.
- **C.** We have no idea who might be calling.
- **D.** Maybe one day I will try to find it and answer it.

GO ON TO THE NEXT PAGE.

PASSAGE II

Breaking Baseball's Color Barrier

A quick perusal of any modern major league

baseball team will reveal a roster of players of multiple

ethnicities <u>from the farthest</u> reaches of the globe.
16

Second only to soccer, baseball has evolved into a

global sport and a symbol for equality among races.

    <u>It's</u> diversity today presents a stark contrast to the
17

state of the sport just 60 years ago. As late as the 1940s,

there existed an unwritten rule in baseball that

prevented all but white players <u>to participate</u> in the
18

major leagues. This rule was known as the "color

barrier" or "color line." The color line in baseball

actually predated the birth of the major leagues. Prior to

the official formation of any league of professional

baseball teams, there existed an organization of

amateur baseball clubs known as the National

Association of Baseball Players, <u>which was the</u>
19

<u>precursor to today's National League.</u> On December 11,
19

1868, the governing body of this association had

unanimously adopted a rule that effectively

barred any team that <u>had, any "colored persons"</u> on its
20

roster. However, when baseball started to organize into

leagues of professional teams in the early <u>1880's; the</u>
21

National Association of Baseball Players' decree no

longer had any weight, especially in the newly formed

16. **F.** NO CHANGE
    G. from the most far
    H. from the most farthest
    J. from farther

17. **A.** NO CHANGE
    B. Its'
    C. Its
    D. Its own

18. **F.** NO CHANGE
    G. to be able to participate
    H. from participating
    J. to participation

19. Is the underlined portion relevant here?
    A. Yes, because it helps familiarize the reader with the range of baseball associations that once existed.
    B. Yes, because it helps clarify the development the author traces.
    C. No, because the names of the organizations are not important.
    D. No, because it is inconsistent with the style of the essay to provide specific historical data.

20. **F.** NO CHANGE
    G. had any, "colored persons"
    H. had any "colored persons"
    J. had any "colored persons,"

21. **A.** NO CHANGE
    B. 1880s, the
    C. 1880s. The
    D. 1880s, and the

GO ON TO THE NEXT PAGE.

American Association. <u>For a brief period in those early</u>
₂₂
<u>years, a few African Americans played side by side with</u>
₂₂
<u>white players on major league diamonds.</u>
₂₂

[1] Most baseball historians believe that the first

African American to play in the major leagues was

Moses "Fleet" Walker. [2] <u>Walker was a catcher</u> for the
₂₃
Toledo Blue Stockings of the American Association

between 1884 and 1889. [3] During that time, a few other

African Americans, <u>including</u> Walker's brother Weldy,
₂₄

<u>would be joining him</u> on the Blue Stockings. [4]
₂₅
Unfortunately, this respite from segregation did not last

for very long; as Jim Crow laws took their hold on the

nation, many of the most popular white ballplayers

started to refuse to take the field with their African-

American teammates. [5] By the 1890s, the color barrier

had fully returned to baseball, where it would endure

for more than half a century. 26

Jackie Robinson would become the first African

American to cross the color line <u>at the time when</u> he
₂₇
debuted for the Brooklyn Dodgers in 1947. For

Robinson's landmark achievements on and off the

22. The writer is considering deleting the underlined portion. Should the writer make this deletion?
- **F.** Yes, because the information is not relevant to the topic of the paragraph.
- **G.** Yes, because the information contradicts the first sentence of the paragraph.
- **H.** No, because the information shows that white players did not object to integration.
- **J.** No, because the statement provides a smooth transition to the specific information about early African-American players in the next paragraph.

23.
- **A.** NO CHANGE
- **B.** Walker, being a catcher
- **C.** Walker, a catcher
- **D.** Walker who was a catcher

24.
- **F.** NO CHANGE
- **G.** which included
- **H.** who would include
- **J.** including among them

25.
- **A.** NO CHANGE
- **B.** joined him
- **C.** were to join him
- **D.** will join him

26. Upon reviewing this paragraph, the author discovers that he has neglected to include the following information:

> A handful of African Americans played for other teams as well.

This sentence would be most logically placed after:
- **F.** Sentence 1.
- **G.** Sentence 2.
- **H.** Sentence 3.
- **J.** Sentence 4.

27.
- **A.** NO CHANGE
- **B.** when
- **C.** while
- **D.** when the time came that

GO ON TO THE NEXT PAGE.

diamond, he will <u>forever be recognized as</u> a hero of the
₂₈

civil rights movement and a sports icon. The path that

he blazed through the prejudices of American society

during the 1940s and 1950s opened the door for the

multi-racial and multi-national face of modern

baseball, and fans of the sport worldwide <u>will be in his</u>
₂₉

<u>debt for all time to come.</u>
₂₉

28. F. NO CHANGE
    G. one day be recognized
    H. forever recognize
    J. be admired by a lot of people for being

29. A. NO CHANGE
    B. will be forever in his debt.
    C. will owe him a lot.
    D. being in his debt forever.

Question 30 asks about the essay as a whole.

30. Suppose the writer had been assigned to develop
    a brief essay on the history of baseball. Would this
    essay successfully fulfill that goal?
    F. Yes, because it covers events in baseball over
       a period of more than a century.
    G. Yes, because it mentions key figures in
       baseball history.
    H. No, because people played baseball before
       1868.
    J. No, because the focus of this essay is on one
       particular aspect of baseball history.

PASSAGE III

The Bear Mountain Bridge

When the gleaming Bear Mountain Bridge officially

opened to traffic on Thanksgiving Day in <u>1924, it</u> was
₃₁

known as the Harriman Bridge, after Edward H.

Harriman, wealthy philanthropist and patriarch of the

family most influential in the <u>bridges</u> construction.
₃₂

Before the Harriman Bridge was constructed, there

were no bridges spanning the Hudson River south of

Albany. By the early 1920s, the ferry services used to

transport people back and forth across the river had

become woefully inadequate. In February of 1922, in an

effort to alleviate some of the burden on the ferries and

31. A. NO CHANGE
    B. 1924; it
    C. 1924. It
    D. 1924 and it

32. F. NO CHANGE
    G. bridges'
    H. bridge's
    J. bridges's

GO ON TO THE NEXT PAGE.

create a permanent link across the Hudson, the New

York State Legislature <u>had authorized</u> a group of private
                       33

investors, led by Mary Harriman, to build a bridge. The

group, known as the Bear Mountain Hudson Bridge

Company (BMHBC), was allotted 30 years to <u>build,</u>
                                          34

<u>construct, and maintain</u> the structure, at which time
        34

the span would be handed over to New York State.

The BMHBC invested almost $4,500,000 into the

suspension bridge and hired the world-renowned

design team <u>of Howard Baird and George Hodge</u>
                          35

as architects. 36 Baird and Hodge enlisted the help of

John A. Roebling and Sons, <u>who were</u> instrumental in
                           37

creating the steel work on the Brooklyn Bridge and

would later work on the Golden Gate and George

Washington Bridges.

Amazingly, the bridge took only 20 months and

33. **A.** NO CHANGE
     B. authorized
     C. was authorized
     D. would authorize

34. **F.** NO CHANGE
     G. build and construct and maintain
     H. construct and maintain
     J. construct, and maintain

35. **A.** NO CHANGE
     B. of Howard Baird, and George Hodge
     C. of Howard Baird and, George Hodge
     D. of, Howard Baird and George Hodge

36. The author wants to remove the following from
     the preceding sentence:

> invested almost $4,500,00 into the
> suspension bridge

If this language were deleted, the essay would
primarily lose:

F. a piece of information critical to the point of
     the essay.
G. a necessary transition between the second
     and third paragraphs.
H. a detail contributing to the reader's
     understanding of the magnitude of the
     project.
J. an explanation of how the group raised
     money to invest in the bridge.

37. **A.** NO CHANGE
     B. who was
     C. a company
     D. a company that had been

GO ON TO THE NEXT PAGE.

11 days to complete, and not one life was lost. **38** It was a technological marvel and would stand as a model for the suspension bridges of the future. At the time of the Harriman Bridge's completion, it was, at 2,257 feet, the longest single-span steel suspension bridge in the world. Therefore, the two main cables used in the
                                                                       39
suspension were 18 inches in diameter, and each contained 7,752 individual steel wires wrapped in 37 thick strands. If completely unraveled, the single wires in both cables would be 7,377 miles longer. The bridge
                                                                       40
links Bear Mountain on the western bank of the Hudson to Anthony's Nose on the eastern side, and it lies so precisely on an east-west plane that one can check a compass by it. It carries Routes 6 and 202 across the Hudson, as well as being the point of river crossing for
                         41
the Appalachian Trail.

In an attempt to recoup some of its investment after the bridge opened, the BMHBC charged an exorbitant
                        42
toll of 80 cents per crossing. Even with the high toll, however, it operated at a loss for 13 of its first 16 years. Finally it was acquired, more than 10 years—a full decade—earlier than planned, by the New
        43
York State Bridge Authority. The bridge was renamed the Bear Mountain Bridge. Today, the Bear Mountain Bridge sees more than six million vehicles cross its
                  44
concrete decks each year.

38. If the writer were to delete the preceding sentence, the essay would lose primarily:
  F. information about how long the project had been expected to take.
  G. a warning about the dangers of large-scale construction projects.
  H. crucial information about the duration of the project.
  J. a necessary transition between paragraphs 2 and 3.

39. A. NO CHANGE
  B. Nonetheless, the
  C. At the same time, the
  D. The

40. F. NO CHANGE
  G. long.
  H. in total length.
  J. lengthy.

41. A. NO CHANGE
  B. and is as well
  C. and is
  D. besides being

42. F. NO CHANGE
  G. opened the BMHBC charged
  H. opened: the BMHBC charged
  J. opened; the BMHBC charged

43. A. NO CHANGE
  B. years and a full decade
  C. years, a full decade,
  D. years

44. F. NO CHANGE
  G. over
  H. even more than
  J. a higher amount than

GO ON TO THE NEXT PAGE.

ACT ADVANTAGE
ENGLISH & READING

© 2007 Kaplan, Inc.

Question 45 asks about the essay as a whole.

45. Suppose the author had been assigned to write a brief history of bridge building in the United States. Would this essay successfully fulfill that requirement?

    A. Yes, because it provides information on the entire process from the initial funding through the opening of the bridge.

    B. Yes, because Bear Mountain Bridge is historically significant.

    C. No, because it mentions only one bridge.

    D. No, because the essay is primarily concerned with the financial aspects of building and maintaining the bridge.

PASSAGE IV

The Dream of the American West

As the sun <u>was slowly rising</u> over the Atlantic Ocean
₄₆
and painted New York harbor a spectacular fiery orange,

I started my old Toyota's engine. At this early hour, there

was still some semblance of the night's tranquility left

on the city sidewalks, but I knew that, as the minutes

ticked by, <u>the streets would flood with humanity.</u>
₄₇

46.   **F.** NO CHANGE
    G. rising slowly
    H. rose slowly
    J. continued to rise

47. The author wants to contrast the statement about the quiet of the night streets with a related detail about the daytime activity. Assuming that all of the choices are true, which of the following best accomplishes that goal?

    A. NO CHANGE
    B. some people might appear.
    C. everything would be different.
    D. the tranquility would be unbroken.

I smiled <u>with</u> the thought that soon all the wonderful
₄₈
chaos of New York City would be disappearing behind

me as I <u>embarked on my trip to the other side of</u> the
₄₉
country.

48.   **F.** NO CHANGE
    G. along with
    H. at
    J. all because of

49.   **A.** NO CHANGE
    B. embarked on this journey across
    C. traveled to the other side of
    D. traveled across

GO ON TO THE NEXT PAGE.

As the morning sun climbed into the sky, I
                                    50
shuddered with excitement to think that my final stop

would be in California, where the sun itself ends its
                                        51
journey across America. Like the sun, however, I still
           51
had quite a journey before me.

I had been planning this road trip across the United

States for as long as I could remember. In my life, I had

been fortunate enough to see some of the most

beautiful countries in the world. However, it had always

bothered me that although I'd stood in the shadow of

the Eiffel Tower, marveled in the desert heat at the
                                        52
Pyramids of Giza, I'd never seen any of the wonders of
      52
my own country, except those found in my hometown of

New York City. All of that was about to change.

As I left the city, the tall buildings began to give way
                                            53
to smaller ones, then to transform into the quaint rows
                                        53
of houses that clustered the crowded suburbs. Trees and
      53
grass, then the yellow-green of cornfields and the

golden wash of wheat were rapidly replacing the
                                        54
familiar mazes of cement and steel. My world no longer
      54

stretched vertically toward the sky, it now spread
                                    55

50. Which of the following alternatives to the underlined portion would NOT be acceptable?
   F. At sunrise,
   G. Watching the morning sun climb into the sky,
   H. The morning sun climbed into the sky,
   J. As the sun rose,

51. The writer is considering revising this sentence by deleting the underlined portion. If she did so, the paragraph would primarily lose:
   A. information about the reasons for the writer's trip.
   B. information about the writer's destination.
   C. a description of the writer's planned route.
   D. a comparison between the sunrise in New York and the sunset in California.

52. F. NO CHANGE
   G. Eiffel Tower and had marveled in the desert heat at the Pyramids of Giza,
   H. Eiffel Tower and marveled in the desert heat at the Pyramids of Giza
   J. Eiffel Tower, and marveled, in the desert heat, at the Pyramids of Giza

53. Given that all are true, which of the following provides the most effective transition between the third paragraph and the description of the Midwest in the fourth paragraph?
   A. NO CHANGE
   B. In fact, there were changes on the horizon almost immediately.
   C. My excitement hadn't diminished.
   D. I realized that people who lived in other areas might feel the same way about visiting New York.

54. Assuming that all are true, which of the following provides information most relevant to the main focus of the paragraph?
   F. NO CHANGE
   G. appearing before me.
   H. racing past my window.
   J. becoming monotonous.

55. A. NO CHANGE
   B. the sky but it now spread
   C. the sky; it now spread
   D. the sky spreading

GO ON TO THE NEXT PAGE.

horizontally towards eternity. <u>For two days</u> I pushed
through the wind-whipped farmlands of Mid-America,
hypnotized by the beauty of the undulating yet
unbroken lines. At night, the breeze from my car would
stir the wheat fields to dance beneath the moon, and the
silos hid in the shadows, quietly imposing their simple
serenity upon everything.

Then, as the <u>night's shadows</u> gave way to
light, there seemed to be a great force rising
to meet the <u>sun as it made its reappearance.</u>

<u>Still,</u> I had no idea what I was looking at. Then, there
was no <u>mistaking it.</u> The unbroken lines of Mid-America
had given way to the jagged and majestic heights of the
Rockies and the gateway to the American West.

56. F. NO CHANGE
G. For two days,
H. During two days,
J. During two days

57. A. NO CHANGE
B. nights shadows
C. shadows from the night
D. night shadow

58. F. NO CHANGE
G. sun as it reappeared.
H. reappearing sun.
J. sun as it was also rising.

59. A. NO CHANGE
B. Even so,
C. At first,
D. Eventually,

60. F. NO CHANGE
G. mistake to be made.
H. chance to mistake it.
J. having made a mistake.

PASSAGE V

Traveling at the Speed of Sound

The term "supersonic" refers to anything that
travels faster than the speed of sound. When the last of
the supersonic Concorde passenger planes made its
final trip across the Atlantic in <u>November of 2003, an
interesting</u> chapter in history was finally closed. The
fleet of supersonic Concorde SSTs, or "Supersonic
Transports," which were jointly operated by Air France
and British Airways, had been making the

61. A. NO CHANGE
B. November, of 2003 an interesting
C. November of 2003 an interesting
D. November of 2003; an interesting

intercontinental trip across the Atlantic for almost 30

years. These amazing machines cruised at <u>Mach 2</u>
₆₂

<u>which is</u> more than twice the speed of sound. They
₆₂

flew <u>to a height</u> almost twice that of standard passenger
₆₃

airplanes. The Concorde routinely made the trip from

New York to London in less than three hours and was

much more expensive than normal transatlantic flights.

Though the majority of the passengers who traveled on

the Concorde were celebrities or the extremely wealthy,

it also attracted ordinary people who simply wanted to

know how it felt to travel faster than the speed of sound.

<u>Some of these,</u> would save money for years just to gain
₆₄

that knowledge.

What is the speed of sound? Many people are

surprised to learn that there is no fixed answer to this

question. The speed <u>that</u> sound travels through a given
₆₅

medium depends on a number of factors. <u>So that we</u>
₆₆

<u>may better begin to understand</u> the speed of sound, we
₆₆

must first understand what a "sound" really is.

The standard dictionary definition of sound is "a

vibration or disturbance transmitted, like waves

through water, through a material medium such as a

gas." Our ears are able to pick up those sound waves

and <u>convert</u> them into what we hear. This means that
₆₇

62.
F. NO CHANGE
G. Mach 2, which
H. Mach 2,
J. a speed of Mach 2, which is

63.
A. NO CHANGE
B. at an altitude
C. toward an altitude
D. very high

64.
F. NO CHANGE
G. Among these were those who
H. Some
J. Some,

65.
A. NO CHANGE
B. to which
C. at which
D. where

66.
F. NO CHANGE
G. In order that we may understand
H. To understand
J. For understanding

67. Which of the following alternatives to the underlined portion would be the LEAST acceptable?
A. change
B. translate
C. alter
D. transform

GO ON TO THE NEXT PAGE.

the speed at which sound travels through gas <u>directly</u>
<u>depends on what gas it is traveling through, and the</u>
<u>temperature and pressure of the gas.</u> When discussing an
aircraft breaking the speed of sound, that gas medium, of
course, is air. As air temperature and pressure decrease
<u>with altitude,</u> so does the speed of sound. An airplane
flying at the speed of sound at sea level is

traveling roughly at 761 mph; <u>however</u> when that same
plane climbs to 20,000 feet, the speed of sound is only
about 707 mph. This is why the Concorde's cruising
altitude was so much higher than regular passenger
aircraft; <u>planes can reach supersonic speeds more</u>
<u>easily at higher altitudes.</u>

    In the years since the Concorde <u>has been</u>
decommissioned, only fighter pilots and astronauts
have been able to experience the sensation of breaking
"the sound barrier." <u>But that is all about to change very</u>
<u>soon.</u> Newer and faster supersonic passenger planes are
being developed that will be technologically superior to
the Concorde and much cheaper to operate. <u>That means</u>
<u>we can expect that in the very near future,</u> supersonic
passenger travel will be available not only to the rich
and famous, <u>but also be for</u> the masses, so they, too, can
experience life at faster than the speed of sound.

68. F. NO CHANGE
    G. depends directly on the type, temperature, and pressure of the gas it is traveling through.
    H. directly depends on what gas it is, and also on the temperature and pressure of that gas.
    J. depends directly on the type, temperature, and pressure of the gas.

69. A. NO CHANGE
    B. with height
    C. with a drop in altitude
    D. at higher altitudes

70. F. NO CHANGE
    G. however,
    H. and so,
    J. even so

71. Given that all are true, which of the following provides the most logical conclusion for this sentence?
    A. NO CHANGE
    B. they're much faster.
    C. they use much more fuel than regular aircrafts.
    D. they're rarely visible because they fly above the cloud cover.

72. F. NO CHANGE
    G. came to be
    H. was
    J. had been

73. A. NO CHANGE
    B. Soon, however, that is about to change.
    C. Soon, however, that will change.
    D. That is about to change soon.

74. F. NO CHANGE
    G. So then, in the near future
    H. Soon,
    J. We can expect, then, that in the near future

75. A. NO CHANGE
    B. but also be available to
    C. but also to
    D. but for

END OF TEST.

STOP! DO NOT TURN THE PAGE UNTIL TOLD TO DO SO.

Reading Practice Test 2

Reading Practice Test 2

This is not the actual test, so don't worry! This is simply a chance to practice skills that will be on the real test. It will also give you and your teacher a sense of your strengths and weaknesses so that you can better prepare for Test Day.

This test is designed to resemble the ACT Reading Test and therefore has the range of topics and difficulty levels that you will see on Test Day. To best accustom yourself to test-like conditions, your teacher will administer the test using the same timing rules as the ACT Reading Test: all 40 questions are to be completed in a total of 35 minutes.

All of the questions are multiple choice. Use the Answer Sheet to mark each answer so you can become accustomed to doing so on Test Day.

If you finish all 40 problems before time is called, review your work.

Reading Practice Test 2

When your teacher tells you, carefully tear out this page.

1. Ⓐ Ⓑ Ⓒ Ⓓ
2. Ⓕ Ⓖ Ⓗ Ⓙ
3. Ⓐ Ⓑ Ⓒ Ⓓ
4. Ⓕ Ⓖ Ⓗ Ⓙ
5. Ⓐ Ⓑ Ⓒ Ⓓ
6. Ⓕ Ⓖ Ⓗ Ⓙ
7. Ⓐ Ⓑ Ⓒ Ⓓ
8. Ⓕ Ⓖ Ⓗ Ⓙ
9. Ⓐ Ⓑ Ⓒ Ⓓ
10. Ⓕ Ⓖ Ⓗ Ⓙ
11. Ⓐ Ⓑ Ⓒ Ⓓ
12. Ⓕ Ⓖ Ⓗ Ⓙ
13. Ⓐ Ⓑ Ⓒ Ⓓ
14. Ⓕ Ⓖ Ⓗ Ⓙ

15. Ⓐ Ⓑ Ⓒ Ⓓ
16. Ⓕ Ⓖ Ⓗ Ⓙ
17. Ⓐ Ⓑ Ⓒ Ⓓ
18. Ⓕ Ⓖ Ⓗ Ⓙ
19. Ⓐ Ⓑ Ⓒ Ⓓ
20. Ⓕ Ⓖ Ⓗ Ⓙ
21. Ⓐ Ⓑ Ⓒ Ⓓ
22. Ⓕ Ⓖ Ⓗ Ⓙ
23. Ⓐ Ⓑ Ⓒ Ⓓ
24. Ⓕ Ⓖ Ⓗ Ⓙ
25. Ⓐ Ⓑ Ⓒ Ⓓ
26. Ⓕ Ⓖ Ⓗ Ⓙ
27. Ⓐ Ⓑ Ⓒ Ⓓ
28. Ⓕ Ⓖ Ⓗ Ⓙ

29. Ⓐ Ⓑ Ⓒ Ⓓ
30. Ⓕ Ⓖ Ⓗ Ⓙ
31. Ⓐ Ⓑ Ⓒ Ⓓ
32. Ⓕ Ⓖ Ⓗ Ⓙ
33. Ⓐ Ⓑ Ⓒ Ⓓ
34. Ⓕ Ⓖ Ⓗ Ⓙ
35. Ⓐ Ⓑ Ⓒ Ⓓ
36. Ⓕ Ⓖ Ⓗ Ⓙ
37. Ⓐ Ⓑ Ⓒ Ⓓ
38. Ⓕ Ⓖ Ⓗ Ⓙ
39. Ⓐ Ⓑ Ⓒ Ⓓ
40. Ⓕ Ⓖ Ⓗ Ⓙ

DO NOT TURN THE PAGE UNTIL TOLD TO DO SO.

READING TEST
35 Minutes—40 Questions

DIRECTIONS: This test contains four passages, each followed by several questions. After reading each passage, select the best answer to each question and fill in the corresponding oval on your answer document. You may refer to the passages while answering the questions.

Passage I

PROSE FICTION: This passage is adapted from *The Age of Innocence,* by Edith Wharton (1920).

It was generally agreed in New York that the Countess Olenska had "lost her looks."

She had appeared there first, in Newland Archer's boyhood, as a brilliantly pretty little girl
5 of nine or ten, of whom people said that she "ought to be painted." Her parents had been continental wanderers, and after a roaming babyhood she had lost them both, and been taken in charge by her aunt, Medora Manson, also a wanderer, who was
10 herself returning to New York to "settle down."

Poor Medora, repeatedly widowed, was always coming home to settle down (each time in a less expensive house), and bringing with her a new husband or an adopted child; but
15 after a few months she invariably parted from her husband or quarrelled with her ward, and, having got rid of her house at a loss, set out again on her wanderings. As her mother had been a Rushworth, and her last unhappy marriage had
20 linked her to one of the crazy Chiverses, New York looked indulgently on her eccentricities; but when she returned with her little orphaned niece, whose parents had been popular in spite of their regrettable taste for travel, people thought it a pity
25 that the pretty child should be in such hands.

Everyone was disposed to be kind to little Ellen Mingott, though her dusky red cheeks and tight curls gave her an air of gaiety that seemed unsuitable in a child who should still have
30 been in black for her parents. It was one of the misguided Medora's many peculiarities to flout the unalterable rules that regulated American mourning, and when she stepped from the steamer her family was scandalized to see that the
35 crepe veil she wore for her own brother was seven inches shorter than those of her sisters-in-law, while little Ellen wore a crimson dress and amber beads.

But New York had so long resigned itself to
40 Medora that only a few old ladies shook their heads over Ellen's gaudy clothes, while her other relations fell under the charm of her high spirits. She was a fearless and familiar little thing, who asked disconcerting questions, made precocious
45 comments, and possessed outlandish arts, such as dancing a Spanish shawl dance and singing Neapolitan love-songs to a guitar. Under the direction of her aunt, the little girl received an expensive but incoherent education, which
50 included "drawing from the model," a thing never dreamed of before, and playing the piano in quintets with professional musicians.

Of course no good could come of this; and when, a few years later, poor Chivers finally died,
55 his widow again pulled up stakes and departed with Ellen, who had grown into a tall bony girl with conspicuous eyes. For some time no more was heard of them. Then news came of Ellen's marriage to an immensely rich Polish nobleman
60 of legendary fame. She disappeared, and when a few years later Medora again came back to New York, subdued, impoverished, mourning a third husband, and in quest of a still smaller house, people wondered that her rich niece had not been
65 able to do something for her. Then came the news that Ellen's own marriage had ended in disaster, and that she was herself returning home to seek rest and oblivion among her kinsfolk.

These things passed through Newland
70 Archer's mind a week later as he watched the Countess Olenska enter the van der Luyden drawing room on the evening of the momentous dinner. In the middle of the room she paused, looking about her with a grave mouth and smiling
75 eyes; and in that instant, Newland Archer rejected the general verdict on her looks. It was true that her early radiance was gone. The red cheeks had paled; she was thin, worn, a little older-looking than her age, which must have been nearly thirty.
80 But there was about her the mysterious authority of beauty, a sureness in the carriage of the head, the movement of the eyes, which, without being in

GO ON TO THE NEXT PAGE.

the least theatrical, struck him as highly trained
and full of a conscious power. At the same time

85   she was simpler in manner than most of the
ladies present, and many people (as he heard
afterward) were disappointed that her appearance
was not more "stylish"—for stylishness was
what New York most valued. It was, perhaps,

90   Archer reflected, because her early vivacity had
disappeared; because she was so quiet—quiet in
her movements, her voice, and the tones of her
voice. New York had expected something a good
deal more resonant in a young woman with such

95   a history.

1.   The author describes which of the following
practices as undesirable to New York society?

    A.   Playing the piano
    B.   Performing Spanish shawl dances
    C.   Traveling
    D.   Adopting children

2.   As a result of her "peculiarities" (line 31), Medora
offends her family by:

    F.   allowing Ellen to marry a Polish nobleman.
    G.   wearing a veil that is too short for mourning.
    H.   returning to New York with no money.
    J.   refusing to dress stylishly when meeting
Newland Archer.

3.   It is most reasonable to infer that, after the death
of Medora's third husband, Ellen did not help her
aunt primarily because:

    A.   Ellen was no longer wealthy, since her own
marriage had failed.
    B.   Medora had become embittered because she
hadn't heard from Ellen for so long.
    C.   Ellen resented the incoherent education she
received from her aunt.
    D.   receiving help from her niece would interfere
with Medora's desire to be eccentric.

4.   Based on the characterization of Newland Archer
in the last paragraph, he can best be described as:

    F.   reflective and non-judgmental.
    G.   likable but withdrawn.
    H.   disinterested but fair.
    J.   stylish and gregarious.

5.   The third paragraph (lines 11–25) suggests that
Medora's lifestyle was primarily viewed by others
as:

    A.   acceptably different from societal norms.
    B.   a terrible example to set for her niece.
    C.   unfortunate and pitiful.
    D.   disturbingly inconsistent.

6.   Which of the following conclusions about the
relationship between Medora and Ellen is best
supported by the passage?

    F.   Ellen is grateful that her aunt unselfishly
adopted her.
    G.   Medora is jealous of her niece's marriage to a
wealthy husband.
    H.   Both women share a distaste for New York
society.
    J.   Ellen has adopted some of her aunt's
unconventional traits.

7.   What does the narrator suggest is a central
characteristic of Medora Manson?

    A.   Arrogance
    B.   Immodesty
    C.   Non-conformity
    D.   Orthodoxy

8.   Which of the following characters learns to do
something otherwise unheard of by New York
society?

    F.   Ellen Mingott
    G.   Newland Archer
    H.   Medora Manson
    J.   Count Olenska

9.   Newland Archer would most likely agree with
which of the following characterizations of Ellen?

    A.   She is confident and poised.
    B.   She is lonely and unhappy.
    C.   She is intelligent and outspoken.
    D.   She is highly-educated and intimidating.

10.   One can reasonably infer from the passage that on
the occasion of the dinner, Newland and Ellen:

    F.   had not seen each other for some time.
    G.   were interested in becoming romantically
involved.
    H.   were both disappointed with New York
society.
    J.   had just met, but were immediately attracted
to each other.

GO ON TO THE NEXT PAGE.

Passage II

SOCIAL SCIENCE: The following passage is adapted from a magazine article discussing the role of the Federalist Papers in the passage of the United States Constitution.

In 1787, just a few short months after the Constitutional Convention was held in Philadelphia, a series of curious articles began to appear in newspapers throughout New York State.
5 The articles, each one signed with the anonymous "Publius," provided a keen and detailed knowledge of the United States Constitution, which was still waiting to be ratified. Over the next year, the articles kept coming, one after
10 another, in newspapers such as the *New York Packet* and the *Independent Journal*. Each article contained a detailed defense of one particular element of the hotly debated Constitution. By the time the articles ended, 85 had been published,
15 marking what was one of the earliest and most important publicity campaigns in U.S. political history.

At the time of its creation, the Constitution was a highly contentious document whose
20 ratification was far from assured. Following the conclusion of the Revolutionary War and the failure of the Articles of Confederation to create a sustainable government, the Constitution was drafted in order to form a stronger central
25 government, one capable of taxing its citizens and keeping the Union united. Its survival was dependent upon its ratification by nine of the 13 states that formed the Union. Following the presentation of the document to the general
30 public, debates began to spring up all across America over what many people saw as its extraordinary powers. The debate in New York was particularly fierce.

Of the 55 delegates at the Constitutional
35 Convention, none played as pivotal a role in its formation as James Madison. It is perhaps only fitting then that Madison, as the "Father of the Constitution," also played a key role in explaining its intention and assuring its ratification. Of the
40 85 articles known today as the *Federalist Papers*, Madison, it is now certain, was the author of 28. Many of his essays tended to focus on the larger benefits offered by the proposed Constitution, most notably its ability to provide security and
45 sustainability even in the face of dissension.

In *Federalist Paper No. 10*, Madison eloquently supports the Constitution on the grounds that the federal system of government is the best safeguard against the threat of internal
50 insurrection, without limiting the liberty of individuals and organizations to dissent. As a young nation, the United States was especially vulnerable to disputes between individual states that could easily have threatened to destroy the
55 Union. Madison's argument in favor of a federalist government is a carefully balanced presentation of the benefits offered by a government that grants a limited measure of authority to individual states, while still allowing for the existence of a stronger
60 federal government.

The strength and importance of Madison's *Federalist Papers* lies not only in their political arguments, but also in Madison's keen understanding of human nature and the role
65 government plays in controlling that nature. In one of the most famous lines from the *Papers*, Madison writes, "But what is government itself but the greatest of all reflections on human nature? If men were angels, no government would
70 be necessary." He defended a federal system of government that promoted the best aspects of human nature and the desire for liberty and freedom, while still guarding the interests of the larger Union from complete dissension.

75 Alexander Hamilton and John Jay joined Madison in writing the remaining *Federalist Papers*. Hamilton, who later served as Secretary of the Treasury, wrote 52 of the 85 essays, while John Jay, the first Supreme Court Chief Justice
80 of the United States, wrote five. Of the 52 essays attributed to Hamilton, seven were devoted specifically to the government's power of taxation, a power previously denied under the Articles of Confederation. As with many of the other
85 *Federalist Papers*, Hamilton's arguments centered on the preservation of the Union, as he believed its fate depended in part on its ability to tax its citizens in order to support its military and cover its domestic expenses.

90 In *Federalist Paper No. 1*, Hamilton raises the question of "whether societies of men are really capable or not of establishing good government from reflection and choice, or whether they are forever destined to depend for their
95 political Constitutions on accident and force." Approximately one year after the Constitution was signed, it was ratified by the ninth state, thereby officially making it the law of the land. It was an enormous victory, not only for the men who
100 wrote the Constitution and defended it to the best of their abilities, but also for the entire nation. Governments, as Hamilton had hoped, could indeed be the products of "reflection and choice."

GO ON TO THE NEXT PAGE.

11. According to the passage, the Articles of Confederation did not give the government the power to:
   A.   pay for an army.
   B.   tax its citizens.
   C.   ratify the Constitution.
   D.   fight wars to defend the country.

12. When the author uses the phrase "keen understanding of human nature" (lines 63-64), he means that:
   F.   Madison could read peoples' minds.
   G.   human nature is difficult to understand.
   H.   Madison had a good understanding of people.
   J.   Madison had known many people in his life.

13. The main purpose of the third and fourth paragraphs (lines 34-60) is to:
   A.   explain the role Madison played in writing the *Federalist Papers*.
   B.   explain the failures of the *Articles of Confederation*.
   C.   discuss the threat posed to the nation by having a weak government.
   D.   provide an insight into Madison's personal motives.

14. The author's attitude towards the writers of the *Federalist Papers* could best be described as:
   F.   deeply skeptical of their intentions.
   G.   antagonistic toward the arguments they presented.
   H.   confused as to their motives for writing the *Federalist Papers*.
   J.   respectful of their commitment to creating a better government.

15. Based on information in the passage, the main argument in favor of ratifying the Constitution presented in many of the *Federalist Papers* centered on:
   A.   giving the government the right to tax its citizens.
   B.   granting the government the power to raise an army.
   C.   creating a government strong enough to preserve the nation.
   D.   keeping the level of dissension to a minimum.

16. The function of the second paragraph (lines 18-33) in relation to the passage as a whole is most likely to provide:
   F.   background information on the Constitution and the ratification process.
   G.   an explanation of the weaknesses in the *Articles of Confederation*.
   H.   insight into the motivations of the Constitution's authors.
   J.   information about the Constitutional Convention.

17. According to the passage, Hamilton wrote seven *Federalist Papers* that discussed:
   A.   the threat posed to the Union by dissension and war.
   B.   the need to create a strong central government to preserve the nation.
   C.   the flaws of human nature and the role of government.
   D.   granting the government the power to tax its citizens.

18. According to the passage, one of the reasons the United States was especially vulnerable to disputes between individual states was:
   F.   its inability to limit free speech.
   G.   it was such a young nation.
   H.   no one could agree on the Constitution.
   J.   the states did not want to be taxed.

19. The author uses the phrase "products of 'reflection and choice'" (line 103) to show that:
   A.   ratification of the Constitution involved serious debate and discussion.
   B.   people did not think much about the Constitution.
   C.   newspapers were used to debate the Constitution.
   D.   writing the Constitution was a long process.

20. According to the passage, Alexander Hamilton wrote that governments are historically:
   F.   the best way of protecting people.
   G.   created by force or accident.
   H.   created with the best intentions.
   J.   created by the will of the people.

GO ON TO THE NEXT PAGE.

Passage III

HUMANITIES: The following passage is excerpted from a book about trends in American art, literature, and music in the 20th century.

America emerged from the wreckage of World War II victorious and, compared to much of the world, relatively unscathed. America had established itself as one of the two world
5 superpowers, the home of democracy and liberty. It had become a nation composed of grand and noble ideals centered around individual freedom and equality, ideals that existed in principle, if not always in practice. The general sense of optimism
10 that followed the conclusion of the war was balanced against the carnage and havoc it had wrought. The wide-scale destruction throughout much of Western Europe, the introduction of nuclear weapons with the atomic bomb, and
15 the haunting legacy of the Holocaust forced artists, writers, and thinkers to reconsider the standard notions of art and its function in society. Traditions and forms long established in music, literature, and painting seemed insufficient to
20 explain what was for many artists an utterly new moment in history, born out of destruction far greater than anything ever imagined. Artists in America had another problem to consider as well: While thousands of American soldiers fought
25 overseas for the causes of liberty and democracy, millions of African Americans continued to live as second-class citizens in a country deeply, and often violently, divided by race.

It wasn't long after the war ended that the
30 artistic explosion came. Its center was New York, which by the early 1950s had become the intellectual and bohemian capital of the country. Artists from all over the world met in New York, laying the foundation for a unique
35 series of experimentations that pushed the boundaries of art even further. Jackson Pollack, a New York–based American artist, redefined what a painting could be when he began to create enormous, swirling abstract canvases that had no
40 discernible shapes or figures. Charlie Parker and Dizzy Gillespie blew away the old jazz standards when they began playing their new form of improvisational jazz in salons and nightclubs throughout New York. Jack Kerouac called for
45 a new form of spontaneous prose writing when he wrote his now seminal novel, *On the Road*, in approximately six weeks, typing it out on one long sheet of paper.

At the center of these artistic innovations was
50 a desire to move beyond traditional conventions. Instead of painting pictures that showed people, houses, and trees, why not paint canvases that instead swirled with emotions and feelings? Instead of writing novels that relied on formal
55 sentence structures and previously devised plots, why not write a narrative that moved as fast and as freely as life itself? Why play standard jazz arrangements with structured rhythms and melodies when one could play music that was
60 more fluid and innovative?

The post-World War II artists were interested not only in creating a new type of expression, but also a purer and more direct form of art. In an essay about his unorthodox style of painting,
65 Pollack summed up this desire when he wrote, "When I am in my painting, I'm not aware of what I'm doing ... I have no fears about making changes, destroying the image, etc. because the painting has a life of its own." On a strikingly
70 similar note, Jack Kerouac, in his essay "Belief and Technique for Modern Prose" wrote, "[I] struggle to sketch the flow that already exists intact in [my] mind." Appropriately enough, one of Kerouac's personal heroes was Charlie
75 Parker, whose radical altering of conventional jazz mirrored Kerouac's prose aesthetic. Parker's innovations led to the creation of bebop, a type of jazz markedly different from the big band swing era that had preceded it. Bebop was faster and less
80 structured, relying on dissonance, fragmentation, and solo performances. In Charlie Parker's music, African-American writers such as James Baldwin found an artistic expression that transformed the frustration and challenge of being black in
85 America into an utterly beautiful and liberating art.

By the start of the 1950s, a new era of artistic expression and innovation had been fully ushered in. The traditions of the old world no longer
90 existed intact, having been torn apart in the war. The new art being created celebrated the best of America's long-held ideas of individual freedom and liberty. At the same time it challenged those ideas by putting them directly onto the canvas
95 and page, and by recording and playing them in studios and concert halls throughout the country.

GO ON TO THE NEXT PAGE.

ACT ADVANTAGE
ENGLISH & READING

21. The passage indicates that post-World War II artists:

    A. were traumatized by the devastation of the war.
    B. wanted to move away from old conventions.
    C. were generally optimistic about the world.
    D. could not move beyond the old traditions.

22. The passage states that most post-World War II artists wanted to:

    F. create a purer and more direct form of art.
    G. create art as quickly as possible.
    H. make art that was difficult to understand.
    J. change the way people thought about art.

23. The author states that Charlie Parker's musical style "mirrored Kerouac's prose aesthetic" (line 76) in order to imply that:

    A. Parker was trying to copy Kerouac's style.
    B. Parker wanted to write stories like Kerouac.
    C. Kerouac and Parker shared similar ideas about art.
    D. both Kerouac and Parker were influenced by the same artists.

24. Based on details from the passage, it is reasonable to infer that Charlie Parker was:

    F. not highly regarded by other jazz musicians.
    G. not popular because he had a difficult time getting people to listen to his music.
    H. the only musician of his kind in New York.
    J. an influence on other African-American artists.

25. The main purpose of the third paragraph (lines 49-60) is to:

    A. explain what artists did in their work.
    B. criticize more traditional types of art.
    C. question the motives of the artists.
    D. express the confusion created by the artists.

26. According to the passage, when did New York become the center of an artistic explosion?

    F. Just before World War II
    G. During the 1930s
    H. After World War II
    J. Near the end of the 1950s

27. Which of the following is NOT a characteristic of the postwar art discussed in the article?

    A. A desire to create new forms of art
    B. A fear of trying new styles of art
    C. A reliance on innovation
    D. A tendency to create abstract works

28. As it is used in line 36, the word *boundaries* most nearly means:

    F. borders.
    G. edges.
    H. norms.
    J. lines.

29. The passage states that Pollack's paintings were:

    A. planned well ahead of time.
    B. full of errors and mistakes.
    C. very large with no shapes or figures.
    D. created quickly without much thought.

30. The function of the second paragraph (lines 29-48) in relation to the passage as a whole is most likely to provide:

    F. information about World War II.
    G. a context for the art that was being created.
    H. examples of the damage caused by the war.
    J. an explanation for why artists moved to New York.

GO ON TO THE NEXT PAGE.

Passage IV

NATURAL SCIENCE: The following passage is adapted from "The Discovery of Pluto" by Maximilian H. Portis. It first appeared in the *Nevada Science Reporter*, June 2006, Volume 164. Reprinted with permission. Copyright © 2006 by Nevada Science Reporter, Inc. All rights reserved.

Today it is common knowledge that there are nine planets: Earth, Neptune, Jupiter, Saturn, Uranus, Venus, Mars, Mercury, and Pluto. Although the classification of Pluto as a planet has
5 become controversial, and there is investigation into the existence of a 10th planet somewhere beyond Pluto, the generally accepted view is that our solar system is comprised of nine planets.

While some planets were recognized by the
10 ancients—picked out by their constancy in the sky and, in some cases, their brightness—three planets have been discovered since the invention of the telescope 400 years ago. The planet Uranus was discovered in 1781, and Neptune
15 was discovered only as recently as 1846. Pluto, however, is the most modern discovery: it was not detected in the night sky until 1930.

Astronomers suspected the existence of a ninth planet as early as the first decade of the
20 20th century. An unknown planet's existence is hypothesized based on observed perturbations of the orbit of a known planet. Only another planet exerts enough gravitational pull to cause such disruptions to a planet's orbit. Based on
25 the known planet's orbit, astronomers calculate coordinates for the possible planet and begin searching the sky to confirm its existence and location. Pluto, however, was difficult to see. It is a diminutive planet far out at the edge of the
30 solar system with a slow elliptical orbit—Pluto's orbit around the sun takes 248 years. While there were excellent telescopes at the time, finding an object that small, distant, and slow posed an unprecedented challenge.

35 Astronomer Percival Lowell began an extensive search for this elusive ninth planet in 1905. He had built a private observatory in Flagstaff, Arizona in 1894, and he used the observatory to search for what was then known
40 as Planet X. By studying Neptune's orbit, Lowell calculated approximate coordinates for Planet X. Along with many others across the globe, Lowell focused on finding Planet X between 1913 and 1915. While he managed to discover 515 new
45 asteroids and 700 stars, he remained unsuccessful in the matter of Planet X. Or so he thought. Unbeknownst to Lowell, who died in 1916, his observatory actually had taken a very tiny photo

of what would later be known as Pluto. But this
50 image would not be found for 15 years after his death.

It was another American working at Lowell's observatory, Clyde Tombaugh, who eventually found Pluto. Tombaugh, a 24-year-old lab assistant
55 who had grown up on a farm in Kansas, was respected in astronomical circles even before the discovery, although most of his work had been as an amateur. Fascinated by astronomy, he had built his own telescope from things he found in
60 the barn. Using this telescope, he drew pictures of planets and sent them to the Lowell Observatory, landing himself a job there.

Tombaugh was hired to find Planet X, which put an end to his amateur status but did
65 not undercut his achievement. After all, he was looking for a needle in a haystack. One reason Lowell failed to find Pluto—or recognize it when he saw it—was that the planet is exceedingly small, far smaller than any other planet in the
70 solar system. While scientists knew that it was also very distant, this didn't help. The extreme distance actually meant that there was an even wider blanket of stars to examine in order to find Pluto.

75 Tombaugh began his search by photographing parts of the sky at weekly or biweekly intervals. He then began a tedious comparison of the images, scanning them for any point of light that had shifted against the background of stars. Such a
80 shift would indicate that the point of light seemed to be standing still relative to Earth. Given the slowness of its solar orbit, that is how the distant planet would have appeared in the photographs.

On the night of February 18, 1930, working
85 at the Lowell Observatory, Tombaugh noticed a minute oscillation of light that fit the description he was looking for. His careful methods had paid off. He had found our solar system's ninth planet. It was later named Pluto, for the Greek god of
90 the underworld, who had the ability to become invisible. It is the only planet ever discovered by an American. On January 19, 2006, NASA's New Horizons spacecraft launched on a mission to study Pluto, promising more discoveries about
95 this mysterious planet.

GO ON TO THE NEXT PAGE.

31. According to the passage, what characteristic of Pluto led scientists to believe in its existence prior to any visible proof?

    A. Its slow orbit
    B. Its gravitational pull
    C. Its tiny size
    D. Its brightness

32. The main function of the second paragraph (lines 9–17) in relation to the passage as a whole is to:

    F. establish that Pluto was the most difficult planet to discover in the solar system.
    G. discuss the impact of the telescope on astronomy.
    H. note that planets have always derived their names from ancient mythology.
    J. state that Uranus, Neptune, and Pluto are the furthest planets from the sun.

33. As it is used in line 73, the word *blanket* most nearly means:

    A. area.
    B. comforter.
    C. layer.
    D. level.

34. Based on the details in the passage, one can reasonably infer that:

    F. early 20th-century telescopes were not capable of seeing Pluto.
    G. Clyde Tombaugh's discovery was initially doubted due to his young age.
    H. very few people ever attempted to locate Pluto prior to 1930.
    J. Pluto's orbit is perceived from Earth as being immobile.

35. According to the passage, Percival Lowell attempted to locate Pluto by:

    A. detecting a great number of previously unknown asteroids and stars.
    B. drawing pictures of other planets and comparing them with what he saw in his telescope.
    C. scanning an approximately defined area with his telescope.
    D. using anomalies in Neptune's orbit to pinpoint its exact location.

36. According to the passage, the cause for the great length of Pluto's orbit is:

    F. Neptune's gravitation.
    G. Pluto's diminutive size.
    H. Pluto's distance from the sun.
    J. the orbit's elliptical shape.

37. When the author writes that Tombaugh was "respected in astronomical circles" (line 56), he most likely means that:

    A. the astronomer performed significant work even as an amateur.
    B. the world of astronomy was a small one.
    C. few people possessed the potential ability to locate Planet X.
    D. Tombaugh's drawings rivaled those of any professional astronomer.

38. The main concern of the passage is to:

    F. argue that the discovery of Pluto was the greatest achievement in astronomy in the last century.
    G. discuss the discovery of Pluto from a historical standpoint.
    H. detail the mathematical equations used to locate the position of Pluto.
    J. illustrate how the greatest scientific discoveries tend to be collaborative efforts.

39. In the passage, which of the following was NOT achieved by Percival Lowell?

    A. The establishment of a private observatory
    B. The discovery of 700 stars
    C. A photograph of Pluto
    D. The design of a new telescope

40. Based on the final paragraph, which of the following can reasonably be inferred about the discovery of Pluto?

    F. Astronomers have adopted Tombaugh's methods in their search for more planets.
    G. Spacecraft can help us discover details about a planet that cannot be seen from Earth.
    H. Pluto periodically disappears from telescopic view.
    J. Subsequent discoveries generally belonged to Americans.

END OF TEST.

STOP! DO NOT TURN THE PAGE UNTIL TOLD TO DO SO.

NOTES

NOTES